SEMPRINGHAM
and
St GILBERT
and the
GILBERTINES

Eric W. Iredale

Pointon, Lincolnshire
1992

Published 1992 by Eric W. Iredale
Fen Road, Pointon, nr Sleaford, Lincolnshire

Reprinted 1996, 2000

ISBN 0 9519662 0 0

Typeset for the author by Yard Publishing Services, Lincoln LN2 1PJ
Cover by Ampersand Design, Lincoln LN5 8PN
Printed by G. W. Belton, Gainsborough DN21 2ED

**Cataloguing in Publication Data for this title is available from
the British Library**

CONTENTS

BIBLIOGRAPHY

Information has been obtained from the following:

BRAUN, HUGH, FSA FRIBA, Report on Excavation 1939 (in Sleaford Public Library)

COOK, CANON A. M., *Lincolnshire Links with the U.S.A.*, 1956, by kind permission of Canon Cook's family

CRAGG, W. A., *Threekingham History* , 1913

DUGDALE, SIR WILLIAM, *Monasticon Anglicanum*, 1717

DE THOYRAS, RAPIN, *History of England*, Vol. 1, 1817

FOREVILLE, R, ed., KERR, G. trans., *The Book of St Gilbert*, 1987

FOREVILLE, R, *St Gilbert of Sempringham, His Life and Achievement*, 1987

GRAHAM, ROSE, *Excavations on the Site of Sempringham Priory*, 1940

GRAHAM, ROSE, *St Gilbert and the Gilbertines*, 1901

GOOCH, E. H., *Place Names of Lincolnshire*, Spalding, 1945

KNOWLES, D. & HADCOCK, R. N., *Medieval Religious Houses in England and Wales*, 1953, by kind permission of Longman Group Publishers

The Lincolnshire Domesday (1924)

Log Book of Sempringham Abbey, in care of Eric W. Iredale, Pointon

MUNRO, J. J. , ed., John Capgrave's Lives of St Augustine and St Gilbert of Sempringham, 1910

NORTH, THOMAS, *The Church Bells of the City and County of Lincolnshire*, 1882

PAGE, WM., ed., *A History of Lincolnshire. Religious Houses*, Vol. II, 1906

POYNTON, E. M., ed., Sempringham Charters, *The Genealogist,* Vols. 15 (1899), 16 (1900), 17 (1901)

Sempringham Parish Magazines, loaned by Mrs L. Holland

RHODES, C. A., *St Gilbert of Sempringham and the Gilbertine Order*, 1966

Ross Charters, Sempringham, Lincoln Library

Visitations of Religious Houses (Vol. 1 1420–1436)

WARD, C. F., *History of Sempringham* [n.d.]

YOUINGS, JOYCE, *Dissolution of the Monasteries*, 1971, by kind permission of Harper Collins Publishers

INTRODUCTION AND ACKNOWLEDGEMENTS

St Gilbert of Sempringham and St Hugh of Lincoln are Lincolnshire's two great saints. Since 1983 when Lincoln Cathedral decided to celebrate St Gilbert's 900th anniversary year, there has been a resurgence of interest in this modest man who lived his whole life in the remote Lincolnshire fens, serving the people among whom he was born. The Cathedral published an exemplary short life of St Gilbert by Raymonde de Foreville for the anniversary year, but many people have asked for a more detailed account of his life and work and of Sempringham itself. In this volume I have collected material, including the earliest life still extant, which I hope will help them know more about this good man.

Unfortunately, for neither this book nor my first book on Sempringham, published in 1983, have I been able to read the Chronicles of Sempringham in the Vatican Library in Rome, mentioned in the *Newbury House Magazine* of 1891, which records the history of Sempringham back to A.D. 400. But I am able to give you St Gilbert's life story, written soon after his death by a canon of Sempringham. From this thirteenth-century Latin original John Capgrave, an Austin friar of Lynn, translated into English the story of the saint. Capgrave's translation was thought to have been lost in the fire among the Cotton Manuscripts in 1731; however his account was edited by J. J. Munro in 1910 and is to be found in the City of Sheffield reference library, bound together with the life of St Augustine, also by Capgrave. I have now translated the *Life* from fourteenth-century English into today's English, but kept it in the manner it was written by Capgrave.

I am very grateful for all who have assisted me with material, especially the following: the Lincolnshire Archives, the libraries of Lincoln, Sleaford, Grantham, Bourne and Peterborough, Mrs C. Arum, Dr D. Roffe for translation of the Charters, and Dom. A. Spencer, Abbot of Pluscarden Abbey, for the seal of the Master of the Order.

My sincere thanks to everyone else who has helped in any way and I hope the result will prove interesting reading and useful for reference.

CHANGES OF NAME

In the Domesday Book of 1066 the name of Sempringham is spelt in three different ways: Sepingeham – Spingeham – Stepingeham – the first two are almost the same as the third, except for the omission of TE.

Celtic :   SE signifies   SIX
                TE   WORSHIP
                PIN   HEAD or MOUND
                GE   ENCLOSURE

Anglo-Saxon: STEPN   THE VOICE, A TRIBE or RACE

SEMPRINGHAM – The enclosure or meeting place of the tribe which consisted of six-hundred.

Latin :   SEMPER signifies ALWAYS,
                (this was adapted by the Priory)

Seal of the Master of the Order of
Sempringham. An artist's
reconstruction from the original in the
British Museum

Church of St Andrew, Sempringham 1983

OUTLINE HISTORY OF SEMPRINGHAM

Sempringham goes back to A.D. 400. Before this the Romans built the Car Dyke canal, which is a mile or so to the east. This canal was about sixty-feet wide, with a broad flat bank on it each side. The Romans also built a road about three-quarters of a mile to the west, at one time called King Street, now known as Mareham Lane.

By the middle of the 5th century the Romans relinquished all possession, power and authority in Britain. After their departure the banks, drains, and sluices which they had constructed were neglected, and a great part of the county which they had brought into cultivation fell into its original fenny state.

The Saxons followed, naming Lincolnshire Mercia. Worshipping the sun and moon, the Saxons adored the god of thunder, had images in their temples, practised sacrifices, and believed firmly in spells and incantations. However, in 590 Pope Gregory I despatched Augustine, a Roman monk, with forty associates to preach Christianity to the Anglo-Saxons and the conquered Britons.

628 Paulinus, another Roman monk, created Archbishop of York, was the first to preach Christianity in Mercia.

852 The first mention of coal in Great Britain was as early as 852, when it was recorded that 'the Abbot of Peterborough let the land at Sempringham to Wulfred, who was to send each year to the monastery 12 loads of coal. Also 30 shillings, one horse, 60 loads of wood, two tons of swete ale, and such other thinges reserved'. These may have been transported to Medeshamstede (Peterborough) along the Car Dyke which is only about a mile away to the east of Sempringham.

1083 Jocelin, a wealthy Norman knight, married a Saxon lady 'of lower rank' who lived at Sempringham. Sometime before their child was born, she dreamed that the moon came down and settled in her lap, and she interpreted this as a sign of her child's coming greatness. Soon afterwards around 1083 she gave birth to a son, and called him Gilbert. Gilbert was born with some repulsive physical deformity.

Land ownership in Domesday Book

1086 Land owners in the parish of Sempringham, from the Domesday Book were:

ROBERT de TODENI. In Sepingeham there is 1 carucate of land (assessed) to the geld. There is land for 1 team. 4 sokemen have 1 team there, and, 10 acres of underwood.

GILBERT de GAND. In Spingeham there are 3 carucates and 2 bovates of land (assessed) to the geld. There is land for 3½ teams. There are 13 sokemen and 1 bordar there, having 3 teams, and half a church, and the sixth part of another church, and 24 acres of underwood.

ALFRED of LINCOLN. In Stepingeham, Morcar had 4 carucates and 2 bovates of land (assessed) to the geld. There is land for as many teams and oxen. Gocelin, Alfred's man, has 1 team there (in demesne), and 14 sokemen on 2½ carucates of this land, and 8 villeins and 2 bordars, and the fourth part of 1 church, and 11 acres of meadow and 7 acres of underwood, and now worth 40 shillings; tallage 20 shillings.

1088 Robert Todini land owner at Sempringham died in August. He built Belvoir Castle and this was his chief seat of his Barony.

Gilbert's early life

1100 Jocelin de Sempringham, a Norman knight, built the Church of St Andrew on the site of a more ancient Saxon Church. The chancel was about the same length as the nave, and there were also transepts.

It does not seem to be known how old Gilbert was when he left home; his father was bitterly disappointed in him, for his deformity unfitted him for the calling of arms and even the household servants openly ridiculed him. It was only his mother's affection and early training which made him good, pure, gentle and considerate towards women. In the end he either fled or was sent to France to be educated as a clerk. While he was there he made good use of his time and opportunities, living a good life and resisting all the temptations of the time.

When Gilbert returned his father accepted him, as he now had an honorable profession and his goodness and learning commended him to everyone. He 'bore himself with all humility' with a 'great desire to gain souls for Christ'. As there were no schools in the neighbourhood he began schools for boys and girls of the village area, and there he taught the children not only rudiments of learning but also morals and discipline, and they lived according to a monastic Rule.

1115 Gilbert was a lover of truth and justice, chastity and sobriety, and a diligent cultivator of the other virtues; wherefore he was revered and praised by all and obtained their favour and reward. Even Jocelin his father, now rejoiced in the goodness of his son, he began to cherish him with fatherly affection, and ministered to his needs out of his own riches. Gilbert would be in his late twenties when his father presented him to the vacant churches of Sempringham and West Torrington, which he had built on his own demesne 'in the custom of his country'. As Gilbert was not in orders, he appointed a chaplain named Geoffrey, and they lived together in a room over the porch of the church of St Andrew. They afterwards built a house for themselves in the cemetery, in which they dwelt apart.

1122 Robert Bloet, Bishop of Lincoln sent for Gilbert of Sempringham to be clerk in his household.

1129 VICAR OF ST ANDREWS – Gilbert de Sempringham was instituted by Robert Bloet, Bishop of Lincoln to the parishes of Sempringham and West Torrington.

1131 Gilbert de Sempringham returned from Lincoln, where he had been ordained by Alexander, Bishop of Lincoln, to continue his work. As his father was now dead he became the owner of a large estate. He continued to 'win souls for Christ' but after a fruitless search for men who wished to serve God by a rule of life he turned to 'seven maidens' whom he had previously taught. With the help of Alexander he built accommodation for them within a cloistered enclosure on the north wall of the Church of St Andrew. This small community attracted much attention and brought others into the community life, and some to serve as lay-brothers and lay-sisters to do the manual work.

1139 Gilbert de Gant was a son of Baldwin, Count of Flanders, whose sister was the wife of William the Conqueror. He was granted a hundred and five lordships, of which the chief was Folkingham, in Lincolnshire.

Gilbert de Gant gave Gilbert three carucates of land nearby on which to build a Priory. This lay in the valley 350 yards to the south and south-west of

3

the parish church of St Andrew, and work of the building began in the same year. In virtue of his gift of land, Gilbert de Gant was held to be founder of Sempringham Priory.

In the same year Alexander, Bishop of Lincoln, gave the marshy island of Haverholme, near Sleaford, to Gilbert 'for the faithful nuns of wonderful religion who serve Christ the Lord in love under the charge and teaching of Gilbert. Seizing on the narrow life, the strict life, the life of the monks of the Cistercian religion so far as the weakness of their sex permits, they strive to keep it, and they do keep it'.

1147 Gilbert shrank from the responsibility of the ruling the nunneries, and he went in the company of Cistercian abbots to the general chapter of their Order at Citeaux in Burgundy. He asked the abbots assembled in the chapter to govern his nunneries. Cistercian nunneries had not yet been founded, and the abbots refused to rule over women. Pope Eugenius III was present at the chapter, taking his place as a simple abbot among the others, and he conferred the charge of the Order of Sempringham on Gilbert. St Bernard, Abbot of Clairvaux, invited Gilbert to go to Clairvaux, and gave him so much help in drawing up the Institutes of Sempringham that in a bull of Pope Innocent III, Bernard and Gilbert are described as the two founders of the Order. St Bernard was acquainted with the Order of Fontevrault which had over fifty houses in France.

1148 Gilbert was still at Clairvaux in the middle of October, when Malachy, the famous Archbishop of Armagh, arrived there on his way to Rome, Malachy presented Gilbert with an abbot's staff in token of his love; St Bernard gave him a stole and a maniple as well as a staff.

The establishment of the Order

Gilbert returned to England and completed the Order of Sempringham by appointing canons to serve as priests and to help him in the work of administration. He gave the canons the Rule of St Augustine and added many statutes from the Customs of Augustinian and Premonstratensian canons. The lay-brothers followed the Rule of the Cistercian lay-brothers. The nuns and sisters kept the Rule of St Benedict. Some of the distinctive characteristics of the Order of Fontevrault and the Cluniac nunnery of Marcigny were adapted for the Order of Sempringham. The canons had their own oratory for the service of the Hours, and neither they nor the lay-brothers came usually to the priory church except for mass.

After the confirmation of the Rule by Eugenius III in 1148, the Order of Sempringham was put under the 'protection' of the Papacy.

1155 The Crown showed great favour to the Gilbertines. As the Order was English and the houses were all in England, no money went from them to the

King's enemies. Thomas Becket was Chancellor at the time.

CHARTER (1) – The friendship of Henry II with Gilbert moved him to grant liberal charters of privileges to the Order of Sempringham. As his 'free and special alms' he took all the houses of the Order, and the nuns and canons, into 'his own hand, custody, and protection' and enjoined that they should hold all their tenements 'well and in peace, freely and quietly, wholly and fully and honourably, in wood and in field, in meadows and pastures, in waters and marshes, in fishponds, in tofts and crofts, in roads and ways, and in all places within boroughs and without'.

1158 Henry II granted CHARTER (4) – In city and borough, in markets and fairs, in crossing of bridges and at harbours of the sea, and in all places throughout England and Normandy', the Gilbertines and 'their men' were quit of toll and all other customs.

1164 The Gilbertines helped Archbishop Thomas Becket to escape from England. The archbishop was summoned before the King's Council at Northampton in October. He returned to the Monastery of St Andrew, in which he gave a great feast to the poor. A Gilbertine brother guided him northwards to Lincoln, they arrived at Grantham where they stayed for a short sleep, they then carried on to Lincoln. There they lodged in the house of a fuller by the name of James, who was a friend of the Gilbertines. Thomas dressed as a lay-brother left by boat down the Witham to a lonely hermitage, belonging to Sempringham called Hoyland-in-the-Fens. He remained there for three days safely hidden. He left there for Boston and then by water to Haverholme near Sleaford. The archbishop left the fens and stayed at the Gilbertine house of Chicksand in Bedfordshire. There he met a chaplain of the Order, Gilbert by name who travelled with him by night, and hiding by day till they reached the coast of Kent, and sailed from Eastry to Oye near Graveline on November 2nd.

PRIOR OF SEMPRINGHAM - Torphin occurs.

1165 Early in the year Henry II's justices summoned Gilbert and his priors to Westminster to answer a charge of having sent money abroad to help Thomas Becket. The Order was in grave danger for the penalty was exile. However, Gilbert said that he would rather suffer it than swear to his innocence, lest his oath should be misunderstood; as a loyal son of the church, he would have thought it right to help the archbishop in every way he could. While his priors were filled with terror, 'thinking that some of them might take the oath, and that it was not right to leave the places of their profession for such a cause', Gilbert 'forgot all earthly fear'. On the last day, when they expected to hear that they must all suffer exile without delay, messengers arrived from Henry II to say that he would judge the case himself on his return from Normandy, in the meantime Gilbert and his priors to go in peace.

Henry revered and loved the saintly Master of Sempringham. Queen

Eleanor too, rejoiced that her sons were blessed by Gilbert.

1170 Gilbert was more than eighty years old, the great trouble of the rebellion of the lay-brothers came upon him. In the Cistercian Order the monks were as numerous as the lay-brothers and shared their work, but Gilbert's few learned brothers could not cope with their resolute resistance. The lay-brothers complained of the harshness of the Rule, and demanded more food with less work.

Henry II, several of the bishops and Cardinal Hugh, the papal legate, took up Gilbert's cause, and they wrote to Alexander III on his behalf. William, Bishop of Norwich, was a most strenuous defender of Gilbert. Roger, Archbishop of York said that he had always heard that the Gilbertine houses in his diocese were 'honestly and religiously ruled'. In another letter the archbishop and Hugh de Puiset, Bishop of Durham, testified to their own knowledge of Malton Priory. Henry of Blois, Bishop of Winchester, the Prior of Bridlington, and Cardinal Hugh wrote to the Pope in like manner.

Alexander was convinced 'by these testimonies and prayers' that he had been deceived by the lay-brothers. He granted to Gilbert and his successors, 'that no one might add to, correct or change their religion, laws, or reasonable institution without the consent of the greater and wiser part of the Order'.

1175 Henry II granted CHARTER (3) – He bade his 'justiciars sherriffs, and all other servants' to protect the Gilbertines and their property, as though it were the King's.

1177 Godwin the Rich of Lincoln, became a benefactor of Sempringham, and was received by Gilbert into full fraternity.

Last years of Gilbert's life

1188 Gilbert wrote this letter to his canons of Malton some time in the last year of his life:

My dear sons – While God gave me power, whenever I came to visit you, I was ever wont to invite and draw you to the Divine love so far as I could and knew how. Would that virtue followed on my care for you! But I am almost destitute of bodily strength, and by putting off this robe of the flesh a way opens up for me to depart hence from life, which has long been bitter and tedious to me. And now since I can not speak to you with my voice, by this letter I cease not to admonish you, for love of God and the safety of your souls, to watch more diligently even than hitherto, to repress vice to exalt justice, to observe the institution and tradition of your Order the more wakefully and strictly since you are free from the occupations with which the lay-brothers busy themselves, and you have the opportunity of exercising the rigour of the Order, that you may check the insolence of any delinquents. For this I have specially gathered you together, that our

Order may be rightly ruled, protected, and exalted by the rigour of your religion. If you think my care for you has been of use to you, do not refuse to consider the hire of my labour, but entreat the clemency of the Lord with your most fervent prayers that He enter not into judgement with me, but by His great sweetness may wipe away my sins and grant me everlasting rest. To you whom I leave behind me, I give the peace and mercy of God, His blessing and my own. By the authority granted me by Him, as far as I may, I absolve all who love our Order and defend it from all accusations which any have brought against its institutions through ignorance or infirmity, negligence or contempt. Let those who imagine mischief and strife against our congregation, know that my absolution cannot avail them, since unless they repent before the Lord, and make worthy satisfaction, they are accursed. None of you do I think guilty of this charge, but I trust in you all that you will be more diligent than formerly in performing all things for the welfare of your souls, with the help of the Saviour, that my joy in your society may increase before the Lord, and that He Himself may be glad whose kingdom and power abide for ever and ever. Farewell.

On Christmas night Gilbert received extreme unction at the monastery of Newstead-on-Ancholme. His companion and chaplain carried him to Sempringham forty miles away, secretly, and as swiftly as they could. They dared not follow the straight road, lest Gilbert should be detained on the way, that his bones might rest in some other church or monastery.

1189 The priors of all his churches came to Sempringham to receive his blessing, Friday February 3rd. On the last day, with only his successor, Roger, Prior of Malton at his side, he lay in a stupor seeing no one, hearing no one. At last he said, 'He hath dispersed. He hath given to the poor, this is thy duty for the future'.

On the next morning, Saturday 4 February, he died about the hour of Matins. Gilbert's biographer could not find words to express the grief of the Order. 'He gathered us together as a hen gathers her chickens under her wing.' 'Kings and princes honoured him, pontiffs and prelates received him with devotion, kinsmen and strangers loved him, all the people revered him as a saint of God. We have seen bishops on their knees asking for his blessing, and coming from a far distance seeking fragments of his clothing.'

He was buried on the following Tuesday, 'in the presence of abbots, of priors of his own and other monasteries, of many of the religious both men and women, of the many noble and rich of the world, and of a countless multitude of the people'. The tomb was placed between the altars of St Mary and St Andrew in the priory church of St Mary, on either side of the wall which divides the men from the women, so that all alike might see him.

Henry II was fighting against Richard and John in Normandy, when he

7

heard of Gilbert's death in February. He sighed deeply and said, 'Truly I knew that he had left this earth, for all these evils have come upon me because he is dead'. He would not be comforted until some of his nobles told him that Gilbert could intercede better for him in heaven than on earth.

Development of the Order

At the time of Gilbert's death, there were in England thirteen religious houses belonging to the Order, with 700 monks and 1300 nuns. Nine were for men and women together, and four for canons only. Besides, he had built hostels for the poor, and the sick, orphans, and widows. Kings and Princes honoured him, prelates were devoted to him, and the people loved him as a Saint of God.

The convent of Sempringham at first suffered poverty, but several benefactors had compassion on the nuns. In 1189 the possessions of the Priory included the whole township of Sempringham, with the parish church and the chapel of Pointon, the granges of Kirkby, Marham, Cranwell, Fulbeck, Thorpe, Bramcote. Walcote, Thurstanton, the hermitage of Hoyland, a mill at Birthorpe, half a knights fee in Laughton (Locton), the mills at Folkingham, the churches of Billingborough, Stow with the chapel of Birthorpe, Hanington, Aslackby, Buxton, Brunesthorp, Kirkby, Bradstow, and moieties of Towell and Laughton. Probably in consideration of this endowment Gilbert limited the number of nuns and lay-sisters to 120, and of canons and brothers to 60.

MASTER OF SEMPRINGHAM – Roger elected 1189.

1193 As the chief source of income was the proceeds of the wool sold to foreign merchants, the Gilbertines must have suffered severely in 1193, when the whole of the wool of the Order for that year was seized for the ransom of Richard. To this was added the plate belonging to the churches, upon the Queen's promise to restore it after the King's release.

1198 Henry II granted his charters to the Order of Sempringham as his 'free and special alms.' Richard I, whose purpose in granting charters was to get money for the Crusade, nevertheless confirmed his father's charter 'in free alms'. In 1198 his first seal was broken up, and a new one, containing the three leopards passant, was cast. Richard then repudiated all the earlier charters of his reign, and ordered that they should be brought to him for confirmation, as he needed money for his war against Philip Augustus. At Chateau Gaillard, on November 11th, he again granted a charter 'in free alms' to the Gilbertines.

1199 Godwin the Rich of Lincoln a benefactor of Sempringham, founded the Gilbertine Priory at Bridgend, Horbling.

1201 Eleven years after Gilbert's death, Hubert Walter, Archbishop of

Canterbury, judged that Gilbert was worthy to be canonised and sent the Abbots of Lincolnshire houses of Swineshead, Bourne, Croxton to make inquisition about him and his miracles.

King John and some of his nobles came to see the tomb of Gilbert on January 9th.

The abbots arrived at Sempringham the same day, and afterwards satisfied themselves by sworn inquisition as to the truth of the miracles. King John, the Archbishop of Canterbury, the Bishops of London, Norwich, Bangor and Ely, the Dean and Chapter of Lincoln, the three abbots and many others, sent letters to Innocent III, asking for the canonisation of Gilbert of Sempringham. Master Roger and the Chapter of Sempringham told how he built many monasteries and cared for the poor, how at his tomb the lame walked, the dumb spake, the deaf heard. Two of the canons set out for the Curia with all these testimonies.

Innocent III received them kindly, and gave them letters for the archbishop and others enjoining a three days fast on the whole Order, and a further inquisition into the life and miracles of Gilbert. The archbishop fixed September 26th 1201 for the inquisition and the fast for that day and the two preceding days. After some delay because they feared the difficulties of the journey, five canons and six men, who had been cured of their infirmities by Gilbert, set out to carry the sealed testimonies to the Pope, with a letter from the Archbishop of Canterbury stating that all alike bore witness to Gilbert's holy and unspotted life.

The canons reached Rome safely on December 31st.

1202 The canons went from Rome to Anagni, where Innocent III then was on January 2nd. When a few of the miracles had been read in the Curia, some of the cardinals said that these alone sufficed, others that they were already more than enough.

On January 11th in the presence of a great number of clergy and people, Innocent made a long speech on the merits of Gilbert and decreed his canonisation. After the return of the canons, the archbishop wrote to the bishops commanding them to keep the Feast of St Gilbert on February 4th. They might be present if they chose, on the Sunday after the Feast of St James. When he had promised the Order to elevate the body of the Confessor with honour and due reverence.

The translation took place on October 13th 1202 before many nobles and prelates and a great multitude of people.

When his body was raised it was found in perfect condition, and was wrapped afresh in fine linen, next in a covering of rich silk given by Hubert, Archbishop of Canterbury, and was finally enclosed in lead, within which was deposited a record of St Gilbert's miracles, and memoranda of his canonisation and translation.

On the leaden coffin was the following inscription: 'Hic jacet sanctus Gilebertus, primus pater et institutor ordinis de Sempingham, translatus in hunc loculum, domino Huberto, Cantuariensi archiepiscopo, per mandatum Innocentii papa tertii, iii idus Octobris anno ab incarnatione Domini MCCll'. The translation from Dugdale's Monasticon: 'Here lyes St Gilbert, the first Father and Institutor of the Order of Sempringham, translated to this Tomb, when Hubert was Archbishop of Canterbury, by order of Pope Innòcent III, three days before the Ides of October, in the year of our Lord 1202'.

The writing put into the tomb was thus:

'In this coffin are contained the relics of St Gilbert Priest and Confessor, first Father and Institutor of the Order of Sempringham; whose Life, tho rendered commendable and renowned on many Accounts, was principally made remarkable by this, that making choice of voluntary Poverty, he assigned all the Temporalities God had given him to supply the wants of the Brothers and Sisters whom he had instituted under a regular discipline, and diligently fostered. To whom in process of time, God added so much Grace and Virtue, that he built four Monasteries of Canons Regular, and nine of Nuns; in which, at the time when he departed to the Lord, besides a multitude before dead, he left 700 religious men and 1500 sisters continually serving God.

'Gilbert died at an old age of around 106 years, in the year of our Lord 1189, the day before the Nones of February, in the Reign of the Renowned King of England, Henry II. His own Merits requiring the fame, many Miracles attesting it, and divine Revelations persuading he was canonised and inserted into the Catalogue of Saints by Pope Innocent III, by the whole Court of Rome, at Anagni, in the presence of the clergy and people, in the year of the Incarnation of the Word 1201, the 3rd. day before the Ides of January, 3rd. year of the illustrious King John, the venerable Archbishop Hubert presiding in the See of Canterbury, he having by Order of the said Pope Innocent III, together with his Collegues, Eustace Bishop of Ely, Acharius Abbot of Peterborough, made diligent Inquisition into the miracles divinely wrought by him, and they transmitted to the See Apostolic their Attestations faithfully reduced into writing, and enclosed under their Seals. Whereby the Pope being certified of this Sanctity and Miracles, he resolved to add him to the Number of Gods Saints, in the 4th. year of his Pontificate. And the same year, by command of the said Pope, he was by the aforesaid Archbishop Hubert translated to this Tomb, on the 3rd. day before the Ides of October, in the presence of venerable Bishops of Norwich, Hereford, Landoff, and many other abbots and prelates of churches, and the great men and nobility of England, and a numerous assembly of clergy and people. To perpetuate the memory whereof, the said archbishop, bishops and abbots, affixed their Seals to this Writing, and

10

placed it in this Tomb.'

To all who should come to the Shrine of St Gilbert, the archbishop relaxed forty days penance and his bishops a hundred and ten days; moreover they were granted a share in the prayers and blessings of all who served in the churches of Sempringham and in the church of Canterbury forever.

1203 PRIOR OF SEMPRINGHAM – Roger de Sempringham.

1204 MASTER OF SEMPRINGHAM – John elected.

1205 MASTER OF SEMPRINGHAM – Gilbert elected.

1218 VICAR OF ST ANDREWS – Gilbert de Sempringham, presented by the master and convent of Sempringham. In the time of Bishop Hugh de Welles (probably about 1218).

1223 A visitation of the Order was conducted by the Abbot of Warden by order of the legate Otho. The injunctions of the Abbot of Warden showed that there was a tendency to relax the rule in somewhat unimportant matters. He directed that the cowl of the nuns should not be cut too long, that fine furs should not be used for the cloaks of the canons and nuns, that the canon's copes should be made *minime curiose*. Variety of pictures and superfluity of sculpture were forbidden. The rule of silence was to be more strictly observed. The proctors were bidden to provide the same food and drink for the nuns as for the canons, and not in future to buy beer for the canons when the nuns had only water to drink.

Honorius III restricted the admittance of any girl or woman into the Order who did not intend to become a nun.

1225 MASTER OF SEMPRINGHAM – Robert elected.

1226 Henry III gave the Master of the Order of Sempringham a present of 100 marks for their support.

1228 Henry III relieved the Priory of the expense of providing food during the meeting of the General Chapter at the motherhouse on the Rogation Days, by his gift of the church of Fordham, which was worth fifty-five marks a year.

1236 The Master of Sempringham was sometimes appointed by the Pope to hear causes which he had been asked to judge. In 1236 Gregory IX sent a mandate to the Master of Sempringham and the Dean of York to hear and bring to an end the cause between Bartholomew, rector of St Kerverne in Cornwall, and the Abbot and Convent of Beaulieu. In the same year Gregory ordered the Master of Sempringham, the Prior of Holy Trinity, London, and the Archdeacon of Sudbury to summon Edmund Rich, Archbishop of Canterbury, personally or by proctor, to Rome, to answer to the Pope, if he persisted in attempting to subject to himself the Abbot and monks of St Augustine's, Canterbury.

1242 PRIOR OF SEMPRINGHAM – Thomas de Sempringham.

1246 Innocent IV, granted that the Order might receive a bishop into their houses and show him hospitality as charity without thereby giving him any rights over them. When the news came of a bishops' approach, all the canons and brothers were summoned to the choir by a bell. They went forth in procession, two and two, and stood outside the gate of the monastery. As the bishop drew near they fell on their knees. The prior kissed his hand and gave him the holy water. A short service in the church, and a sermon from the bishop in the chapter, took place before he went to his lodging.

The annual payment of forty marks was felt as a grievous burden by the Abbot and convent of Paisley, and seems to have been ignored in several years, for in 1246 the Prior and convent of Sempringham appealed to Innocent IV to right them. They were obliged to pay the whole of the expenses of the suit and remit half the arrears of the debt on condition that the Abbot and convent of Paisley should make regular payments from that time onwards.

1247 The poverty of Sempringham was probably due to the papal extortions; 'there were two hundred women living at Sempringham and often needed the necessaries of life, and suffered in health for lack of them'.

Innocent IV, granted to the Master of Sempringham the right to appropriate the church of Horbling because of this. The legal expenses of the Order at the Papal Curia perhaps accounted for their poverty.

1251 MASTER OF SEMPRINGHAM – William de Sempringham, elected.

1253 The prior and convent obtained a grant of free warren in all their demesne lands.

1254 The spiritualities of Sempringham were assessed at £170, the temporalities at £196.9s.1d.

1256 The Gilbertines were dependent on the bishops 'for the ordination of their canons, and the benediction of their nuns'. Alexander IV, granted that 'any catholic prelate' might perform the function, 'should the bishop of the diocese make difficulties about doing it'.

A small counter seal
in use in 1261

Seal of Patrick
1262

12

1259 Alexander IV, sent an indulgence 'to the Master and brethren of the Order of Sempringham: that they shall cause their churches and chapels, in which vicars have not been appointed, to be served as heretofore by their own chaplains, and the vicarages shall not be taxed nor perpetual vicars appointed against the will of the said Master and brethren, notwithstanding any indulgence granted to the Archbishop of York, or any other in regard to such taxation and appointment'.

1262 MASTER OF SEMPRINGHAM – Patrick de Sempringham elected.

1268 VICAR OF ST ANDREWS – Gilbert Wade, chaplain, presented on the resignation of Gilbert to the vicarage of the church of St Andrew of Sempringham. Patron —Prior and convent of Sempringham. Instituted 14 kal March, in the 11th year of Bishop Gravesend (16 February 1268-9)

In King Henry III's reign there was a charter granted to the monks of Sempringham, to hold a fair at Stow Green, which, doubtless in those early times, would be a great source of revenue.

A very important papal visitation was undertaken when Cardinal Ottoboni was legate in England from 1265 to 1268. He went to Sempringham in person, but delegated the duty of visiting other houses of the Order to members of his household.

After careful study of the reports of the visitors, a series of injunctions was drawn up by Ralph of Huntingdon, a Dominican chaplain in the service of the legate, with the aid of Richard, chief scrutator of the Order. Principles of the Order had been violated, the master and heads of houses had shown arbitrary tendencies. It was necessary to insist that the master should strive to rule by love than fear, and to threaten the priors and sub-priors who were stern to the verge of cruelty and deposition. The lucrative practice of collecting wool and selling it with the produce of their own flocks, was strictly, though in vain, forbidden. Lay-brothers who were skilled in surgery might only practise their art by the priors leave, and if the patients were men. The master was to see that they were not stinted in clothes or food.

1247 VICAR OF ST ANDREWS – William de Gayton, priest on the death of Gilbert Wade. Patrons – Prior of the Blessed Mary of Sempringham. Instituted 7 kal November in the 16th year of Bishop Gravesend (26 October 1274) at Stowe.

1275 An Inquisition taken by the Justices Itinerant in the third year of Edward I, shows that the Monastery of Sempringham held three carucates of land of Gilbert de Gant, on which the Priory was founded, being the gift of Gilbert de Gant, and they were not geldable, also three carucates in the same town, the alms of Reginald de Baworth, £20 per annum. One carucate at Kirkby, the gift of Adam St Leonard; and 100 acres of wood in the Manor of Aslackby, of Hubert de Ria; half a knight's fee of 340 acres at Horbling, of Roger Goylin; 15 plough-lands at Stow, of Robert Pikeson; and one carucate

13

or 60 acres at Welthorp, worth 30s. a year to Lawrence Preston; Hugh de Bajocis afterwards gave them land in Sempringham; Robert Luterel at Stamford, Ketton, Cotesmore, Casterton, and Irnham, to maintain three Chaplains to say masses for his soul, viz., one at Sempringham, one at Irnham, and one at St Mary's at Stamford.

1276 In the time of Edward I, the immunities of the Gilbertines and other Orders had become a general grievance. The jurors of the wapentake of Aswardshurn in Lincolnshire said before the justices, sent down by Edward I, on special commission in the fourth year of his reign, 'that the Order of Sempringham had liberties granted to it by the kings of England which hindered common justice and subverted the royal power, because of those liberties they would not answer any one in pleas about forbidden distraint or any other pleas before justices except the King himself and his chief justice'.

MASTER OF SEMPRINGHAM – John de Homerton elected.

1277 On October 16th, Edward I sent a mandate from Shrewsbury 'to all bailiffs and others not to take from the Master and Prior of Sempringham against their will any of the grain which they have for their support, although the King has commanded provision of grant to be made in the various counties of the kingdom for himself and his army in Wales, and to restore to them whatever grain has been taken already'.

1278 VICAR OF ST ANDREWS – Gerinus, priest on the resignation of William de Gayton. Patrons – Priory of the Blessed Mary of Sempringham, Instituted 5 kal March, 21st year of Bishop Gravesend (26 February 1278-9) at Stamford.

1280 Mattersey Priory was appropriated to the house of Sempringham to repair the losses by sudden fire; in this sudden fire many writings are reputed to be lost.

1281 VICAR OF ST ANDREWS – Benedict de Ringesdon, chaplain, on the resignation of Gerin de Stowe. Patrons – Semplingham Priory. Instituted 6 kal March in the 2nd year of Bishop Sutton (25 February 1281-2) at Leicester.

Roger, Prior of Sempringham, who sued Walter de Poynton of Stow, and Alice his wife, for a toft and two bovates in Stow by Trikingham as the right of his church of Sempringham. The jury said that Hugh de Trikingham, Knight, gave this land to the house of Sempringham, in free alms together with Peter, then tenant thereof in villenage, with all his chattels and issue. Therefore judgement was given for the Prior.

1283 VICAR OF ST ANDREWS – John de Herlauston, priest, on the resignation of Benedict de Ringesdon. Patron – Semplingham Priory. Instituted 8 ides April in the 3rd year of Bishop Sutton. (6 April 1283) at Milton.

MASTER OF SEMPRINGHAM – Roger de Bolingbroke elected.

On November 11th, Edward II wrote to the prior and prioress asking them to admit the child of Prince Llewellyn of Wales, Princess Gwenllian to their Order and habit, 'having the Lord before our eyes, pitying also her sex and age, that the innocent and unwitting may not seem to atone for the iniquity and ill-doing of the wicked and contemplating especially the life of your Order'.

1284 VICAR OF SEMPRINGHAM – Robert de Bilingburg, chaplain, on the resignation of John de Herlauxton, because of his admission to the vicarage of the prebendal church of Keton. Patrons — Sempringham Priory. Instituted 4 nones March, 4th year of Bishop Sutton (4 March 1283-4) at Lincoln.

William and Alice de Poynton quit claimed to William, Prior of Sempringham, for the sum of £10, a messuage and two bovates of land in Stow.

The seven daughters of Prince David of Wales, were, on their falling into the hands of King Edward I, consigned to the charge of the nuns of Sempringham Priory.

1287 Four years after the admission of Gwenllian to Sempringham, Edward issued a mandate to Thomas Normanvill 'to go to the places where the daughters of Llewellyn and of David his brother, who have taken the veil in the Order of Sempringham, are dwelling, and to report upon their state and custody by next parliament'. He allowed Sempringham Priory to aquire certain lands in mortmain because he had charged it with Gwenllian.

1288 VICAR OF ST ANDREWS – Peter de Birthorp, chaplain, on the resignation of Robert de Billingburg (sic), chaplain. Patron – Semplingham Priory. Instituted 3 kal September, 9th year of Bishop Sutton (30 August 1288) at Lincoln.

1290 The twelfth century priory church was reported to 'threaten ruin' and the building was already causing anxiety, when Pope Nicholas IV granted an indulgence of a year and forty days to penitents who visited the priory church on four feasts of the Blessed Virgin and those of St Andrew and St Gilbert. The papal indulgences were intended to attract the offerings of pilgrims and penitents, and may have enabled the prior and convent to undertake urgent repairs to the church.

Nicholas IV granted a licence to the prior and canons to have within their house a discreet and learned doctor of theology to teach those of their brethren who desired to study that science. For some years the master had sent certain canons of the Order to study at Cambridge, so a house of residence was secured in the town, and contributions were afterwards levied from all the houses of the Order for the support of the canons as scholars.

1291 On January 2nd the prior and convent secured indulgences for those who visited each of the following chapels: St John the Evangelist, St Stephen, and St Catherine on the feast and octaves of the saints and the dedication of the priory church.

VICAR OF ST ANDREWS – Henry de Carleby, chaplain, on the resignation of Peter de Birthorp, for the sake of his institution to the vicarage of Stow. Patrons – Semplingham Priory. Instituted 8 ides May, 11th year of Bishop Sutton (8 May 1291) at Stow Park.

The assessment of the temporalities had risen to £219.17s.11½d. The property continued to increase, as several licences were obtained subsequently to appropriate numerous small grants of land in mortmain.

1292   VICAR OF ST ANDREWS – John de Folkyngham, chaplain, on the resignation of Henry de Carleby for the sake of institution to the vicarage of Stow. Patron – Semplingham Priory. Instituted 2 kal May, 12th year of Bishop Sutton (30 April 1292) at Elnestowe.

Robert Luterel, Rector of Irnham, near Stamford, 'gave the Manor in the parish of St Peter at Stamford to the Priory of Sempringham, desirous to increase the numbers of the convent and that it might ever have scholars at Stamford studying divinity and philosophy'. Robert Luterel stipulated that the master should provide a chaplain to minister to the spiritual needs of scholars in the chantry of our Lady at the Manor in Stamford.

1293   The right of holding a fair in the Manor of Wrightbald was conceded.

1294   John de London petitioned the King for a licence to assign some property to the priory and convent of Sempringham.

1295   'That that which concerns all might be approved by all', Edward I summoned the master of Sempringham, with archbishops and bishops, abbots and priors, earls and barons, and representatives of shires and towns, to the great Parliament, which met at Westminster on November 13th 1295. In that year the King granted a licence for the prior and convent of Sempringham 'to stop a lane called "Cheke Lane", in the parish of St Sepulchre's in the suburb of London, adjoining their houses of the west side, and to enclose the same for the enlargement of their site'. There, not far from Smithfield, the master of Sempringham lodged when business drew him to London.

1296   In August, the abbot of Paisley acknowledged for himself and the convent that a sum of forty marks was owing to the master of Sempringham. He promised to pay ten marks on August 30th and thirty marks at Michaelmas. The ten marks were paid, but there are no later receipts.

1298   MASTER OF SEMPRINGHAM – Philip de Burton, elected.

1300   Robert, son of Robert Coffin petitioned the King for a licence to assign some property to the prior and convent.

Hugo, son of John, son of Ralf de Rippinghale petitioned to the King for a licence to assign some property to the prior and convent.

1301 PRIOR OF SEMPRINGHAM – John de Hamilton occurs.

The building of a new and larger church at Sempringham was begun under Prior John de Hamilton. It is probable that imminent danger to the structure induced the prior and convent to begin building. It was soon apparent that a fresh source of income for a fabric fund was essential.

VICAR OF ST ANDREWS – Robert de Braiceby, chaplain, on the institution of John de Folkingham to the vicarage of Buckeston in the diocese of Norwich. Patrons – Semplingham Priory. Instituted 3 ides June, in the 1st year of Bishop Dalderby (11 June 1301) at Buckden.

On December 13th Edward I in consideration of his kindly affection towards the Order of the Gilbertines of Sempringham, and because we have charged the Priory of Sempringham with Gwenllian, daughter of Llewellyn, late Prince of Wales, granted a licence in mortmain to Master Robert Luterel to grant 4 messuages, 2 plough-lands, and 12 marks rent in Ketene and Cotesmore, and a messuage, 1 plough-land, and 10 marks rent with the appurtenances in Stamford and Castreton to the prior and convent of Sempringham.

Robert de Kirkston and others have petitioned the King for a licence to assign some property to the prior and convent.

Master Robert petitioned the King for a licence to assign some property to the prior and convent. He also assigned a second lot.

1302 VICAR OF ST ANDREWS – Adam de Lavington, chaplain, on the resignation of Robert de Braiceby, Patrons – Semplingham Priory. Instituted 6 ides October, in the 3rd year of Bishop Dalderby (10 October 1302) at Bikelswade.

1303 The prior held in Lincolnshire half a knight's fee in Horbling, half in Irnham, half less one-twelfth in Laughton and Aslackby, a quarter in Cranwell, a quarter in Bulby, one-fifth in Bulby and Southorpe, one-eighth in Fulbeck, one-eighth in Scredington, one-sixteenth in Osbournby, one-twentieth in Bitchfield.

A canon named Robert Manning of Bourne began to write, in the cloister of Sempringham, his book called 'Handlyng Sinne', which was an English version of Waddington's Manuel des Peches, a satire on the failings and vices of English men and women of all classes of society. He had previously studied at Cambridge.

On November 3rd John Dalderby, Bishop of Lincoln, in a letter addressed to the prior and convent, reciting 'Whereas Mr Robert Luterel has granted you a manor which he had in the parish of St Peter's, Stamford, by way of charity, wishing that scholars, proportionate to the augmented number of your convent studying the scriptures and philosophy, may live in the same manor together with a secular chaplain to celebrate in the chapel of Our Lady in the same manor, commending this pious deed, though there has been a chantry founded in the said chapel for a long time past, yet to confirm the wishes of the said Mr. Robert and for the solace and quit of the students', granted special licence for them to hold the manor for these purposes.

It can hardly be denied that this is nothing less than the foundation of a university hall at Stamford, where members of the Gilbertine Order were to go and study theology and philosophy.

Difficulties in the Order

1304 The financial liabilities of Sempringham were now increasing. At the General Chapter of the Order which met this year, it was decided, on account of frequent and continuous royal and papal tenths, contributions and exactions, that in priory a grange, church, or fixed rent should be set aside to meet these demands. Owing to the Scottish wars the payment of £26.13s.11d. from the abbey of Paisley for the wardrobe of the nuns ceased altogether, it had been made irregularly since the Gilbertine house at Dalmulin, on the north bank of the Ayr, founded and endowed by Walter FitzAlan about 1221, was abandond and its possessions transferred to the abbot and convent of Paisley for an annual rent.

The prior and convent of Sempringham sent a petition to Pope Clement V for help to secure a fabric fund, and thus to override possible obstruction by the bishop of Lincoln.

A constitution by Cardinal Ottoboni forbade bishops to assign a parish church to the uses of a monastery unless it was overwhelmingly burdened by poverty. Almost all the parish churches in the patronage of Sempringham Priory had already been appropriated to the uses of the monastery. These were Sempringham with the chapel of Poynton, Stow with the chapel of Birthorpe, Billingborough, Horbling, Walcot, Cranwell, and Kirkby-la-Thorpe. Thrussington in 'Leicestershire and Norton in Lincolnshire, each assessed for taxation at £13.6s.8d. were still rectories, and therefore a possible source for a fabric fund.

In the petition to Clement V the prior and the convent declared that their church was in dangerous condition and they had begun to rebuild it or to build it anew, a most costly undertaking, and they sought help from the Pope and others.

1306 Clement V gave permission to the prior and convent to appropriate the churches of Thrussington and Norton Disney for the purpose of finishing the building of the new church and as a perpetual fabric fund for repairs and maintenance. The papal bull was to take effect on the death or resignation of the rectors, and without requiring the consent of the bishop of Lincoln, on condition that the prior and convent found suitable priests to serve the parishes. These appropriations would eventually form the nucleus of a fabric fund.

Sempringham needed to appropriate the church of Fordham to meet the expenses of the General Chapter.

1307 At the request of a knight, John de Avernia, Pope Clement V gave permission to the master of the Order of Sempringham, the prior and convent for the enclosed nuns of the Order to have grated windows made through which they might see and worship mass. Hitherto a solid screen of stone or wood had separated them from the altar during celebration of mass.

The prior and convent had the support and sympathy of the new lord who had come to Folkingham. The last descendant of that Gilbert de Gant of Folkingham who had given the site of the priory had died childless in 1298.

Edward II granted Folkingham and other lands in Lincolnshire to Henry de Beaumont. He was the younger son of Louis de Brenne, Viscount of Beaumont and Maine, and had attended Edward I in 1302 in the Scottish War.

He was grandson of John of Brienne, King of Jerusalem and Emperor of Constantinople. Edward also gave him the Isle of Man.

1309 In 1308 Sir Henry de Beaumont was appointed joint warden of Scotland, south of the Forth, and his first act as a benefactor of Sempringham was to get Edward II's consent this year to the alienation by the Scottish Abbey of Lindores (county of Fife) of the advowson of Whissendine (county of Rutland) to Sempringham Priory. Lindores had drawn a pension of £6.13s.4d. from Whissendine since 1237-8. It seems probable that John Dalderby, Bishop of Lincoln, was unwilling to agree to the appropriation of yet another parish church, and one assessed for taxation at £36.13s.4d. to Sempringham.

1310 It was practically impossible to refuse loans to the King, though the Order must sometimes have been put to considerable inconvenience in parting with the money. Edward II frequently applied to the master of Sempringham in his financial difficulties. In June this year he asked him to aid him 'by way of a loan', with victuals for his Scottish expedition, and 'to take his request so great and so hastily made to heart and to perform it willingly, as he esteems the honour and profit of the King and his realm'.

1311
Seal of Philip de Burton
MASTER OF SEMPRINGHAM

1312 John, Prior of Sempringham, rode off with his canons and servants to the park at Birthorpe, to recover the goods which Roger de Birthorpe and Geoffrey Luterel of Irnham had seized when they broke the doors and walls of

19

Sempringham.

PRIOR OF SEMPRINGHAM – John de Hamilton occurs.

1313 King Edward II applied to the master of Sempringham for a loan of a thousand marks for his Scottish expedition.

1315 King Edward II asked for a loan again from the master of Sempringham in March this year, the loan demanded from the Order for the purchase of provisions for the expedition to resist the Scottish invasion was two thousand pounds, although the whole revenue of the Order scarcely exceeded three thousand pounds. The Gilbertines suffered with the rest of the nation under the burden of Purveyance.

1317 Edward II wrote to Pope John XXII telling him that sometime since the prior and convent of Sempringham had begun to build another church of marvellous greatness (mire magnitudinis), and that he himself knew well, the costs were far beyond their resources, and he prayed the Pope to decree the appropriation of Whissendine for the completion and maintenance of the new church and to provide other necessaries for the numerous nuns, daughters of nobles, among them he mentioned Gwenllian the daughter of Llewellyn, the last King of Wales, who had been brought thither in her cradle in 1283. He pleaded that the Order of Sempringham was English and therefore the dearer to him.

1319 This year the Pope sent a mandate to the Archbishop of Canterbury to appropriate Whissendine to Sempringham, and the archbishop duly executed it; the reason given in the bull was the payment from Paisley of £26.13s.4d. had ceased for over fourteen years, and it was never resumed. The rector did not resign until 1327 or 1328, only the pension of £6.13s.4d. was received, and it is probable that the fabric fund received little or nothing from Whissendine. The maintenance of two hundred nuns was indeed a heavy charge on the resources of the monastery and extreme variations in prices are noted in the Annals of Sempringham.

Walter, Archbishop of Canterbury, blessed fifty-two nuns of Sempringham, twenty-five of Haverholme, five of Cattley, and one General Scrutatrix, at Sempringham on April 17th.

A visitation of Archbishop Reynolds to Sempringham on October 5th.

1320 Financial liabilities were piled up at the priory, and the prior had recourse to money-lenders. This year he was indebted to Geoffrey de Brampton for £1000.

1321 The Master of Sempringham was summoned to Parliament at Westminster, in July, in which the DeSpencers were condemned to forfeiture and exile. Three months later Edward took up arms.

From 1315–1321 (seven years), the greatest famine known in England prevailed everywhere and large numbers of people died for want of food. This dearth greatly affected the monasteries. The prices of corn then was abnormally high. A quarter of wheat sold at 24s. and more; barley at 16s; oats at 20s. If these prices were compared with prices in 1287 – a year of plenty – it would be seen how high they were during the time of the famine, for wheat was 1s.8d. per quarter; barley 2s.2d.; and oats 2s.

1322 The master of Sempringham was requested to send as many foot soldiers as he could muster at Coventry on February 28th, to march against the rebels of adherents of the Earl of Lancaster. The Annals of Sempringham contain an account of the rising. The writer recorded Edward's victory at Boroughbridge and his terrible vengeance on the conspirators, giving without any comment, a long list of knights who were hanged, drawn, and quartered, showing the characteristic medieval indifference to human life.

In the Parliament which met at York on May 2nd, Margaret, Countess of Cornwall, wife of Sir Hugh de Audley and niece of the King, was judged to continue in guard at Sempringham among the nuns, where she arrived on May 16th and continued there.

1324 The prior borrowed £100 from Antony Maloisel of Genoa.

Joan, the daughter of Sir Roger de Mortimer of Wigmore who escaped out of the Tower of London, was sent to Sempringham by the King, whither she came on Whitsun Eve, 2nd June.

1325 PRIOR OF SEMPRINGHAM – John of Glinton occurs.

The prior borrowed £80 from Annotus Grimaldi of Chieri.

1326 The prior borrowed £40 from Bartolomeo Richi of Chieri.

The annals of the Gilbertine House were recorded in French from 1290-1326, 'Le Livere de Reis de Brittanie'.

1327 When Edward III stayed some days at Sempringham, he granted Gwenllian a yearly pension of twenty pounds for life, a very liberal allowance compared with the payments made by Edward I for the Scottish captives.

1328 The Gilbertines struggled repeatedly against the bishops' visitations. In the characteristic way of the Middle Ages, the bishops strove to break through the privilege of the Order and to establish a precedent for the rights which they claimed as due to their office. John XXII sent 'a commission and mandate to Henry, Bishop of Lincoln, to annul the sentence of excommunication issued by the President of the Order of St Gilbert, against Roger de Stanes, canon of the Priory of Sempringham, on certain unsworn charges made against him which he denied on oath'.

1329 The prior was owing to Thomas de Holm, a merchant from Beverley £300.

1330 VICAR OF ST ANDREWS – John Barn, priest, on the death of Sir Adam de Lavington. Patrons – Brother John the prior, and the convent of Sempringham. Instituted 2 ides June (12 June 1330) at Thame.

The priors at Sempringham and Haverholme accompanied by several of their canons and other persons, were charged by William of Querington and Brian of Herdeby with raiding a close at Evedon, cutting down trees, carrying away timber, and depasturing and destroying corn with the plough cattle.

1331 John de Glenton, prior, acknowledges for himself and his convent, that he owes William de Kendale of Glenton £20.

The prior lodged a complaint against Brian of Herdeby and others who had assaulted a canon and a lay-brother at Evedon, consumed his crops and grass at Burton, hunted in his free warren there, and carried off hares and partridges.

1332 The prior and convent sought for more funds from indulgences. They secured one from Henry Burghersh, Bishop of Lincoln, for those visiting the image of the Blessed Virgin Mary in Sempringham Priory Church.

MASTER OF SEMPRINGHAM – John de Glinton elected.

The Master of Sempringham was regularly summoned to Parliament up to this year.

In the midst of their embarrassment, the King requested the prior to grant a subsidy in aid of the expenses incurred for the marriage of the King's sister Eleanor to Reginald, Count of Guelders, the granting of which subsidy should not be drawn into a precedent to his prejudice.

PRIOR OF SEMPRINGHAM – John of Glinton occurs.

1333 The prior of Sempringham received a mandate to send to York by the morrow of the Ascension at the latest a stout cart, well bound with iron, and five horses for the King's service against the Scots.

1337 The King excused the prior and convent from a payment of £39.15s.4d., their contingent for the tenth of the first year for the last three yearly tenths, granted by the clergy of the province of Canterbury.

Gwenllian daughter of the Prince of Wales, died, after fifty-four years of life in the Order.

A grant of £20 a year to Joan and Eleanor, nuns of the priory, daughters of Hugh de Despenser, senior.

1341 The Master of Sempringham pleaded that he ought not to be summoned to Parliament and was exempt for the future. Attendance at Parliament was so great a burden and expense that the priors and abbots diminished in number from 80 in 1301, to 27 the normal number after 1341.

John de Glinton resigned as Master of the Order.

MASTER OF SEMPRINGHAM – Robert de Navenby elected.

1342 The prior and convent sought indulgences from Bishop Thomas Bek, Bishop of Lincoln, in which the great expense of the new church still in building was mentioned.

1345 The King excused the prior and convent again from payment of £39.15s.7d., their contingent for the tenth granted by the clergy of the province of Canterbury.

'Queen Philippa, Henry, Earl of Lancaster and Leicester, Steward of England, his son Henry, Earl of Derby, Thomas, Earl of Warwick. Marshal of England, Hugh Despenser, the King's kinsman, Lord of Glomer and Morgan', signified to Clement VI, 'that although the Master, priors, brethren, and sisters of the Order of Sempringham, immediately subject to the Roman Church, are exempt from ordinary or legatine authority, nevertheless certain ordinaries endeavour to enforce jurisdiction over them. The aforesaid persons therefore pray the Pope to confirm the said privilege and exemption, and to declare the said Order to be free from all ordinary jurisdiction for ever'. Clement VI granted 'full exemption to the Master, priors, canons, lay-brothers, nuns, and sisters, present and future, and to the monasteries'.

The Order of Sempringham was paying a pound of gold every two years to the papal treasurer in 1345; at the request of King Edward and Queen Isabella, his mother, the pound was reduced to a mark.

1346 The prior held a knight's fee in Stragglethorpe, one-sixth in Walcote, and one-thirty-second in Aunsley.

1348 It was a disastrous year of the Black Death.

On November 6th Edward III granted a licence to Sir Robert Tiffour to alienate the advowson of the parish church of Hacconby to the prior and convent of Sempringham and a licence for its appropriation 'towards a more abundant subvention of the clothing of the nuns in return for a perpetual chantry to be founded in the priory church'.

1349 On the eve of Trinity Sunday there was a great storm and flood, the water in the church rose as high as the capitals of the pillars, and in the cloister and other buildings it was six feet deep. Many of the books were destroyed. According to the Institutes of the Order books were in the charge of the nuns, and as in other Orders they were probably kept in a cupboard in the cloister or in a book-room opening out of it. Eighteen sacks of wool were damaged, a heavy loss; at the beginning of the fourteenth century the annual sale of wool amounted to twenty-five sacks varying in price from £20.6s.8d. a sack to £6, according to the quality.

The Black Death

The Black Death had swept over England from 1346 and into 1349, slaying its thousands. This was most disastrous at Sempringham, for at least half its members perished, and none were forthcoming to fill the empty places. Sheep were affected by it, and died in thousands, and the harvest rotted for lack of labourers to reap it.

VICAR OF ST ANDREWS – John de Irnham, priest, on the death of Sir John Barn. Patrons – the prior and convent of Sempringham. Instituted 8 ides October (8 October 1349) at Gosberkyrke.

1351 VICAR OF ST ANDREWS – John de Stowe by Trikyngham, priest, on the resignation of John de Irnham. Patrons – the prior and convent of Sempringham. Instituted 7 kal June (26 May 1351) at Hupwode.

1361 VICAR OF ST ANDREWS – Thomas Caworth of Irnham, priest, on the resignation of John de Stowe. Patrons – prior and convent of Sempringham. Instituted nones March (7 March 1361-2) at Lidyngton.

1363 There are indications of a decline in discipline and morals, as well as in numbers. The Master, Robert of Navenby, was seeking to obtain from Urban V the rights of a mitred abbot that he might himself give benediction to his nuns. The Bishop of Lincoln however protested.

1364 MASTER OF SEMPRINGHAM – William of Prestwold, elected.

PRIOR OF SEMPRINGHAM – William of Prestwold occurs.

1366 PRIOR OF SEMPRINGHAM – William Cusom occurs.

PRIORESSES OF SEMPRINGHAM – Edusia of Pointon, Elizabeth of Arderne, Natilda of Willoughby.

Many nuns of Sempringham had not received benediction, and as the Master, William of Prestwold, refused to listen to the Prioress, they petitioned Bishop Bokyngham, who came to Sempringham, to right them. The number of nuns had then fallen to sixty-seven.

1369 It is probable that gifts to the fabric fund were made by members of the Beaumont family, the Lords of Folkingham. Henry de Beaumont was buried in the priory church this year.

1370 The central Norman tower of the Parish Church was taken down sometime between 1350-1370 and the present tower was built in the style of that period on the original foundations.

1372 VICAR OF ST ANDREWS – Roger de Camelton of Sempringham, priest, on the resignation of Thomas de Chaworth of Irnham. Patrons the prior and convent of Sempringham. Instituted 5 May 1372 at Lidynton.

1382 Richard II granted a licence for the master and priors of the Order to seize and detain all vagabond canons and lay-brothers, due to the Order being short of these men.

1383 Mandates were issued to the sheriffs and others to arrest an apostate canon.

1388 VICAR OF ST ANDREWS – John Crees, priest, on the resignation of Roger de Camelton. Patrons – the prior and convent of Sempringham. Instituted 4 March 1388-9 at Sleaford.

1390 Mandates were issued again to the sheriffs and others to arrest any apostate canon.

1392 The church was still unfinished for lack of money, and the prior and convent sent a petition to Pope Boniface IX, asking for the appropriation of the parish church of Hacconby, assessed for taxation at £16 a year: they pleaded that their former church was ruined and prostrated to the ground with age, and they had begun to rebuild it at no little expense, they had been hindered by their poverty and the malignity of the times. In response to this appeal Boniface IX sent a mandate for the appropriation which took effect on the resignation of the rector in or before 1395.

1393 MASTER OF SEMPRINGHAM – William de Beverley elected.

A knight, Sir William Marmyon, who died this year, had willed to be buried at Sempringham Priory church near the tomb of Elizabeth, his second wife, but in a codicil he desired to be buried near his first wife at Lavington.

VICAR OF ST ANDREWS – William, son of William Peretson of Coryngham, priest, on the resignation of Sir John Crece. Patrons – the prior and convent of Sempringham. Instituted 3rd August 1393 at Sleaford.

1396 On September 8th, Henry de Beaumont's son John made his will on the day before his death at Stirling; in it he left his 'little cross made of our Lord's Cross' to Sempringham Priory church where he desired to be buried 'near the tomb of his most honoured lord and father'.

The licence for the appropriation of Hacconby church did not take effect until this decade, when the revenues of Hacconby church, after a provision for a vicar, were asssigned to the building fund of the still unfinished church.

1397 Pope Boniface IX sent a mandate to the Archbishop of Canterbury and York and the Bishop of Ely, to investigate the charges against William of Beverley, who was elected master in 1393. It was reported that on his visitation he took immoderate procurations, burdened the houses by the excessive number of the members of his household and of his horses, and committed many grievences and enormities against the statutes of the Order. The bishops were to punish him if guilty, to visit the houses, correct and reform what was amiss, to revise the statutes of the Order, and frame others if expedient.

1399 Pope Boniface IX gave permission to the master, priors, canons, lay-brothers, nuns and sisters of the Order of Sempringham to farm, to fit lay-men of clerks for a fixed time, their manors, churches, chapels, stipends, and possessions, without requiring the licence of the ordinary. Thus they lost their profits from the wool trade, which had probably exceeded their revenues from all other sources. The sheep died in thousands from the pestilence, and it was in fact impossible for the Gilbertines to carry on their former occupations of farming and trading with any success.

1400 Pope Boniface IX granted one of his most noted indulgences in the

Catholic world, known as the Portiuncula, which took its name from the little church about a mile from Assisi which was rebuilt by St Francis. All those who visited the Priory Church of Sempringham from first to second vespers on the Feast of the Annunciation and the two following days, and gave alms for the conservation and repair of the church, and were contrite, confessed, and absolved, were liberated (*a culp et a pena*) in heaven and on earth from the time of baptism up to the moment of entrance into the church.

Crowds were anticipated when the indulgence of the Portiuncula was granted; the prior and six other confessors of his choice, regular canons or secular priests, were given power to hear confessions and grant absolutions except in cases reserved to the Pope himself.

1405   The Pope issued another mandate, stating that William of Beverley, Master of the Order, had dilapidated divers goods, movable and immovable, had enormously damaged it, reduced it to great poverty, and continued in the same course. If found guilty he was to be deprived. However, whether the Order obtained any redress is not known.

1407   MASTER OF SEMPRINGHAM – John Hanworth elected.

1409   Work on the bell-tower over the crossing was in progress, when John Huntyndon remembered it with a legacy in his will dated June 17th.

VICAR OF ST ANDREWS – Sir John Cham, on the resignation of William Peretson, for the sake of an exchange with the church of Flokton in the diocese of Norwich. Patrons – the prior and convent of Sempringham. Instituted 6th August 1409 at Sleaford.

1412   The first bell in the Abbey Church was probably founded around 1412, by Anketel de Mallorby? The inscription on the bell is 'Sancte Gabriel Ora Pro Nobis', translated 'Holy Gabriel Pray for Us'. This bell has a mouth diameter of 32 inches, with an approximate weight of roughly 6 cwts. 1 qr.

1413   Henry, son of John de Beaumont of Folkingham was buried in the Priory Church.

VICAR OF ST ANDREWS – Nicholas Horne on the resignation of Sir John Cham for the sake of an exchange with the vicarage of Amwyk. Patrons – the prior and convent of Sempringham. Instituted 3rd January 1413 at Sleaford.

1416   John Marmyon, Esq., who died this year, desired to be buried in Sempringham Priory Church, and he left an annual rent of £1.6s.8d. to his daughter, Mabel, who was one of the nuns.

1417   VICAR OF ST ANDREWS – William Peretson, priest, on the death of Sir Nicholas Horne. Patrons – the prior and convent of Sempringham. Instituted 12th January 1417, at Sleaford.

1428   The prior held one-quarter of a knight's fee in Thrussington, Leicestershire.

1431 VICAR OF ST ANDREWS – Richard Semon, priest, on the death of William Peretson. Patrons – the prior and convent of Sempringham. Instituted 28th September 1431 at Lincoln.

1432 A visitation from Bishop Gray to Sempringham on Friday 2nd May.

1435 A visitation from Bishop Gray to Sempringham on September 24th.

1445 During the fourteenth and fifteenth centuries the Order fell into great poverty. On February 23rd, Henry VI exempted Nicholas Resby, Master of the Order of Sempringham, and all the houses, for ever, from all aids, subsidies, tollages, and payments of every kind. He granted that they should never pay any tax contributed by the whole body of the clergy, nor any tenths or fifteenths levied on the whole realm. Four months previously, on October 26th 1444, he had granted this exemption to Watton Priory.

MASTER OF SEMPRINGHAM – Nicholas Resby occurs.

1449 VICAR OF ST ANDREWS – Sir Thomas Browne, priest, on the resignation of Richard Seyman. Patrons – prior and convent Sempringham. Instituted 8th August 1449, at Bukden.

The seal attached to a deed of 1457 is in the shape of a pointed oval, and represents the 'Annunciation of the Virgin'; in the base there is a carved corbel.

1494 VICAR OF ST ANDREWS – Sir Thomas Clyffe, priest, on the death of Sir Thomas Browne. Patrons – the prior and convent of Sempringham. Instituted 2nd April 1494, at Sempringham.

Decline and Dissolution

1500 With the abandonment of farming, except on the immediate demesne, the need of the Order for lay-brothers disappeared. They probably died out altogether in the fifteenth century, as there is no record of any. Servants, too, probably very largely took place of the lay-sisters.

1501 MASTER OF SEMPRINGHAM – James occurs.

At the General Chapter held at St Catherine's, Lincoln, it was resolved that the number of canons, which in those days was less than usual, should be increased. The priors were to seek suitable persons, that with greater numbers religion might prosper. This attempt at revival was to some extent successful, for in several houses, as at Sempringham itself, the number of canons fixed at this chapter was reached before the dissolution.

1503 VICAR OF ST ANDREWS – Sir Richard Hansby, priest, on the resignation of Sir Thomas Clife. Patrons – the prior and convent of Sempringham. Instituted 27th April 1503, at Lydington.

1508 MASTER OF SEMPRINGHAM – Thomas occurs.

1509 VICAR OF ST ANDREWS – Sir John Durhaunt, priest, canon of Sempringham, on the resignation of Sir Richard Hensby. Patrons – the prior and convent of Sempringham. Instituted 22nd October 1509, at Lydington.

1522 Henry VI could not bind his successors forever. An annual grant was to be made by the spirituality, for the King's personal expenses in France for the recovery of that crown. The grant of the Prior of Sempringham was fixed at £40, that of the Prior of Chicksand £20.

PRIOR OF SEMPRINGHAM – John Jordan occurs.

1526 VICAR OF ST ANDREWS – Sir John Raketh of Rakes was vicar.

1529 PRIOR OF SEMPRINGHAM – John Jordon occurs.

1535 In 1535 the clear yearly value of the house was £317.4s.1d. Of this sum £128.16s.7d. was drawn from the rectories of Sempringham with the chapel of Pointon, Stow with the chapel of Birthorpe, Billingborough, Horbling, Walcote, Laughton, Cranwell, Norton Disney, and Hacconby in Lincolnshire, Whissendine in Rutlandshire, Fordham in Cambridgeshire, Thurstanton in Leicestershire, and Buxton in Norfolk. The remainder of the property included granges or lands and tenements at Sempringham, Threekingham, Stow, Pointon, Dowsby, Ringesdon dyke, Billingborough, Horbling, Walcote, Newton, Pykworth, Osbournby, Kysby, Folkingham, Aslackby, Woodgrange, Kirkby, Bulby, Morton, Wrightbald, Brothertoft, Wilton, Kirton Holme, Wrangle, Cranwell, Stragglethorpe, Carlton, and Fulbeck and a few other places in Lincolnshire; Ketton, Cottesmore and Pickwell in Rutland; Thurstanton and Willoughby in Leicestershire; Bramcote, Trowell and Chinwell in Nottinghamshire; and Walton in Derbyshire. Six granges appear to have been farmed by bailiffs for the monastery and the rest were let on lease. The demesnes of Sempringham were worth £26.13s.4d. a year.

MASTER OF SEMPRINGHAM – Thomas de Hurtesley occurs.

PRIOR OF SEMPRINGHAM – John Jordan occurs.

1536 MASTER OF SEMPRINGHAM – Robert Holgate.

As is clear from the commissioners instructions (Doc. 11) the decision was reached as early as April this year to exempt the whole of the Gilbertine Order from the Dissolution of the Monasteries. This may have been due to an anticipation of the problem of finding alternative accomodation for the seven

28

smaller communities of this Order which contained both men and women, but is far more likely to have resulted from the influence of the Master of the Order of St Gilbert of Sempringham, Robert Holgate, President of the Council of the North.

1538 By early autumn this year, the pace of the dissolution had quickened. In September William Petre was in Lincolnshire and Nottinghamshire, where, in the course of just over two weeks, he received the surrender of nine Gilbertine houses, including Sempringham itself, each of the deeds surrendered carrying the seal not only of the priory but also of the Grand Master of the Order, Robert Holgate, who barely two years earlier had obtained for his Order complete exemption from parliamentary suppression. Like all the small houses which were given formal exemption from the act of 1536, these Gilbertine convents followed the normal course and surrendered by deed of gift.

The surrender of the monastery to the King

On September 18th Robert, Master of the Order of Sempringham, Roger, Prior of Sempringham, and sixteen canons surrendered their house. The general form of surrender to which they set their common seal was drawn up by the commissioners. 'Know' said the canons, 'that by unanimous assent and consent with deliberate purpose, with certain knowledge and free impulse, for some just and reasonable causes, being especially moved by our minds and consciences, we have of our own will and desire, granted the Priory of Sempringham to our most illustrious Prince and Lord, Henry VIII, Supreme Head of the English Church'.

A detailed enumeration of all the possessions and rights of the house followed, and then the canons again declared that they made the renunciation of their own free will.

On 3rd October, John Freeman, Augmentations Receiver for Lincolnshire, furnished Cromwell with a summary of the proceeds, namely revenues of £1,407. Out of this there had been allowed £547.6s.8d. in pensions, but Freeman added, there were many benefices, and as these became vacant they could be bestowed on the former religious and pensions saved accordingly. In addition, he put the value of goods, sold and unsold, at £4,729.3s.0d.

PRIORESSES OF SEMPRINGHAM – Agnes Rudd and Margery Marbury.

In all the houses of the Order there were, in 1538, only 143 canons, 139 nuns, and 15 lay sisters.

The prior received Fordham rectory and £30 a year, the canons and prioresses and sixteen nuns were also pensioned.

1539 The site of the priory was granted in January to Edward Fiennes, Lord Clinton and Saye and his wife Elizabeth, who were expressly discharged in their letters patent from all 'encumbrances' except certain specified rents and fees.

John Smythe, Organist at Sempringham.

'THIS INDENTURE made the second day of March in the 25th year of the reign of our sovereign Lord King Henry VIII, between us, John, the prior of the monastery of Sempringham in the county of Lincoln of the Order of St Gilbert and the convent of the same place, of the one part and John Smythe, servant to the said prior, of the other part, witnesseth that the foresaid prior and convent as well by their whole assent and as by the special licence of Thomas, the chief and head prior of the said Order of Gilbert, have given and granted to the said John Smythe our servant, for his true and diligent service that he hath done and with God's grace hereafter shall do, a certain corrody or annuity during his natural life in the manner and form following: That is to say, a mansion or a dwelling house in the East Court of the said monastery, with an orchard and all other grounds as they be enclosed within the walls of the said house, with the appertenances. Also 40s of money yearly to be paid at two terms in the year, that is to say at the Feast of the Annunctiation of Our Lady and the Archangel, by even portions.'

Sempringham in the 16th and 17th centuries

VICAR OF ST ANDREWS – Sir Hugh Gryssington, chaplain on the death of the last incumbent. Patron – Thomas, Duke of Norfolk, Great Treasurer of England and Earl Marshal, by reason of a grant from the late dissolved priory of Sempringham. Instituted 14th May 1539, at London.

1541 VICAR OF ST ANDREWS – Sir Robert Baker, chaplain, on the death of Sir Hugh Gressington. Patron – Edward Clinton, Lord Clynton and Saye. Instituted 17th October 1541, at Sleford.

1547 The English were fighting against the Scots, and the English fleet

The stamps of Robert Newcombe, bell founder

consisting of sixty-five vessels were approaching Newscastle, of which Sir Edward Clinton of Sempringham was Admiral.

1550   The second bell of Sempringham Abbey Church bears the stamp of Robert Newcombe, Mayor of Leicester around the year 1550? This bell has the inscription of 'BE NOT OVER BUSIE', the diameter of the mouth of the bell is 27 inches, with an approximate weight of 4 cwts. 2 qrs.

1552   Lord Clinton was married in the parish church of Sempringham to his third wife, Elizabeth, the widow since 1548 of Sir Anthony Browne. Lord Clinton, Earl of Lincoln held high offices of State; he obtained a grant of Tattershall Castle in 1551, but it has been suggested that Sempringham was his usual seat when in residence in Lincolnshire.

1556   Robert Holgate, Master of Sempringham between 1536-1538, then became Archbishop of York, died.

1558   The register was started at the Abbey Church.

1565   The monastery of Sempringham owned land in Threekingham to a yearly value of 18s. and it was in the tenure of John Bell. This was granted to Lord Clinton and Saye and to Sir Henry Clinton, his son and heir 'to be held in free and common socage of the manor of East Greenwich'.

1566   The churchwardens reported that 'a handbell', which belonged to the church in Queen Mary's time, had been sold and defaced.

1569   In the 11th year of Queen Elizabeth's reign, the English were fighting the Scots and Lord Clinton of Sempringham was at the head of Twelve thousand men near Carlisle.

1572   Lord Clinton, High Admiral, was created Earl of Lincoln by Queen Elizabeth.

In the middle of the year the Queen sent the Earl of Lincoln to France, to see the treaty sworn between herself and the King of France, who shall mutually assist one another against all persons who shall attack them under any pretence whatsoever. The treaty shall remain in force till a year after the death of either party.

1581   Edward Clinton, Earl of Lincoln, Lord Admiral of England was amongst the Ambassadors to meet the Ambassadors of France when they arrived to agree the conditions of the marriage of Queen Elizabeth to the

The arms of Edward Lord Clinton

31

Duke of Anjou, brother to the King of France.

The inscriptions on the north face of the north-west tower wall in the parish church are interesting. They read 'Singe praises unto the Lorde O ye saintes of His, 1581' and 'In Te Domine Speravi Non Confundar In Aeturnum'. These inscriptions are said to have been carved here by a canon of Sempringham who returned some years after the Dissolution, to visit the site of the destroyed Priory.

1585 On the death of the Earl of Lincoln, Edward Lord Clinton, his son Henry Lord Clinton second Earl of Lincoln chose to reside at Tattershall Castle.

VICAR OF ST ANDREWS – Sir Roger Rodiat was curate in 1585, ordained by the Bishop of Coventry and Lichfield, 23rd September 1567. Against his name is written 'servinge man'.

1602 Henry Lord Clinton, second Earl of Lincoln as lay impropriator of Sempringham, Billingborough, Horbling, Threekingham, and Swaton received the great tithes of those parishes and was therefore responsible for the repairs of the chancels of those churches; nevertheless, in returns of the Bishop of Lincoln's commissaries, it is stated that the chancels of all these churches were ruinous or in great decay through the default of the Earl of Lincoln.

1613 Henry VIII despoiled these parishes so utterly that, for seventy years, not even so small a sum as three shillings and sixpence a year could be raised for a payment of a King's due! (Vide the 'Composition Books'). In 1623 the Lessees re-endowed the benefice with £20 per annum.

1614 VICAR OF ST ANDREWS – John Wood was Curate.

1616 Henry Lord Clinton, second Earl of Lincoln died at his manor house of Sempringham on September 29th; he may have resided there for some years.

1617 VICAR OF ST ANDREWS – Samuel Skelton.

1619 Thomas Lord Clinton, third Earl of Lincoln died at Tattershall Castle, leaving a widow and three sons.

He was succeeded by his son Theophilus, a young man of nineteen years of age. To help the young earl to administer his vast Lincolnshire estates, Lord Saye and Sele, cousin to the late earl and a man of strong Puritan inclination, sent Thomas Dudley, one of his most capable administrators to Sempringham.

1620 The widow and three sons of Thomas Lord Clinton were living at Sempringham.

Bridget, daughter of Lord Saye and Sele was married to the young Theophilus Clinton, Earl of Lincoln, and went to live at Tattershall Castle, while his mother and the rest of the younger folk settled down at Sempringham in a large old house which had once been part of the Priory property.

Soon after her brother's marriage Lady Frances Clinton Fiennes, eldest girl, was married to John Gorges, second son of Sir Ferdinando Gorges, Governor of the English Plymouth.

1623 Lady Arabella Clinton Fiennes the second daughter became the wife of Rev. Isaac Johnson, a young and wealthy clergyman, born at Stamford, educated at Emmanuel College, Cambridge, a hot centre of Puritan doctrines.

1626 Arabella Fiennes, infant daughter of Theophilous the fourth Earl of Lincoln, was baptised in the parish church of Sempringham.

At this time the unfinished great house which had never been occupied was pulled down and the site converted into a garden for the smaller house.

Sempringham and the Americas

Lady Susannah Clinton Fiennes, third daughter, had married John Humphrey who was related by a previous marriage to John Winthrop who had been responsible for funding money for John Endicott's voyage to America in 1624 and the fitting out of his ship. It was these alliances and the common religious outlook which they shared which brought so many relatives and friends to the house of the Earl of Lincoln at Sempringham. The author of *The English People on the Eve of Colonisation* writes: 'Sempringham, the seat of the Earl of Lincoln, became a centre where men gathered and discussed plans for furthering the emigration to Massachusett. Among them were John Winthrop, his brother-in-law Emmanuel Downing, Rev. Isaac Johnson and others'.

1628 The Rev. Samuel Skelton, who was Vicar of Sempringham in 1617 and chaplain to the Earl of Lincoln, sailed to America, and on the same boat were some unnamed servants of the Rev. Isaac Johnson. There is no doubt these men went to see the conditions prevailing and to report back to Sempringham and so to lead to later and larger migrations.

1629 In July two ships sailed from Gravesend for Salem in America taking with them the Rev. Mr Higginson, a separatist minister who appears to have been engaged by Sempringham.

The Massachusetts Bay Company received its Charter from Charles I but not before John Winthrop, Isaac Johnson, Thomas Dudley and others of the Sempringham group had applied as to the terms on which they were allowed to join the Company. Once they had joined, they took leading parts. Within a matter of months Winthrop was elected Governor of the Company and at once began to equip a fleet for the journey to America.

1630 The immediate consequence of the weddings of the Fienne's family was of great importance. Sempringham became the centre of the long discussions and cautious scheming which led to the fuller formation of the Massachusetts Bay Company and the sailing of Winthrop's great fleet this year. The Winthrop fleet of eleven ships sailed in April, with Isaac Johnson and his wife Arbella, Charles Fiennes her brother, Thomas Dudley, his daughter Anne and her husband Simon Bradstreet and others of the Sempringham group.

The vessel in which they sailed, formerly the *Eagle*, was renamed *Arbella* before sailing.

1631 Lady Susannah Fiennes with her husband John Humphrey and their four children left for Massachusetts in America.

1633 The Rev. John Cotton, vicar of St Botolph's, Boston, felt it wise to leave his parish and spend sometime at Sempringham, while awaiting the opportunity to join those who had previously sailed to America.

1638 VICAR OF ST ANDREWS – Samuel Stoneham, clerk M.A. Commission for induction dated 22nd December 1638. Patron – The King.

1662 VICAR OF ST ANDREWS – John Marshall vicar.

1676 VICAR OF ST ANDREWS – Thomas Morton, clerk B.A. on the death of the last incumbent. Patron – Charles Bates, esq. in full right. Instituted 12th February 1676-7.

1693 Under the will of the fifth Earl of Lincoln, who died without issue, the Lincolnshire estates were divided and Sempringham passed ultimately to the ninth Earl of Lincoln who succeeded to the dukedom of Newcastle-under-Lyme.

1697 VICAR OF ST ANDREWS– Mr Henry Brerewood was curate.

The 18th and 19th centuries

1705 VICAR OF ST ANDREWS – Mr Samuel Galley (Vicar of Helpringham) was curate with the consent of the Bishop, and there was a service once on Sunday.

1719 The third bell in the Abbey Church was founded, and marked THO ESSINGTON C W. The diameter of the mouth of the bell was 36inches, with a weight of approximately 8cwts.1qr.

1725 VICAR OF ST ANDREWS – M. Rowlandson curate.

1726 Between 1724 and 1726 Daniel Defoe travelled the English countryside making notes on where he visited and one place was that of Sempringham. He was on his way from Peterborough to Ancaster when he called at Sempringham and saw 'two pieces of decayed magnificence; one was the old demolished monastery of Sempringham, the seat of the Gilbertine nuns, so famous for austerity, and the severest rules, that any other religious order have yielded to. The other was the ancient house of the Lord Clinton, Queen Elizabeth's admiral, where that great and noble person once lived in the utmost splendour and magnificence; the house, though in its full decay shows what it has been, and the plaister of the ceilings and walls in some rooms is so fine, so firm, and so entire, that they break off in large flakes, and it will bear writing on it with a pencil or a steel pen, like the leaves of a table book. This sort of plaister I have not seen anywhere so very fine, except in the Palace of Nonsuch in Surrey, near Epsom, before it was demolished by Lord Berkeley.'

1745 VICAR OF ST ANDREWS – Mr Miles Robinson was curate, and also curate of Horbling and vicar of Little Steeping.

1747 VICAR OF ST ANDREWS – Johnathan Lancaster, curate.

1748 Thomas Wilberfoss was sequestrator.

1752 VICAR OF ST ANDREWS – Johnathan Lancaster was curate up to March.

1758 VICAR OF ST ANDREWS – Edward Edwards, curate.

1770 VICAR OF ST ANDREWS – John Towers, curate and minister, several marriage entries by him.

1771 VICAR OF ST ANDREWS – Ri: Ward, curate, three marriages conducted by him.

1778 VICAR OF ST ANDREWS – Irton Murthwaite was curate, and also curate of Horbling.

1786 VICAR OF ST ANDREWS – John Shinglar, curate.

1788 The Norman chancel which 'had become very ruinous owing to the default of the Earl of Lincoln' and which was about the same length as the present nave, was demolished this year together with the transepts. The

The Abbey Church before the chancel was demolished in 1788. Copyright by kind permission of Lincolnshire County Council Recreational Services.

transepts were never rebuilt, but a small chancel about seven feet in length was then erected. When the Norman chancel was taken down the Priest's door was removed to Threekingham where it was built into a doorway for a pidgeon-cote.

When the north wall was being repaired, the foundations were discovered belonging to the cloistered enclosure in which Gilbert accommodated his first seven nuns, against the north wall of the Abbey Church.

The Priest's doorway

1791 In June, Sempringham was visited by Lord Torrington, who wrote in his *Diaries*, 'Tradition reports that St Gilbert was buried under a large blue slab at the top of the middle aisle, which I should be tempted to remove and discover any stone coffin or a crozier, etc. that might remain.'

1813 VICAR OF ST ANDREWS – William Thomas Walters, clerk M.A. on the death of the last incumbent, John Shinglar. Patron – The King for this turn only by lapse. Instituted 13th April.

St Andrew's Church, Sempringham,
from an engraving in The Church of England Magazine, *1846*

1826 VICAR OF ST ANDREWS – Thomas Latham, clerk M.A. on the resignation of William Walters, clerk. Patron – Earl Fortescue in full right. Instituted 18th February 1826.

1846 VICAR OF ST ANDREWS – Samuel John Hillyerd, clerk, on the death of Thomas Latham, clerk. Patron – Hugh, Earl Fortescue, in full right. Instituted 12th August 1846.

1855 The site of Sempringham Priory was included in the conveyance dated 20th March 1855 by the Earl of Fortescue and Viscount Elerington, to the Crown when the Billingborough Estate was purchased.

1861 The Rev. Samuel John Hillyerd died on 29th June, vicar of Sempringham.

VICAR OF ST ANDREWS – John Charles Kitching Saunders, clerk, M.A. on the death of Samuel John Hillyerd, clerk. Patron – Hugh, Earl Fortescue of Castle hill, South Moulton, County Devon, in full right. Instituted 13th September 1861.

Restoration of the church

1862 The venerable Abbey Church, despoiled of its fine Chancel, Porch, and South Transept had been left to go to ruin until 1862 when, through zeal and devotion, the Rev. J. C. K. Saunders began its restoration. Until then, there had been only one service in the Abbey Church (situated nearly a mile from the nearest house) each Sunday, for, it is said, a handful of people out of a population of six hundred. And at that date there was neither schoolroom nor vicarage house.

1867 April 29th, the Right Reverend the Lord Bishop of Lincoln visited Sempringham Abbey Church in reference to the proposed restoration.

When the Rev J. C. K. Saunders proposed restoring Sempringham Abbey Church he said, 'Considering that it is the Church in which St Gilbert was baptised, in which he worshipped as a youth, at whose altar he ministered as a rector, and within whose walls his remains were deposited, considering that it is the Church in which the first Gilbertines worshipped, and where their successors also worshipped for more than 500 years and also considering that the Gilbertine was the – ONLY WHOLLY ENGLISH MONASTIC ORDER – this old Abbey Church assumes the character of a NATIONAL MONUMENT.'

1868 This is how the interior of the Abbey Church was described.

'No two seats in the church were of the same size and shape. Some few of the handsome old carved seat ends remained, but the greater part of them had been removed to serve as sleepers for the floors, or used as supports for seats and the gallery stairs. Some of oak seats had been repaired with deal, and deal with oak. Some were low, some were high, some with doors, others without, some with a portion of the seat gone, many with large holes in the floor, and one without a floor.

'The roof was very unsound, the rafters being split or worm eaten. The slabs with which the aisles were formerly paved had in many instances been replaced with brick tiles and even with common stable pitching. The walls had been thickly covered with successive coats of, white-wash, blue-wash, yellow-wash and pink-wash.

'The lofty and noble tower arches leading to the north and south transepts had been filled in. The chancel arch was obscured by the chancel roof, which was several feet below it, while a fourth arch to the west was hidden by a hideous painting of the royal arms and decalogue, occupying a space of 10 or 12 feet.

'In a word, the interior of the church presented a melancholy scene of delapidation and decay such as is seldom witnessed.

'By the energetic and persevering exertions of the vicar, Rev. J. C. K. Saunders M.A. he began to restore this interesting Abbey to a condition more befitting its hallowed association and sacred use.'

On August 10th the restoration of Sempringham Abbey Church began. Mr Edward Browning of Stamford was architect and Messrs C. & W. B. Wilson of Donington were contractors for £910.

1869 The restoration had begun on the Abbey Church with the help of the following donations:

'Her most gracious Majesty, who is the impropriator and owner of half the parish, has contributed £500, and Earl Fortescue (patron) £50, the Bishop of London (late of Lincoln), Earl Brownlow (Lord-Lieutenant), Lord Kesteven, Lord Monson, the Ven. Archdeacon Kaye, the Ven. Archdeacon Trollope, Rev. W. J. Conant, Wm. Parker, Esq. of Hanthorpe, Brasenose College, etc., have added various amounts in aid of the good work, making in all the sum of £900, and leaving about £100 yet to be raised.

'Great is the change now presented. The dilapidated roof is replaced by a new one and substantial. Uniform and handsome seats with bench ends beautifully carved in scrupulous accordance with the existing originals have been substituted for the heterogeneous and unsightly pews. Tiles laid in becoming patterns now occupy the places of the broken slabs and stable pitching. The north wall has been rebuilt from its foundations, and extended so as to occupy the site of the old north transept. The walls and piers and arches have been denuded of their various coloured washes, and the beautiful mural decorations have once more been brought to light. Three out of the four tower arches are now opened, and that on the south has had a new and consistent window inserted, which has been filled with stained glass, containing the sacred monogram and medallions with Alpha and Omega, the gift of Mrs Saunders, the lady of the Vicar. There is another window of stained glass on the south side of the nave, the gift of the Rev. J. C. K. Saunders and Mrs Saunders, in memory of their two daughters. The subject is our Lord's ascension, most admirably executed by Mr W. H. Constable of Cambridge, in a style of surpassing richness and overpowering impressiveness. A third window, exquisite in design and colour, representing the Saviour as lovingly inviting the weary and the heavy laden to come unto Him, has been kindly presented by Mr W. H. Constable.

'The chancel has been re-built by the Crown at a cost of £400. It is in the Early English style, with an apsidal termination, having three lancet windows at the east end, between which are pilasters of red Mansfield stone, resting on beautifully carved corbels, and surmounted with deeply sculptured capitals. The floor is laid with Minton's tiles. The furniture of the chancel consisting of altar cloth, communion plate (including flagon, chalice, and paten), alms dish, chairs, stools, service books and kneeling carpet, is the generous gift of Mrs Casswell (late of Pointon) and family. The pulpit is of oak elaborately carved and a stone base, with the appropriate inscription, "We preach Christ crucified".

'On the 13th July the ceremony of the re-opening of the Abbey Church took place at which were present the Bishop of Lincoln, the Ven. Archdeacon of Lincoln, the Rev. J. Dodsworth (Rural Dean), the Revs. C. Whichcote, E. Alderson, C. Bullivant, S. Craven, F. S. Emly, J. D. Grenside, H. Harris, T. M. Jackson, G. W. Keightley, H. Knapp, J. Kynaston, H. Latham, O. Luard, E. H. Parry, J. P. Sharp, B. Snow, J. Tagg, J. Topham, and P. S. Wilson. There was a large attentive congregation both morning and afternoon. Between the services there was a public luncheon in an extensive marquee erected outside the churchyard, at which 150 persons were regaled. The total collections from the two services amounted to £43.'

In October, the Rev. J. C. K. Saunders had been appointed to the Rectory of Thornton-le-Moor, by the Bishop of Lincoln. He had prepared for the press an article on 'The History of Sempringham and the Gilbertines'.

VICAR OF ST ANDREWS – Robert Keith Arbuthnot, clerk M.A. presented by Hugh, Earl Fortescue, Patron. On the cession of John Charles Kitching Saunders, clerk. Instituted 17th December 1869.

1874 VICAR OF ST ANDREWS – John James Hodgson, clerk M.A. presented by Hugh, Earl Fortescue, patron. On the cession of Robert Keith Arbuthnot, clerk. Instituted 18th June 1874.

1877 On August 30th the Rev. John James Hodgson, vicar of Sempringham was buried in the churchyard. 'Owing to a serious accident he dislocated his neck and was wholly paralysed, he lived for a few days only.'

39

VICAR OF ST ANDREWS – Thomas Charles Litchfield Layton, clerk M.A. on the death of John James Hodgson, clerk. Patron – Hugh, Earl Fortescue, in full right. Instituted 23rd November 1877.

1887 VICAR OF ST ANDREWS – Edwin Wrenford, clerk on the resignation of Thomas Charles Litchfield Layton, clerk. Patron – Hugh, Earl Fortescue of Castle Hill, in the parish of Filleigh, Co. Devon, in full right. Instituted 10th December 1887.

1891 Church land now let for £15 per year.

1893 'This historical Abbey Church of Sempringham was, on Saturday June 17th the scene of an interesting gathering, the occasion being the consecration of an addition to the burial ground of its churchyard by the Lord Bishop of Lincoln, and the crowning, in part of some of the important Church work which the Vicar (Dr Wrenford) has accomplished during his short incumbency.

'A new and substantial wall has also been erected around the church-yard at Sempringham Abbey. Despite the oppressively hot weather which prevailed, and the somewhat inconvenient time for a Church service – Saturday morning – the ceremony was very largely attended. The clergy present were the Rural Dean the Rev. H. M. Mansfield (Bourne), the Rev. W. W. Layng (Rippingale), the Rev. J. P. Sharp (Edenham), the Rev. E. E. Hodson (South Kyme), the Rev. P. Wilson (Horbling), the Rev. W. M. Thomas (Billingborough), the Rev. W. C. Houghton (Walcot) and Dr Wrenford. The bishop was attended by his chaplain, the Rev. C. W. Baron, and the procession from a tent outside the east gate of the church, in which the clergy robed, to the chancel, was led by the church-wardens, Messrs. Tom Casswell and J. Tomlinson.

'Subsequently a public luncheon was provided in the school-room at Pointon.'

The South Door 1898

The SEMPRINGHAM ABBEY GOLF CLUB was established. Messrs. B. Smith, T. Casswell, Lieut-Col. de Burton and Mr A. G. Fletcher were mainly instrumental in forming the club, and the Earl of Ancaster became president. The nine-hole course was laid out on undulating pasture land and embraced the site of what was formerly the Gilbertine monastery of Sempringham.

1899 A new porch was erected as a memorial of Queen Victoria's Diamond Jubilee, it was dedicated in November. This was built to preserve the beautifully ornamented Norman door and doorway.

1900 The Rev. Edwin Wrenford, vicar of Sempringham died at Grantham on December 19th. He was buried at Sempringham December 22nd.

1901 VICAR OF ST ANDREWS – Edward Ernest Harrison, clerk M.A. on the death of Edwin Wrenford, clerk. Patron – Hugh Fortescue, commonly called Viscount Ebrington of Exmoor, Co. Somerset, patron for this alternate turn. Instituted 6th May.

1902 The vicar devoted the marriage fees taken during his first year in the parish, towards providing an oak and tapestry reredos for the Abbey Church.

June 1st saw peace proclaimed ending the South African war, and on Sunday June 6th a special service was held at the Abbey Church.

An extract taken from the Sempringham Parish Magazine: 'For some years past this has been known as the Royal Parish of Sempringham, and on Wednesday last we showed ourselves to be loyal and sympathetic subjects, as a telegram from the United Parish was sent to the King's secretary expressing our sorrow for His Majesty's illness, and hoped for a speedy recovery. This telegram was acknowledged the same day by Sir Francis Knollys by another telegram thanking the parish for its kind message, which would be placed before the King.'

A special service was held on Sunday August 10th to commemorate the coronation of King Edward VII when the Abbey Church was crowded with a congregation from Church and Chapel.

The improvements made to the Abbey Church during the year were the moving of the pulpit and prayer desk more to the sides, bringing the altar rails more forward, the addition of a stove for the heating of the church, and also the provision of a new gateway for the porch.

1903 Sunday June 21st, the Bourne and Billingborough Volunteers attended a service at the Abbey Church. The weather was fine and people came from all parts of the district to see the parade, which was the first ever held at the village. The church was consequently crowded, many being unable to gain admittance. The Volunteers assembled at the gate-house on the Billingborough–Pointon road, the Bourne and Corby contingents being conveyed in traps and other vehicles. In addition to the attraction provided by a Sunday Parade, the men were headed by the company's Band. The Vicar

41

the Rev. E. E. Harrison conducted the service.

After the service, the Volunteers marched to Billingborough, where they paraded in front of the Fortescue Arms Hotel. Here Captain Bell presented the long service medal to Colour-Sergeant J. Yarrad of Swaton. Afterwards the men were entertained to luncheon, provided by Mr & Mrs Houghton, in a marquee erected in the hotel yard. Later in the afternoon the Volunteers marched to the Sempringham Abbey Golf Links, where they went through a series of field exercises and some practice in signaling. The proceedings were watched by a large number of interested spectators, and the band, which played at intervals, greatly contributed to the success of the gathering.

On Saturday June 27th a sale of work and Garden Fete was held in the Vicarage grounds to raise money for a new roof for the Abbey. They realised between £300-340. A total of between £70-£80 was required for the new roof.

An extract from the December magazine: 'Abbey Church Alterations. The church-wardens have made a great improvement in the Church by moving the Organ and the Choir seats into the Chancel. Not only does the church now look better furnished, but the singing of the choir sounds as well again.'

1904 Another sale of work and Garden Fete took place on June 16th, at Pointon to help towards the restoration of the Abbey roof. Total takings were £32.10s.5d.

In October a bad attack of Scarlet Fever had broken out in the district.

The SEMPRINGHAM ABBEY GOLF CLUB was dissolved, most of the seventy members joining the new Blankney Park Golf Club.

1905 A gift of two oak and brass Choir Book Rests had been given by the Rev. O. A. Garwood of Willingham Rectory, Gainsborough, of which one was placed in the Abbey Church and one at the Pointon Mission Church.

'All the windows in the Abbey Church have been thoroughly overhauled and renovated by Barnes of Sleaford, as it has been considered by many that the draughts which had been experienced during the winter months, had been caused by the faulty conditions of nearly all the windows.'

1906 Several windows in the north aisle had been damaged by stones.

Although the Abbey Church had never been known to suffer damage through lightning, still it was thought it wise to adopt a means to prevent any future electrical damage to the historic building. The steeplejacks of Messrs. Phillips (London) were to fix four conductors on each pinnacle. It was discovered that the pinnacles were in an unsafe condition, so it was decided they be strengthened.

'The following repairs to the Abbey Church had been made, the roof where necessary; reflooring the belfry tower; releading all the windows where in need of it; reglazing all the west window; taking out stained glass and releading the whole window; inserting new glass where damaged; new choir seats; new carpet for the sanctuary; and new door with glass panels, which

Right: damage to church, 1908

Below: damage to chancel, 1908

had been fitted to the porch in order to preserve the very fine old Norman arch and doors.'

1907 'The Abbey Church accounts showed receipts of £17.8s.2½d. and expenditure £22.0s.1½d., a deficit of £4.11s.11d. The Abbey Church Fabric Fund showed receipts of £64.0s.3½d. and expenditure of £52.12s.3½d., leaving a balance of £11.8s.0d.

'Miss Junius Stallard (London) has once more shown her generosity to the Abbey Church, by making and presenting a handsome Purple Altar Frontal, which would be used in Advent, Lent, and Rogation Seasons.'

1908 The Abbey Church was severely damaged in a storm on February 22nd. The parish clerk was in the church at the time but was unhurt. The destruction was caused by lightning causing the three pinnacles on the south side of the tower and the gargoyle, to be completely destroyed, and the roof of the chancel terribly smashed. A quantity of heavy masonary fell on the altar smashing it, as well as the altar step and tiling.

The Norwich Union Insurance Company accepted the claim made by the church-wardens, which meant the expense of restoring the tower and pinnacles, as well as the altar, reredos and curtains would be borne by the Company. The Crown restoring the chancel.

The restoration was carried out by Messrs. George Otter & Sons, Billingborough and the architect was Mr Wilfred Bond of Grantham. The main portion of work was the rebuilding of the pinnacles, the old stonework used as much as possible. The extreme top of the tower was completely smashed in; this was renewed and covered with Collyweston slates. The chancel was so badly damaged as to necessitate new ribs and principals to the Gothic roof. Inside the ediface considerable repairs were necessary. The steps leading to the altar were badly damaged. An improved lightning conductor was fitted. Everywhere the renewed parts were in keeping with the original architecture.

Mr Tomlinson, Birthorpe presented the Abbey Church with a handsome brass candlestick for the pulpit, and two brass candlesticks for the organ.

On Sunday July 19th the Abbey Church was re-opened after undergoing extensive repairs which were rendered necessary by the severe storm.

1909 'At the Reformation, Henry VIII took possession of all the said Revenues, and bestowed them upon Lord Clinton and other courtiers. Their annual value then was £396. That value in 1909 has increased thirty-fold, under the skilful management of Her Majesty's Commissioners for Woods and Forests, and that portion of them lying in Sempringham, Pointon, Birthorpe and Billingborough purchased by the Crown in 1855 from Earl Fortescue, the lessee, is estimated to yield £6,000 per annum, of which it is understood £4,000 a year arises from the Rectorial Glebes and other property in these Royal Parishes.'

1910 The Sempringham Glebe Lands in the county of Huntingdon were sold for £576 on the 11th February. They were invested: £204 in the Great Western Railway at 5% guaranteed stock; and £372 in the South Eastern Railway at 3% preferred stock.

On the day of the funeral of King Edward VII Friday May 20th a specially appointed Commemoration Service was held in the Abbey Church at noon, and so large was the congregation who wished to do honour to the memory of their late Sovereign, that the building was not large enough to hold all who came.

In June the Lincoln Diocesan Guild's Union held a festival at the Abbey Church, 'A Lecture of the Gilbertine Order'. The vicar of Sempringham, the Rev. E. E. Harrison, conducted the first portion, and the Rev. N. C. Marris, Vicar of Morton, said the concluding prayers, the lesson being read by the Rev. Canon Layng, Rector of Rippingale. The sermon was preached by the Rev. Canon Heygate, Vicar of Boston. Upwards of two hundred members of the Guild attended.

The old organ in the Abbey Church was past repair, so another one was bought from Morton Church and thoroughly renewed and placed in the church.

Interior of Abbey Church 1911

1912 Due to the heavy rainfalls in August and September there would be only a Harvest of Thanksgiving. The church was not decorated or any special music due to the great losses to the farmers throughout the country.

1913 A list of the Vicars of Sempringham from St Gilbert onwards, framed in oak, was hung on the west wall of the Abbey Church.

This item was taken from an old magazine for July. 'Rather more then eighteen months ago the late Col. de Burton of Buckminster Hall, Billingborough, spoke to the Vicar of Sempringham about an old stone font which was on his premises, and which he stated came from Sempringham Abbey Church, this font the Colonel said should be restored to the church from which it was removed. Owing to serious illness of the vicar and the Colonel last year no action was taken for the removal of the font, but early last month, acting upon what has proved to be a mistaken message, the vicar gave instruction for the removal of the font into the Baptistry of the Abbey Church. This was done to the delight of many in the parish. It now seems we had no authority to move it, and the solicitors acting on behalf of the heir presumptive and the trustees of the late Col. de Burton have ordered the font to be returned at once and so we have lost what we feel we have a right to. The only present use this sacred relic is put to is as a pump trough in a stable yard, and its intrinsic value is nil, while its historic value in Sempringham parish is immense.'

1914 VICAR OF ST ANDREWS – Rev. T. Bolton on the resignation of the Rev. E. E. Harrison. Instituted February 5th 1914.

1915 List of fees at Sempringham were: Weddings –Publication of Banns 1s. After Banns 5s. After Licence 10s. Certificates 2s.7d. Clerks Fees - Publication of Banns 1s. After Banns 2s.6d. Licence 5s. Funerals - Ordinary and Parishioners 2s.6d. Clerk 5s. Out of Parish 5s. Brick Grave £5. New Grave 13s.4d.

Reginald de Burton Esq. of Buckminster Hall, Billingborough, heir to the late Col. de Burton offered the old font lying at Buckminster Hall and which originally belonged to Sempringham Abbey Church. It was then returned to the church.

1918 VICAR OF ST ANDREWS – the Rev. L. G. Allum appointed temporarily, due to the retirement of the Rev. T. Bolton. April 2nd 1918.

August 4th, the fourth anniversary of the outbreak of War, was kept as a special day of prayer and remembrance of those who had laid down their lives for their country. In the evening was held a special service of Remembrance at the Abbey Church to which members of the congregation brought flowers which they placed on the altar, after which the whole congregation stood in silent tribute while the Dead March in Soul was played. The church was full, and the service was reverent, heartfelt and beautiful.

On November 11th came the glad news of the signing of the Armistice. Joyful peals were rung out on the church bells all round.

1919 VICAR OF ST ANDREWS – The Rev. Thomas Edward Pritchitt, M.A. was instituted April 1919.

1924 VICAR OF ST ANDREWS – Rev. William Thomas H. Bradley, on the resignation of Thomas Edward Pritchitt. Instituted 23rd December 1924.

1927 VICAR OF ST ANDREWS – Rev. Percy Jules Hulbert. Instituted on March 24th 1927.

1928 The Processional Cross – This was the gift of the vicar and was made from oak taken out of the belfry of Horbling Church on restoration. It was made by Messrs. Carpenter and Sons, and was dedicated and first used at Evensong to lead the Rogation procession round the churchyard on Sunday May 13th.

Furnishings for the Font – The Ewer – the copper ewer was the gift of a parishioner as a thanks-offering for the recovery of one of his sons after an accident. It was specially made by the Craftsmen's Guild of London, and was dedicated at Evensong on Sunday July 1st.

Linen Cloth for the Altar – was a gift from Miss Casswell before leaving the parish.

A red damask Burse and Veil and a Corporal was given to the Abbey Church by Mrs Barbara Van Geyseghui of Croydon, neice of the Rev. E. E. Hodgson.

1929 The Font furnishings – The Cover – was the gift of the Rev. E. E.

Hodgson of Trusthorpe in memory of his brother who was Vicar of Sempringham from 1874-77. It was made by Messrs Carpenter and Sons of Horbling and was dedicated by the Rev. E. E. Hodgson at Evensong on Sunday April 21st.

Mr Bellamy of Billingborough became organist.

A choir stall had been offered from Heckington and was placed on the organ side.

1931 VICAR OF ST ANDREWS – the Rev. Albert Edward Parsons on the cession of the Rev. Percy Jules Hulbert. Instituted November 1931.

1932 Two more bells were added to the Abbey Church belfry. The founder was Alfred Bowell of Ipswich. The approximate cost of renovation and new bells was £266. The Bishop of Lincoln officiated at the service on Sunday April 24th.

1933 At a service in the Abbey Church on Sunday September 24th the Vicar of Billingborough, the Rev. S. Skelhorn dedicated a tablet in memory of a former vicar of the parish, the late Rev. Edward Pritchett.

1937 VICAR OF AT ANDREWS – Rev. Leonard Garnier Pilkington was instituted February 1937.

1938 Having received the approval of the Crown, which is the owner and tenant of the site of Sempringham Priory. Members of the Lincolnshire Architectural and Archaeological Society proposed to conduct a careful excavation there, begining as soon as possible in the year. The small executive committee was composed of Col. W. King-Fane as chairman, Captain A. W. Cragg, Professor R. de la Bere, M.A., Mr G. S. Dixon, and Miss F. E. Mann.

Excavating at Sempringham

47

Dr Rose Graham, at that time probably the greatest authority on the Gilbertines, would be taking an active interest in the excavation. A fund was opened up to help to cover the expenses. They thought a total of £150-£200 would be needed.

During the excavation a large number of carved stones had been found, a stone coffin, which is now in the Abbey Church, some various stained glass, a lead fleur-de-lis, Edward III and James I silver coins, and one of the Priory exchequer counters. The most interesting find perhaps was part of a caricature jug of Cardinal Bellarmine, a 16th century notability, and a portion of a 17th century glass bottle, bearing the arms of Chaworth of Annesley. Due to the winter season coming on the excavations ceased. The work had already proved that this monastic institution must have been one of the architectural glories of Lincolnshire of its day.

In December the Abbey Church had sufficient funds to install two additional bells. These were founded by Alfred Bowell of Ipswich. One bell was inscribed with Rev. L. G. Pilkington, Rev. E. E. Harrison and Mr T. Casswell. The second one has an inscription PAULINE.

1939 March saw the dedication of the two treble bells that had been installed, bringing the peal up to six. The dedication was made by the Ven. K. C. H. Warner, Archdeacon of Lincoln.

One of the bells was a gift of a former vicar, the Rev. P. J. Hulbert of Lancing, Sussex, and his brother Mr W. H. Hulbert of Johannesburg, to commemorate a life of unselfish service by their sister Pauline.

The cost of the other bell was borne by public subscriptions. Campanologists were present from Donington, Edenham, Bourne, Morton, Rippingale, Aslackby, Folkingham, Billingborough, Grantham, Heckington, Sutterton, and Thurlby, including ringing masters from Algakirk and Edenham.

Taken from a local newspaper:

'Excavation at Sempringham. Remains of a Big Church Discovered. Further excavations by the Lincolnshire Archaeological Society at Sempringham Abbey have disclosed a building of cathedral proportions, and, unlike the majority of the great churches of this county it consists of two churches side by side, with a wall separating the church of the monks from that of the nuns.

'The building so far explored is believed to be that of the monks. Its nave of five wide bays has a north aisle, beyond which is a long transept with three chapels in the eastern aisle, and the choir was on these bays.

'This unusually wide-spanned building must have been very lofty, as it is flanked by enormous buttresses, which take the thrust of the high stone vaulting on either side of this church or its counterpart, believed to be the church of the nuns.

'The building now being explored, and the sections will include the cloisters, refectory, dormitories, chapter house etc. As the work proceeds, a number of carved stones are being discovered, and one particularly interesting example has a recumbent lion carved upon it. The remains of a 13th century crypt has also been found, and one of the columns, a very fine example remains in position.

'The hopes of the committee responsible for the work are concentrated upon discovering the actual site of the burial place of St Gilbert, between the choirs of the monks and nuns, and possibly within the base of the shrine which was subsequently erected on the spot. If this is discovered, it is hoped to erect a memorial'.

1946 VICAR OF ST ANDREWS – the Rev. Wilfred Fardell Howard.

1949 VICAR OF ST ANDREWS – the Rev. Leslie Ronald Swingler. Patron the King.

1958 VICAR OF ST ANDREWS – the Rev. Charles Francis Ward. Patron the Queen.

1959 In July most of the footpaths around the Abbey Church had been concreted.

On October 13th the Rev. C. F. Ward commenced the celebration of St Gilbert's Day with an Evensong service at Sempringham at 7pm.

1960 New carpets were provided by the Womens Fellowship for the Abbey in time for the Easter service, these went from the main aisle and from the north to south door, also the north aisle, these were dedicated at the morning service on Palm Sunday.

June 20th Grantham Local History Society visited the Abbey where the Rev. J. D. Smart, Vicar of Wilsford, gave a talk on the Gilbertine Priory of Alvingham.

An autoscythe was purchased to keep the churchyard grass cut.

Four facsimile Seals of the Priory and Masters which had been obtained from the British Museum. The smaller seal depicts the Annunciation, a counterseal *c* 1261, a seal of Patrick, Master of Sempringham 1261, and Philip de Burton, Master 1311.

A small booklet produced by the Rev. Ward was put on sale at the Abbey.

A quantity of stained glass from the Priory of Sempringahm which was recovered during the excavations has been offered for use in the Abbey. It dates from the 13th century.

1961 A gift of fourteen dollars has been received from Mr E. H. Skelton of Winter Park, Florida. He is a descendant of the Rev. Samuel Skelton, Vicar of Sempringham 1619-1628 who sailed to Massachusetts a year before the Winthrop Fleet, and became the first minister in Salem and Chaplain to Governor Endicott. The value was about £5 which will buy something for the

Abbey.

A Confirmation Service was held at Sempringham Abbey which was conducted by the Lord Bishop of Lincoln with about 30 candidates.

A legacy of £200 had been left by Mrs Andrews for the upkeep of the graves, cleaning of the Bell Chamber and upkeep of the churchyard.

October 13th was the annual Service commemorating the life and work of St Gilbert given by the Rev. J. H. Jacques, Vicar of North and South Witham who had considerable knowledge of St Gilbert and the Gilbertine Order. The Rev. C. F. Ward spoke. 'As St Gilbert was born at Sempringham and founded the only English Monastic Order within the walls of our own Abbey Church it is fitting that we should do all we can to keep his memory alive in the age which we live. He was one of the earliest pioneers in the field of rural education if not the first, he founded many Religious Houses where the Faith was taught, vocation encouraged, the sick the poor and the lepers were tended – indeed of all the Religious Orders existing in England his was the one held in highest regard. As we go up to Sempringham it is interesting to remember that kings, statesmen, and leaders have gone there before us seeking counsel and blessing, and after Gilbert's death pilgrims in their thousands.'

Calor gas heaters were installed at the Abbey and, on the two occasions they were used on St Gilbert's Day Services, have proved to be most successful. Also the Abbey was floodlit. So striking and effective was this floodlighting, that the churchwardens have decided to buy four lights to use on special occasions.

A Carol Service was held for the first time at the Abbey on Christmas Eve and attended by a large congregation.

1962 Thirty new red leather hassocks have been given to the Abbey by the Womens Fellowship.

SEMPRINGHAM VILLAGE SITE: In April several pieces of pottery picked up in the fields surrounding the Abbey have been indentified as Roman, Saxon and up to fourteenth century. This shows continuous occupation of the village there, for at least one thousand five hundred years. This can be extended for a period of another two hundred forty years, as there is documentary evidence to show that Sempringham Manor House was pulled down just after the property was sold to Lord Fortescue in 1743. The main part of the village had, however, disappeared long before this.

In May an anonymous donor gave a gift of a really fine white festal Altar Frontal for use in the Abbey.

On St Gilbert's Day Service in October, the service was taken by the Rev. Father Clement Mullinger of Kelham, Society of the Sacred Mission. An interesting feature of this service was the inclusion of a hymn written in the mid-fourteeth century especially for the festival of St Gilbert's Translation. This hymn was specially translated for this occasion, and it was the first time

50

it had been sung here since 1538.

The Abbey Chancel Roof is in need of repair.

On December 17th, the death of the Rev. C. F. Ward was announced and he was later buried at Sempringham Abbey. He was vicar of Billingborough and Sempringham with Pointon.

1963 The late R. W. Atkinson left a legacy of £50 for the upkeep of Sempringham Abbey.

In April, Mrs Ward gave a new chalice to Sempringham Abbey in memory of her husband. It was dedicated at the Holy Communion Service after Mattins on Easter Sunday.

'A Flower Festival was held for the first time on June 22nd-24th in the Abbey with about forty decorations. The Bishop of Lincoln preached at the Sunday Evensong. It was regrettable that everyone present was unable to get into the Abbey for the service. Provisions were made for it to be relayed outside and this came over loud and clear. We have been honoured by the visit of some very great men.

'May the seeds that were sown by St Gilbert during the 12th century and revived in a very quiet way by the late Vicar the Reverend Frank Ward, live and grow in the hearts of each one of us and blossoms as the rose for many centuries to come!'

Mr Peter Dearden of Newton gave to the Abbey Church a copy of Leonardo da Vinci's 'Last Supper' beautifully carved in wood and perfect in detail. This has been placed beneath the stained glass window in the South Aisle.

1964 VICAR OF ST ANDREWS – The induction of the Rev. Peter Hearn to Sempringham by the Archdeacon of Lincoln on April 10th at the Abbey assisted by the Rural Dean.

A book had been received from Mr George Graham, a copy of his sister's (the late Miss Rose Graham), *St Gilbert of Sempringham and the Gilbertines*. Published over sixty years ago this book is still the main source of our knowledge of Sempringham and its history. The book is the property of the church.

1965 On April 4th a quarter peal was rung at Sempringham as a compliment to Mr J. Rolt on his 82nd birthday, Mr Rolt himself took part.

1966 In June a Diocesan youth pilgrimage to Sempringham was held with the Bishop of Grantham.

October 13th, St Gilbert's Day Service with the Bishop of Grantham.

1967 Mr & Mrs D. Burges leave Pointon and Mr F. Gould takes over as churchwarden from Mr Burges.

Work on the tower at Sempringham will cost over £1100.

Mr & Mrs Burges were presented with a silver cigarette box with the coat of arms of Sempringham engraved on it.

1968 In April a gift of a copy of Dugdale's *Monasticon* was given to Sempringham by Mr John Covell. Much of our information about Sempringham and the Gilbertines comes from this book, which is a history of Abbeys and Monastic Orders in England. The edition Mr Covell has presented dates from the eighteenth century and was the property of Miss M. Smith of Horbling.

At the evening service during the Flower Festival in July, a new altar book was dedicated for use in the Abbey Church. The previous book was dated 1888 and had served well. The book was presented in memory of Mrs Edna Swales by the family.

1970 Clergy of the Rural Deanery met at Sempringham for Corporate Communion on July 8th at 8.30am, with breakfast at Billingborough afterwards.

At a Rural Deanery Eucharist at Bourne the Bishop of Lincoln referred to the Abbey as 'perhaps the most precious of all churches in this County'.

1971 On January 21st to between 23rd several of the stained glass windows were damaged at the Abbey; only the previous year £300 had been spent on having the windows cleaned and repaired.

1973 The Rev. P. B. Hearn took up his living in September at Flixborough, South Humberside. The priest in charge was the Rev. R. H. Moseley, vicar of Horbling and Swaton.

October saw the Rev. R. H. Moseley leave for the living at Soberton near Portsmouth.

The Rural Dean, Canon G. J. Lanham in charge until a new priest takes the living.

1974 Judith Stokes donated a beautiful Altar Frontal to the Abbey Church.

VICAR OF ST ANDREWS – May 24th, the Rev. G. E. Wood's induction at Billingborough Church by the Bishop of Grantham with the Archdeacon of Lincoln.

1975 The Lord Bishop of Lincoln instituted the Rev. G. E. Wood to the Benifice of Sempringham on 18th February.

1976 Gales which brought the New Year in, caused extensive damage to the Abbey. Temporary protection covering was provided till repairs could be done. The north-east pinnacles had blown down and damaged the chancel roof.

1979 A further £2000 was required to complete the final repairs to the Abbey.

April saw the death of Mrs Alice Bullock at ninety-four years old, organist for forty-five of those years at Sempringham and Pointon.

The Lord Bishop of Lincoln preached at Evensong on June 17th.

A Flower Festival was held to raise money for the final repairs to the Abbey on June 22nd-24th.

After years of struggling to pay for repairs to the Abbey Church after the 1976 gales, the Crown Estate Commissioners agreed to pay £3000 towards the cost.

1980 The Rev. G. E. Wood retires from the Benifice of Sempringham. The Rev. C. N. Ogden retired priest officiates at Holy Communion services until a new priest arrives.

The bells at Sempringham have been repaired and rehung and ready for use again.

1981 VICAR OF ST ANDREWS – The Rev. H. J. Theodosius. Instituted 15th May.

July 14th saw the Rev. H. J. Theodosius instituted to the parish of Sempringham and Pointon by the Archdeacon of Lincoln.

The monks of the Community of the Glorious Ascension occupied the Abbey for a certain time where they held a service each day except on a Thursday.

1983 Marked the 900th Anniversary of St Gilbert's birth at Sempringham, and was celebrated with a Flower Festival at the Abbey Church in June and a service in Lincoln Cathedral. The Flower Festival was a success with takings amounting to £1000.37, some of this money going to restore the original South Door.

1984 This year for the first time, the St Hugh's Gathering did not take place in Lincoln Cathedral but at Sempringham Abbey on July 14th, when between 600-700 people took part in the day's services. The Bishop of Grantham and the Bishop of Grimsby officiated with about twenty priests.

1985 By the end of the year, the workmen had started to remove and replace the new wooden flooring in the Abbey.

1986 In March the death of Raymond Wesley was announced; he had been churchwarden for over forty years at Sempringham and Pointon.

August saw the renovation of the North Aisle and the Centre flooring completed at the Abbey at a cost of over £1500, this now leaves the South Aisle to be renewed.

A donation of a hundred dollars to the Abbey Funds was received from the St Julian Order of Norwich in America.

A candle-light Carol Service was held on Christmas Eve with the Abbey floodlit outside by Calor Gas.

1987 The renovation of the South Aisle of the Abbey has now been completed at just over £300.

The Rev. H. J. Theodosius appointed Rural Dean of Aveland, Ness and Stamford.

1989   Saturday February 4th, 1189 St Gilbert of Sempringham died at the Priory Church. Saturday February 4th, 1989, 800 years later, in his Parish Church, a special celebration of Holy Communion was held at 12.00 noon with the celebrant the Lord Bishop of Lincoln the Rt. Rev. Robert Hardy. In the region of 100 people attended from all denominations and from various parts of Lincolnshire, including St Gilbert's other parish church at West Torrington.

It is hoped a permanent memorial to St Gilbert will be placed at Sempringham at his Parish Church, as there is nothing to be seen on the actual site of the Priory. The initiative for this has come from a group of archeologists, historians and priests, both Anglican and Roman Catholic, and the parochial church council is represented on the Committee. The cost will be in the region of £6500 and the memorial will consist of three slate plaques on the south side of the tower and a preaching plinth in front.

Also to celebrate St Gilbert's death, a Flower Festival on July 7th–9th in the Parish Church at Sempringham, in September a pilgrimage from Lincoln Cathedral to Sempringham with the Community of Communities, and in October a Roman Catholic Mass.

Facsimile of first paragraph of John Capgrave's Life of Gilbert, taken from J. J. Munro, John Capgrave's Lives of St Augustine and St Gilbert of Sempringham, *1910*

THE LIFE OF ST GILBERT
BY JOHN CAPGRAVE

JOHN CAPGRAVE'S PROLOG

To my well beloved in our Lord God master of the Order of Sempringham, which order is entitled unto the name of St Gilbert, I friar John Capgrave, amongst doctors last, send reverence as to such dignity, desiring cleanliness to your soul and health to your body. Now with in a few days it was notified unto me that the life of our father St Augustine, that which I translated in our tongue at the instance of a certain woman, was brought to your presence, which you liked well, as it is told, except you would I shall add thereto all thou religious that live under his rule. But to this I answer that it was not my charge, but if men like for to know this matter diffusely they may learn it in a sermon that I said at Cambridge the year before my opposition, which sermon perhaps I will set in English at the end of this work.

Then after you had read this life of St Augustine you said to one of my friends that you desired greatly the life of St Gilbert should be translated in the same form. Thus he made instance to me, and I granted both your petitions, this for I would not frustrate him of his medicine. To the honour of God and of all saints then, we will begin this treatise, namely for the solitary women of your religion which can not understand Latin, that they may at vacant times read this book of the virtues of their great master. For there may they look as in a glass, who they shall transfigure their souls latch on to that exemplary in which they shall look.

GILBERTUS, of the interpretation of his name, what it should mean in English, for we have it not readily in our books of interpretations, we will speak in such manner of authority which divides names in parties. GILA, they say, is a word of Hebrew, as much as to say as he that passeth from one country to another. And BER is a well, or a pit, also derived from Hebrew tongue. TUS is a Latin word, in English a sweet gum, which we throw in our incense when we shall do a special honour to God. This holy man was a walker here on earth that passed from the well on to the sweet saviour.

The sweet saviour name my holy opinion of this man which savioured so sweetly in this land that it made many men to sell all that they had and to follow the steps of poverty. Of this saviour spoke the blessed apostle when he said: 'We be the good odour of our Lord Christ in every place, both to him that shall be saved, and also to them that shall perish. To some be the saviour of life and to some the saviour of death.' So seems it that the clean life of St Paul, and the devout preaching of him, was unto him that were reprobate a saviour of everlasting pain. All this is said to according of St Gilbert's name, that all his life from his baptism on to his death ran in such a sweet saviour that yet at these days the devout virgins of his Order bare witness that of the root of his doctrine sprang all these fair flowers of virginity. This is the introduction or else the prologue of St.Gilbert's life, which life I have taken on hand to translate out of Latin right as I find before me, save some additions I will put thereto which men of that Order have told me, and else other things that shall fall to my mind in the writing which be pertinent to the master.

CHAPTER I   HIS PARENTS

This man was born in that same place called Sempringham. His father was born in Normandy, his mother a lady of Sempringham. His father, as they say, was a Norman knight which came to this land with King William at the Conquest and married the lady of Sempringham, so that by the heritage St.Gilbert was very ever of this possession and of many other.

That this is likely to be true, I allege a testimony which I have the information of my Lord Beaumont, John, that now liveth. He said that his kindred came first out of France with this same King William, and one of them, a notable knight, wedded the lady of Folkingham at that time, and so of her issue came all the Beaumonts that have been since. Such many other might we rehearse and make the book over long and tedious to be read.

Then was this man mingled with two bloods, Norman of the fathers side, English of the mothers side. What authors write of these two nations and what commendation they rehearse of them is pertinent to set here in magnifying of this man. The Normans they say, they came from Norway and conquered the land where they dwell, a people gentle of condition, wise and ready in battle and great tillers of corn. The description also of this nation must much accord hereto, because they conquered us and at this day their succession dwells with us. So it seems that this man was not born of no wretched nation nor of no servitude, but of people gentle and freemanly and large, both on the fathers side and the mothers.

He was in his young age, and in his simpleness full of grace like unto Jacob, whom for his cleanliness and innocence the mother Rebecca, through inspiration of God, preferred to be lord of all his bretheren, like as this man is preferred to be master of all this religion. And also, as it is said in the book of Job: 'The lamp which was despised in the thoughts of rich men was arrayed again another time; in which you shall understand that those virtues which grew with this child in young age, then despised of the world, were ordained for to be held in more reverence in time command'.

He was at that age sent to school and learned groundly in thoughts, sciences which they call liberal, as grammar, rhetoric, logic and such other. But his courage at that time was more inclined to learn good manners than subtle conclusions, also because afterward that he was ordained to be a teacher of virtuous living, it was convenient that he should first be a disciple in the school of honesty. In all his young age was he clean from such vices as children use, as lying, wanton raging, and other stinking conditions. Even then he began to be like a religious man, to which life he was applied by God. For in all his life, as they bear witness that say his conversation, he never touched a woman. Touching I call vicious handling in self or such manner circumstance of bodily approximation by which any man might deem evil.

CHAPTER II   HIS YOUNG AGE

In that same secular life and in that tender age, he followed, as he could and might, the rules of religious life, and to them all of which he had any power he full benignly gave example the same rules to follow. For first, he was a master of learning to the small children such as learning to read, spell and sing. The children that were under his discipline he taught not only their lessons on the book, but besides this, he taught for to play in due time, and here games he taught that they should be honest and merry without clamour or great noise. For those he had not at that time experience of the good customs which be used amongst religious men in monasteries, yet had our Lord God at that age put in his breast these holy exercises, for he taught those disciples that he had to keep silence in the church, all and one hour to go to bed and also to rise to their lessons; all went they together to their play or any other thing.

His most labour and greatest desire was to win souls to God with word and also example, for the best sacrifice unto God is the jealous love of souls. Like unto this man was the holy Athanas in his young days, that same Athanas which made Quicuque Vult. We read of him that in his childhood he would gather together many children of his aquaintances, and lead them to the waterside, and this was at great Alexandria. Then he would enquire of them whether they were christened or not, and if they were not christened, he made his fellows, as in a game, to make the child naked and so dip him thrice in the cold water, he standing sadly and saying the very sacramental words of baptism. This noise came to the bishops's ear, which at that time hit Peter; he sent after the children and enquired of them what Athanas said unto them, what they answered, under what form he washed them, and what he said that thus all things was doing right as the church useth, he determined that though children were baptised, notwithstanding that it was done in play, commanding his priests to take the children and say over them the other orisons which the church useth. All this is said for our Gilbert, that in so young age had so sad conditions and so great zeal to lead souls to heaven.

When he was promoted to the order of priesthood, and had souls in governance and also had received power to make ministration of the spiritual gifts which be virtue of our Lord's blood are left in the church, then, as a true steward of his Lord's treasure, he departed his Lord's whete to them that dwell in the household of our faith, to each of them as it needed. That is to saint, the word of good exhortation was not hid in him, but he dealt it out freely to them that would learn. For his auditory was so endowed with learning that it seemed in all her governance they had been nourished in the monastery amongst the servants of God.

They used no insolent drinkings, nor no long sitting there, nor used not to run to wrestlings, bear baiting and such other unthrifty occupations, which some men now on days prefer before divine service; this used they nought, but they used to pray devoutly in church, to pay truly their tythes, to walk about and visit poor men, to spend their good in such a way as in pleasure of God and comfort to the poor. Who so had seen them within the church he might soon discern whether they were Gilbert's parishioners or not, he had taught them so well to bow their backs and their knees to God and so devoutly to bide their beds.

CHAPTER III
HIS CONDUCT AS PRIEST UNDER ROBERT, BISHOP OF LINCOLN

In his first promotion he was in the household of the Bishop of Lincoln, called Robert Bloet. Thither was he drawn first and made a chaplain half against his will, for he was special with the Lord, and to him was committed to ransack all the grevious crimes or sins throughout the diocese, he to correct after his discretion. For he was a general judge, as it seems, to make his remission and commination right as he listed. In all this authority he was not proud of bearing , nor found in no costly array, but the higher he was in dignity the lower was his soul, for in all his movements nothing secular, but like a canon regular or a cloisterer, seemed he ever.

In so much that while he was in this service in court he was fasting greatly, he woke as to other men's waking insupportably, prayed ever, and also other spiritual exercises were never left behind. He was so well occupied in that administration that he would complain of himself afterward when he had begun this religion, that he was more perfect in life before that conversation to religion than he was after, notwithstanding that after time he had taken this holy habit he was enemy great enough unto his own body. But that he did less penance to his body after he had taken religion, it is not to ascribe to sloth and negligence, but rather unto charity, which intended more to other men's profit than his own.

So we read that St Martin had less virtue gave unto him after his promotion to the bishopric than he had before. This man which we talk of now, before all virtues loved poverty, for a great and a good archdeaconry preferred to him by the same Bishop Robert, he fully refused. For he would say some time these benefices of great expense be often time a ready way to lose of man's soul. For which cause all the goods which left of his benefices beside his necessary living, he gave it freely unto the profit of the poor men. When he was out of his own possession he received every Christ as his guest in fatherless children, in widows, in old folk, in sick and feeble, whom he sustained with his proper goods, and also with the churches revenues, clad them and fed them.

And that he should go unto the greatest some of perfection, all that he had he gave to poor men such as he, though the inspiration of our Lord, had chose and made to live in wilful poverty, which hereafter for his temporal goods that he spent in worship of our Lord, should receive him into everlasting tabernacles, as the gospel bare witness. Thus, of true dispencing of worldly goods and great love which he had to souls, he was worthy of our Lord to receive a double reward.

CHAPTER IV   HIS FIRST NUNS

Then he thought among other things that virginity was a great authority, one of the greatest virtues that may please God, which fruit bore by them is most allowed in heaven, for this cause he ordained first seven maidens which, was his teaching, were inflamed in love of God, that they should be closed up from the vanity of the world and serve our Lord in quiet contemplation. So under the wall of the church of St.Andrew he made them cells where they might pray and have part also of all divine service, both in saying and in hearing. After that he joined unto their service other certain women that were not learned, and men also that were converted to religion, but no clerks; these all were ordained to the service of the aforesaid virgins.

After this doing he ordained certain monks, lettered men and bound to straight rules, that they should have the governance of all these people aforesaid. Unto these all ordained he gave meat, drink, cloth, and other necessaries from his rents and of other goods lawfully got. To their souls also ordained he spiritual meat, unto the nuns the rule of St.Benedict, unto the monks the rule of St.Augustine, beside these certain institutions he ordained, as the holy anointing taught him, which by the Holy Ghost sent from heaven. Thus he set them laws meddled with such attemperance that amongst divers kinds, divers habits, divers degrees, he exhorted them in our Lord they all should have but one soul and one heart fixed in God.

What shall we say more of his congregation. Beside those alms houses which he made for poor men, for sick men and women in languor, for lepers, for widows, for fatherless and motherless, which houses he set in divers degrees and in divers disposition, beside all these, he edified in his life thirteen conventional churches with all other houses pertinent, four of canons dwelling by themselves, nine of nuns with their bretheren and monks, and persons that were unlearned ordained to service of the nuns, as we said before.

And verily, as we suppose, he left at his death such persons dedicate to God upon two thousand two hundred, beside them that were dead ere that time he passed from us. And many more monasteries might he made, nor had by the straight conscience which he had in receiving of worldly, goods, for with full great dread and much heaviness received he worldly riches which were proffered him; sometime he was compelled for to take these gifts, sometime he refused them, so was honest poverty rooted in his heart and so well beloved. Thus seemeth it that he was set in the poor way, as was Solomon that said unto God: "Give me Lord, neither riches nor poverty, but grant me such thing which is needful unto me". So this man had desire to the poor, neither to the rich, nor for to want, but to have such things as was necessary to the great number newly gathered by him, that they should not fail of their daily provisions. His purpose was ever to dwell amongst them that were humble, therefore it pleased our Lord for to exalt him that himself so humbled.

CHAPTER V   THE INCREASE OF HIS ORDER, AND HIS VIRTUES

Who that he behaved in his prelacy and who fatherly he was at all times unto his subjects, I suppose, verily, that it is now not unknown unto the kingdom of England, in so much that his children be so increased and grown to such a number as we may see at the eye, that rightfully we may apply through words of scripture to him which were said to Job: "Thy seed" he said, "shall be multiplied and thy kindred increased as herbs on the earth". This multiplying of his religion, the wise men that live now suppose verily it be the miracle of his good life.

The man stood in a manner of marvel to all that knew him for the great prerogative of good deeds with which he was endowed, also for the new plants of mercy and charity which he had grafted in the garden of Christ's church, moreover for the great multiplying and wise governance of the same. For he that poured wisdom in his breast for to think and to begin such things. He gave them virtue in the administration and conservation of the same. It is open at this day what cunning Saint Gilbert had and what holiness, for and these gifts had not come from God, there should never have risen unto so perfect an end, for the man taught nothing but that he did, for in all his life his doctrine was according to his works; his holy doctrine expressed his clean life and his holy life brought his doctrine unto effect, that is to say, a perfect end.

After time that he was preferred to have governance in dispensing of God's gifts, he doing the part that belong unto his office, he left just nought that belong his spiritual health or else to the charge that belong to governance of his brethren. The man was pleasant and merry, was in words and of used eloquence fulfilled, having nothing in his words that was likely to be blemished, wherefore with great reverence was he beloved both of his own familiar people and also of strangers. In all his behaving outward he was conformed unto his brethren: he was, if I should not lie, the form and example in which they might look for to transfigure their life to that exemplary.

Humble he was amongst them as one of them, as it is said in Solomon: A prince have they made was with them as one of them; for all that ever he commanded his subjects to do he fulfilled himself, his clothes were not whiter than other of his fellow, his meat was not prepared more deliciously than it was for the convent, he had no special chamber for to sleep in, but in the dormitory he took rest, his board was not aught of the refectory, least that a guest caused it. In his riding he had no costly horse, no wasteful array, not many horses, nor many servants, but one of the unlearned of his Order and two of the clerks which should be privy and seal his conversation, at all time they went with him. In his riding he spent not the time with vain tales or flying tidings, but with Psalms and prayers persued he all the way, ever having a purse ready to give alms to poor men which he met. His inn to which he should come was filled with abundance of victuals full discreetly not only for himself but for them that would ask it and had need thereof. At meat he was merry, he talked more than eat, and, with solace countenance would gladden his guests.

CHAPTER VI   HIS MANNER OF LIFE

He would complain sometimes when he rose from the board that he had sinned in unmeasurable eating or drinking, when they that were conversant with him had marvelled how that a man might live with so little meat and drink; when he should sit to eat oftentime he would weep for because, he said, "that our nature every day is compelled of every need to receive meat and drink that he fail not". From flesh and all that longeth to flesh abstained he ever, lest that he were sick, then through counsel of his friends he would eat some. Fish he ate through the year, save in Lent and in Advent, then he would eat none; his meat were worts, lettuce and other herbs, which he ate as they had been delicacies; when he was feeble they were fain to prepare him fish in such manner that he knew it naught. This did his servants for pity of his feebleness and when his meat came before him the first part would he give to God, which was bore to some poor man; nearly all the other part he onto them which sat about him. In his refection he took more heed that his soul should be fed with holy scripture than his body with delicate meats. After meals would he have some bodily labour, and then read and pray, and so occupy his time.

Throughout the year was he clad equally; he wore no more clothes in winter than in summer; with a coat he went and no more, for furs he never wore. Thou should had marvel if thou had seen the members of that old body, who the bones and the skin might scarcely hang together, his shoulders crooked, his teeth out of the mouth, who that such an old body might live when all heat was drawn from him, both natural and accidental, that for discomfort sometime his body was nigh contract. Between the linen and the hair he chose the midway, and all for he would have a conformity between his subjects and him, and also for he would flee the vainglory of the world which make men often to lose their reward. This midway call we, that he used, woollen cloth next his body, for hair wore he none, nor linen would he none wear. When he was compelled by the provocation of nature to go to bed and to rest he would say first certain Psalms which he knew of use, first for himself and for his brethren, then for Kings and bishops, and all Christian folk.

This was his usage, at seven o'clock he would go to rest, seldom would he lay on his bed, but he sat thereon communely. His clothes which he wore on the day he put them not from him at eve, but lay with them all night; nor under his bed would he no pillow have, so that when he slept his head hung down without sustainment and touched sometime his breast. We read in the old fathers lives of Egypt that they called sleep, their enemy because at that time, as they thought, they ceased from the service of God. So did our Gilbert, as I suppose; he would not lay soft that he should not sleep long, for they that have much meat must have much sleep. And therefore that on measurable diet and that diuturnal sleep was forbidden by Christ when he said to his apostles."Beware", he said, "that your hearts be not greaved with over much meat or drink, or sleep". On his bed had our master Gilbert no clothes but of wool and no bolstering but straw. When he was set there should no man there him speak a word till the morning.

CHAPTER VII   HIS MANNER OF LIFE

After that lauds were said in the church then would he rehearse certain saints lives; then would he say certain prayers for them that are dead and assoil them; after this would he make a humble and a long confession, not only for himself but for all his, asking of his brethren of all his defaults forgiveness, and he assoiling them all and giving them all his blessing, like as Saint Job did that every day offered unto God for health of his children.

This master Gilbert was never idle, but all the day occupied, either in reading, or in prayer, of in lesson, or in contemplation, or in other holy works, now and then changing from one to another, after time and leisure that he had. And though he had much to do yet went he from no matter till it had a perfect end, nor he hindered never no circumstances of his perfection for any strange matter, that is to say for no temporal profit he put not God's service behind, nor the holy observances which belonged to the cloister were not hindered with business which was outward. In compassion he was a father to all men, in contemplation more raised up than other men.

Often would he weep in hymns and psalms reading, and in the sweet songs of the church when he heard the melody, so was his soul replenished with sweetness, but yet had he more delights in the words than in the notes. And again these vain thoughts that come suddenly on us, avoiding the sweet devotion that we would have, a marvelous usage had he. For in as much he knew well there might no man want them, he set certain marks of his fingers and his joints in what place of the psalm he was, that soon after the temptation dismissed, he might return again unto the same place of his prayer.

And yet moreover, that he should fulfil all righteousness, he chose one of his subjects whom he knew be the Holy Ghost, that he should succeed in his office after his death. This man chose he specially, and to him made his profession and permitted his stableness unto the house of Sempringham, and so of this same man's hands took Gilbert the habit of profession.

What constant and manhood was in this man's heart is full manifest in to manner things. One is that the great causes he went about he sped them without any vexation or perturbation of soul. Another is that the wrong which were done to him or his at the time, he bare them so patiently that he was never moved for them. Beside all this vexation that he had outward, there was another thing which stood near his heart, the great business in spirit, for those houses which he had reared, for the souls which he had gathered, for the great fear that he had that he should hear no evil tidings of them.

And when it happened that any evil report was made he would bless God, and speak some merry words and turn all into solace. He loved truth and righteousness so well that when he was vexed with any matters, either without the religion or within, he would say sometime he had willingly chosen to be exiled, or else his throat to be cut, than he should suffer in his time the laws of the church and the good customs of religion should fail.

CHAPTER VIII   HIS MANNER OF LIFE

In the last end of his age, notwithstanding that he was blind, yet the great strength of his soul was not impaired, for as great zeal and great business had he at this age to increase of religion and rebuking of vices as ever he had he in his young days. His wit as fresh, his understanding as ready, his mind as tough, his reason as clean wore at that hour, and all other things that belonged to the soul as ever they were, which was marvel to see, especially in a man that had a hundred winters in age. He might hear with the best. His tongue failed not of his office. His hand quaked not with palsy. His feet were stable to bear his body, and his other members. Non of them denied his service to the body; like he was unto Caleph and Moses which too at great age had the use of all their members, save this difference is there, that this man had lost his sight.

It is worthy, as some men think, they which serve God with due obedience should have their members obedient to them. For in the mind of this man of which we speak now was full great heart of charity, both unto God and to all men, for in his heart Christ wanted never, men might know by his mouth which was ever speaking of Christ. Also his tongue and his hands were ever ready to help of his neighbours. This was the course of his life; this was the manner of his living; these by the experiment of his virtues; these by the good array of his characteristics with which he was magnified with great men; for in virtue he was greater than they and nought only was he follower of the blessed life of religious men, but he had a life in himself which religious men may follow; let see what man at those days was so commendable of good works that he might be set as equal to this man; what man could now gather so great riches with such poverty, yet most marvel of all, a secular man, dwelling in court, serving in court, and newly drawn out of the world, which taught never of no man the rules such as belonged to the monastery, that he should be perfect so soon and so soon know those rules.

Moreover that he should make rules in which so many persons should rise to perfection, of this had men wonder. Wherefore this man for his holiness was beloved, and for his magnificence stood in marvel to men, but both to God and man he stood in great worship. Kings and princes they honoured him, bishops and prelates they received him full devoutly. They that were near him and also that dwelt far from him, they loved him, and shortly to say, all the people held him in great reverence. Also the virtue of our Lord which gave him all this grace added thereto full great joy, for he that set these good works in him made the same works to shine with virtues.

CHAPTER IX
MIRACLES DONE THROUGH HIM, & APPROACHING HIS DEATH

And though it be so that these days be not used with miracles as the former days were, in which were done many miracles, for as the psalm saith, we see now no tokens, now is there no prophet for to tell us what shall befall; and though it be so that Saint Gilbert be more worthy to be in worship for his meritorious deeds than for doing of miracles yet unto the witness of his good works, beside the great business he had in winning souls, which is of more virtue than curing of bodies, yet were there, through the great merit of his holy life, doing many tokens through which his doctrines were commended and his holiness confirmed. And even as through his words and his deeds the rudeness of many a soul was reformed, right so be the touching of his clothes, his hose, or his girdle, or such other things which he touched in his life, many a body was restored to health after the faith which they put in him.

There was bread kept sixteen years after his death, un-corrupt, un-mould, which he blessed and sent to a devout woman which asked that in God's name, of which bread many men have ate and be healed of divers sickness. Thus after he had fulfilled the great merits of his perfection and set in a perfect stableness all his congregation, also when our Lord had disposed to reward his labours with everlasting joy and the time of his calling was nigh, he began to wax more feeble than he was wont to be and said unto his brethren, he should not long live with them, for that the members of his body began to fail, and nature, which is propitious to health, had withdrawn somewhat her favour. Thus, sickness growing, and age of an hundred year touching, he was in party compelled for to pass from this life in which he was greatly broken for penance which he had endured in God's service, but yet were all his members whole as we said before, save his sight.

Then he sent letters unto all the churches of his Order, in which he notified unto them that his day was come in which he shall leave his body here and go to God's mercy, praying them devoutly in those same letters that they should recommend his soul with their prayers to God, most specially at that time when it should forsake the body. Also in those same letters he gave God's blessing and his to all that after his decease should love the Order and keep those congregations in perfect love and charity, and defend the same Order from their enemy. Moreover to all that this commandment fulfilled he sent plenery absolution of all those defaults in which they had trespassed either against the rule or his institutions. And in those same letters he wrote unto all those that in the Order should make any discord or any schism that this present absolution shall never favour them but that they should know themself, but if they did penance that they were reprobate of God.

CHAPTER X APPROACHING DEATH

Thus when the time was come in which that holy soul should leave the In of his body; in the night in which our Lord Jesus was born, it happened him to be at a house of his in an island, which house they called Cadney, for in that same house at the beginning of his sickness he received the sacraments of penance and of housel, and thus many days after that abode the time assigned by our Lord in which his soul should pass from his body great advisement and full ripe devotion. Though they that were with him, his chaplains and brethren, thought they would remove him from that place, for if it so happened that he had died there, they were afraid that some man of great might would arrest the body by the way in his journey and take their treasure from them.

Therefore they carried him while he was alive by other ways than the common way, and brought him to Sempringham, for it was convenient, as they thought, that his body should lay there which he had set a place, head of all his monasteries. And in this space from Christmas till that day which he died our Lord granted him such a space that all the soveriegns of his Order and all the provosts of his churches might come and visit him, for so they did come unto him and also many a disciple of his, for there had they his blessing and noble exaltations of peace and unity of the rigour also, and the hardness of the Order, who it should be kept after his days, and thus instruct they went home from him.

The last day of his temporal life, when all were out of the house, he sat by his bedside, he that was successor in his office, taking heed at him what he would command. And after he had long been still in silence as man that should soon pass, he no man seeing, no man hear, but with the Holy Ghost replete, thus spake in the ghost. For though his bodily sight were rest from him, yet understood he in his soul that his successor was nigh, wherefore these words of the Psalm, distinctly, openly, and with sad advisement he said in this wise; 'He departed, he gave to the poor men. And then he rehearsed: He departed to many men, He gave, and not seldom, to poor men, not to rich men'.

And then last he said thus. 'To thee shall this long hereafterward.' Then spake he other things to that same man which we cannot rehearse. These words, as I suppose were full convenient unto our master, which departed all his goods to many folk which he had called to the service of our Lord, and gave all these goods for pure charity, for he sold them nought, hoping to have of them any worldly profit. To poor men he gave these goods, non to rich, for those gifts gave to poor men, they that live in wilful poverty for the love of God, should receive him into everlasting tabernacles. To rich men he gave him nought, for they need not and also for it is full hard unto them to enter the kingdom of heaven. For these things that he did there, now is he in joy and this that should be his successor, he learned for to do like as he said.

CHAPTER XI   HIS DEATH

The last day of St.Gilbert's life was a Saturday; we should call it a Sabbath-day be the congruous name. Sabbath is as much to say that day when men rest of their works. This day was convenient to his death, for then rested he of all his labour which he had on this mortal body. He might say at his death: 'Night is gone and day shall come; the darkness shall not take me nor trade me'. The hour of his death was while the convent was at Lauds, at Mattins, for at that time as Job saith: 'Praise God, the morrow stirs'. That same Sabbath-day, that is to say, the fourth day of February, the year of the Incarnation of our Lord, one thousand one hundred, and eighty and nine, such time as night changed into day, while that the Lauds were said in the convent this man passed from the darkness of this life, from the labours of this world, full of age more than a hundred years.

Whither that he went ye shall hear, for to dwell in the house of God, for to praise God there forever, where he is set in his Order, that is to say, amongst the circle and the dance of virgins, as we hope, and as revelations were made to some folk afterward, there hath our Lord granted him his seat. After his death were certain visons and revelations made to persons of great credence, through which visions they that were dwelling far from him had very knowledge of that hour and very certification that he was joined unto the fellowship of angels in heaven.

For though it be so, as we believe, that every man receiveth reward after his works, and as truth sayeth, those freinds that be the god of riches, receive the makers into everlasting tabernacles of great righteousness this man is to believed that he is joined to virgins, for as much as he made both body and soul and made in faith persevered ever, and also all his earthly goods gave unto virgins, and for the virginity of many folk laboured at his life. For even as he that receiveth a rightful man in the name of a rightful man shall take the reward of a rightful man, even so he that receiveth many virgins in the name of virgins shall receive the reward of virgins. Also for as much as this man was prelate and beginner of much number, both of men and women which should avow chastity, and because the number century is applied as for a special reward both to prelates and to maidens, therefore hath this man for those too this special reward.

CHAPTER XII   HIS BURIAL AND CANONISATION

Thus was the soul of this blessed man translated unto heaven and the dead body kept upon the ground four days with exequies and masses after the good customs of the church. In that same time all the Priors and Sovereigns of the Order were sent after to be at the burying of their Master. When they were gathered together and numbered, the sum of his progeny came to two thousand and two hundred. The fourth day after his death, that is to say on the Tuesday, were gathered together many prelates, both of his Order and also of other religions, with much folk of the country that came thither for reverence of the man, and after time the mass was said, they washed the body with water, which was kept, for they that drank thereof were restored to bodily health.

After his washing they arrayed him like a priest, and those, they buried him between two altars one of Our Lady, St Mary, the other of St Andrew the apostle. He was so laid at that time that the women might come to the grave on the one side and the men on the other side. The stone above was not laid until the time that all men which were present, as for their last leave, might come and touch the body with what thing they would, and kiss it for reverence of his holiness. Children, maidens, nor no degree, had no fear, nor horror in kissing of that dead body, for faith gave them boldness to touch it and love sent them boldness to kiss it. What mourning there was of all folk, what lamentation of clerks, what weeping of maidens, for as much as they have lost their head and their principal, their father and their shepherd, and for they should no more have him to their consolation, were long to tell. But our Lord God that wrought all these works in his servant, by whom this same servant Gilbert had great prosperity in all his works, this same Lord would neither defraud his workman of his reward nor the good works of their perfect end, as it shall be shown in this next declaration.

Beside those miracles which were done the day of his burying, and beside the miracle done in substitution of his successor, there fell many other great, of blind men, deaf men, bedridden, dropsy, fevers, madness, and other great sickness, which were cured, some by water in which he was washed, some by other relics of him, some by dreams and visions, some in the same place of his burying, some in other places. It is no doubt that his works were full pleasant unto our Lord, wherefore that he should stand in the more worship amongst men, our Lord made his works to be magnified after his decease, in so much that, by the commandment of Pope Innocent III, Hubert, Bishop of Canterbury and another bishop of Ely, also the Abbot of Peterborough, with many other, made diligent inquisitions and arranged in writing all this in a form and sent it up to the court.

CHAPTER XIII   CANONISATION AND TRANSLATION

And when our holy father the Pope had received this information with council of his brethren, the cardinals, he made this man, this St Gilbert to be numbered and ascribed in the catalogue of saints. A catalogue is a short writing of saints, in which writing is contained of what country the saint was and also his holy life. The Pope commanded also that same time his feast to be solemnised in the church and made collects to be said in his commemoration. He commanded also his body to be translated, as it was fulfilled afterwards. For these causes this father's day should be solemnised with more devotion and with more business, because his life was holier, his doctrine more wholesome, his labour more fervent, his fruit more plenteous, his death more provable, his miracles more evident than some other, and therefore he, be likeliness, hath before God more joy and before men more worship.

Joy be made by our mother the church of the joy to which her son is now newly brought, and to her worship and profit of her children sing she the praising of God and her own, that through the prayer of her merits she might make peace with vices, put away adversity, bring in the strength of virtues, the profit and increase of true religion, our lands and countries, God our maker granting, dispose in everlasting peace, confirming that our Lord Jesus Christ, to whom with the Father and the Holy Ghost ever be worship and joy. Amen.

HERE IS THE SECOND PART OF
ST GILBERT'S LIFE

CHAPTER XIV

Because that a great part of justice is for to do no evil, and the profit of the same justice is for to do good, and also for it is not enough to our health that we take not other men's good wrongfully, or desire it wrongfully, but we be bound for to give our own goods for the love of God freely. For this cause this very priest Gilbert studied every day to bare strips of wood to the holy fire which burnt in the tabernacle, both night and day, for the fire of charity that was in the tabernacle of his breast burnt himself, a full delectable offering to our Lord.

And that he should not run in blind presumption, nor use manners without consideration, but that he should run and take the sum of his merits, the best manner of perfection and the truest way to perfection with great business, he both sort and took. The first ground of his work he set in height of meekness, which virtue despiseth in every man his own excellence, for the very place of meekness is in heaven. Therefore he put away the matter of all earthly goods from himself, for those same goods set a man in false excellence and through a man all underfoot. He threw from him all pride which should rise of virtues that were within him.

He took full great heed to the voice of our Lord that sayeth: 'If thou wilt be perfect, go sell all that ever thou hast and follow me'. This man did this. He gave his goods to poor men, not for vanity but for charity, and for that gift the mind of his righteousness shall without an end. When he had determined in his heart that all his goods should be departed unto the poor men, then chose he such poor whose poverty was honest, knit with the dread and also the love of God, for his desire was to sow his seeds in the blessings of God, that he might reap in those same blessings.

In that same time, that is to say, in the reign of King Henry II, as he writeth in the book made of the construction of Monasteries, in that same time where in the town of Sempringham certain maidens secular, whose souls the seed of God's work, sown by this same Gilbert, had so touched that they were ripe unto religion like as corn is to harvest. these same maidens, desiring to be victorious of their kind and also of the world, every day intended to no other thing but to please and to be knit to that spouse which is in heaven.

This, aspired by St Gilbert, specially when he had in his vow made a promise that his possession of Sempringham and of Torrington should be gave to God, furthermore that he would give this to the poor, and also he found no man at that time would live so strictly as these women were disposed, for this cause, he determined to give these goods to such poor which were poor in spirit and might challenge the kingdom of Heaven for them and for others. This man Gilbert made him friends with such riches as he had, which friends should receive him into everlasting tabernacles. The first friends that he made were not men but of women. Women chose he first for the similitude which our Lord rehearsed in the gospel of a woman that had lost a dram and found it, who she called her friends to joy with her for her dram that was found.

So these maidens first chosen were cause that many other should be called afterwards. A dram is a certain money of gold weighing the seventh part of an ounce. Our Gilbert began his perfection at the feebler kind, for to the feebler kind nature teaches that we should do our benefits. The counsel of God is such also to help that thing which is most feeble, also the reward for this help is the greater, furthermore our Lord in the gospel to the feeblest kind applied the greatest reward, the hundred fold fruit to virginity. Gilbert nourished this estate, and therefore hath he part of her reward. Beside all this, our Gilbert, after the right order of almsgiving, gave his goods to them that were rightful after the counsel of Solomon where he sayeth: 'Give thy goods unto good men and receive not these sinners to thine alms'.

CHAPTER XV   THE BEGINNING OF HIS ORDER

Seven maidens, as we said before, fulfilled with heavenly desires in worship of that number of seven gifts longing unto the Holy Ghost, those were beginners of this holy religion under our father Gilbert. These seven bodily virgins offered to be number of these seven gifts, made their virginity the more meritorious because they were array with virtues. What profiteth a lamp that hath no oil? What profiteth clean flesh when the soul is corrupt? What profiteth a body and a heart defouled? Be this way should these heathen men be virtuous whose life is all sin. Therefore, that these maidens should be clean in soul and body; to their souls he ordained clean instruments, their bodies with which they should work their own health.

And because that no man which serveth God may serve well God and be occupied with temporal business, also because virginity is a tender thing and may soon be tempted of the subtle deceits of the serpent, the devil, which is full old of time and full subtle of kind and soon deceiveth virginity, namely, when it is set so open that it is shown to the world – for treasure openly bore is put in great peril – for this cause he closed these virgins from the noise of the world, from sight of men, that they which should enter into the privy chamber of the spouse they should only enter unto the sweet embracing of the same spouse. He would not that they should walk to see vanity, as did Dinah, but that they should hide them in her tabernacle, as did Sarah, or in her conclave, as did Our Lady.

And for it is not enough for to abstain from evil but if we do good, therefore he made to them a law of holiness and taught them that same with which they should please to the heavenly spouse and cleave to his chaste embracing in all manner cleanliness. This gave he them a law of life and of love, of chastity, of meekness, of obedience and charity, and all other virtues which led to everlasting life, he commanded them to keep. They, as good disciples, joyfully received them and devoutly fulfilled them. There shone, or else shined, in the soul of these women, a fair beauty of precious pearls of such spiritual richness as our Lord telleth in the gospel, that a man should sell all that he hath for to possess this.

And though they lived in flesh and not after the flesh, yet know he well as long as they were in flesh, beside such neccessaries as belongeth to the flesh, they might not live, therefore all things that is needful to our fleshy feebleness as meat, or drink, or clothing, or houses, all these ordained he to these maidens and their servants in best manner, in measure and discretion, that is seen, such houses as belong to religion, with a cloister, walled about, and in those houses he closed the handmaidens of our Lord, ever for to dwell there in solitary life; and this work was under the wall of the church of St Andrew, in the street or town of Sempringham, on the north side, first asked and had the counsel and the help of Alexander, then Bishop of Lincoln.

Door was there none made in the wall but one, and that was not open but such time as shall be touched afterward; there made he a window through which they might receive such neccessaries as belong to their life, for though they were in the world he would put them out of the world, from their land, from their kindred, from their father's house, that thus exiled from all these, like a church, and they have a church, that is to say, a congregation in one faith and one charity, forgetting their people and their father's house, from all curiosity and all covetousness, or concupiscence, from all pride, thus clean roused to the high king, should make a complaisance in desiring of her beauty. Thus bound he their bodies within those walls at that same place Sempringham.

CHAPTER XVI   HIS FIRST CONVENT

But he would not, though he prisoned their bodies, bind their souls from God, but this was his intent to close them, because that conversion in the world is won to depart many men from that familiarity which should have with God. Alas because that they might nowhere go out, therefore he ordained unto their service certain maidens not learned, in a poor secular habit, which should bring unto that window made in the wall all things that was neccessary for them, and receive of them at that same hole such things as were convenient to bare out.

That same hole left he open, but not ever open, for it was opened but at certain times which were assigned, for he would have closed it for ever if it had been so that man or woman might have lived without meat or drink or other neccessaries. For a door was made beside, but never open without his special commandment, not for the maidens to go out, but for him to enter unto them for spiritual comfort, or teaching of religion, or visiting of the sick, or such other neccessary causes; also of that door was he jailor himself; no man bore that key but he. Whither that he went, where ever he dwelt, the key of that door was with him, so was he jealous lover of their cleanliness.

After this he studied sorely that there should nothing outward break that peace which these solitary folk had in their cloister. He learned also of religious men and wise men that it was not convenient, nor certain, that secular maidens running about the world should serve such solitary persons for evil speech often time impair full good manners, and also they that run so about should bring chattering tidings, which might impair the souls of the nuns, for this cause those same secular maidens, with the good counsel of their father Gilbert and partly with their own devotion, desired to have a religious habit and so dwell with the nuns, so had they. For there, when they were in full poor life, they served the nuns and lived in full honest conversation.

Thus of one kernel which our founder threw in the earth grew now err beside the first spring which was the nuns. Then when St Gilbert say the good zeal at these secular maidens, this changed unto God, he was full merry for devotion of their faith, but because they were inexpert, not used in such, and simple and unlearned as touching literature, for such idiots all day promise more things than they may fulfil, therefore would not he, our father Gilbert, give them no hard precepts nor lay no grievous burden on their shoulders which they should throw away afterward and repent to great shame of himself and great villainy to religion.

Therefore these neophytes are for to prove that Satan transfigures not himself into an angel of light that the wolf did not on his back have sheeps wool; that the ostrich take not the wings of a hawk; that the ass have not the lions members. All this is said by the author of this life which is of this Saint, that he calleth them neophytes that he newly converted to religion; for neophytes were called in old times folk newly converted to the faith and all these transubstantiations following rehearseth our author to this intention, that men of religion should not have fair conditions outward and evil inward, as malice in soul like a wolf and innocence in words like sheep's wool, and so may man expound all the other transubstantiations.

For this same cause that these folk should understand what they do, and also that they should prove as their age grew, what they should answer, this noble master told them before all these perils and learned them all the sharpness of religion, all that ever they had learned by experience or by telling of other men. To his sisters he preached that they should despise the world, and cast from the hearts all manner of property, that is to say, they should think nothing was theirs, but all commune, as religious folk must do: he taught them the manner who they should chastise their flesh to travail and to occupy them from idleness, and never to sit quiet from labour in prayer or occupation.

He taught them for to wake and not to sleep much, to fast long and not to use meats out of time. Wretched meat, sharp cloth; this would he they should have; no gay array, but closed in cloister as in prison, that they should do no evil, to keep silence, that they no evil speak, but be occupied with orisons and meditations to avoid evil thoughts. They answered unto him at that time that all these precepts pleased him well, to take hardness for softness, labour for ease, heaviness for sweetness, all these things would they gladly suffer, so they might come where they desired.

The need of poverty constrained them, and labour in begging, for to desire to bare high things, to that intention that they might be certain of everlasting reward. The love of God also, that drew them to this same intention, and health of their souls through which they might deserve everlasting rest. So of needs they made virtue and though in some of them were not the very intentions of perfection, yet it hindered not but it got them the end of good work. But this holy man would not bind them suddenly to this perfection, but let them have a year of advisement that of that great dilation should grow the desire of religion.

CHAPTER XVII   HIS FIRST MEN AND GROWTH OF THE ORDER

Then say our father in his inwardly consideration that, without men's solace and purveyance, woman's business profiteth but little therefore chose he certain men which should oversee their possessions and governance of all those great matters which belonged unto them. Some of these chose he of his ploughmen and of his servants some of poor men's children and beggars which he had nourished from their childhood. He was like the servant of which the gospel speaketh, that at the commandment of our Lord went into the lanes and streets of the city, and such as he found poor or feeble, brought and compelled them to enter, that his Lord's house be full.

To these men, thus newly gathered, which he say were inflamed with the love of everlasting life, to these same, at their petition, he ordained a token of meekness, a habit which signified to them that they should despise this world and forget the vanity that longeth thereto. And those same precepts, full hard and not easy, of which we spoke before, he wrote unto them, and taught them that they should not fall from mind. He taught them furthermore other virtues that belong properly to the soul, as meekness, obedience, patience, and such other, whose exercise is hard and made great, and they, as devout disciples, took those precepts gladly and made their vow to fulfil them forever.

Thus is the treasure, or else the talent, doubled, that our Lord took him (Mathew 25), for our Lord put first in his mind to make a congregation of women, and now newly he hath doubled this gift when he gathered their men. Thus is the juncture of women and men joined as brooches for the crown of spouse, thus made by the hands of the high workmen. Now in the time come that the well beloved masculine with the well beloved feminine should go out into the field of this world, for to dwell in the villages and the cities of people. Now was the day come that the vine which our Lord planted should fulfil the earth with his roots, and spread his palms to the sea, and his branches to the other floods; that is to say, that the members of this order should spread the branches of good example,that it should be known wide.

Thus by process of time, by the will of our Lord God, the seed which he had sown by the first fathers of this way many rich men; noblemen of England, that is to say, Earls, Barons, and others, saying and appraising this work which God had begun, and saying before what goodness was disposed after, they offered many possessions to our father Gilbert, and monasteries, in many provinces, under his rule and governance, they begun to edify, of which help Alexander bishop of Lincoln was first, and King Henry II, he confirmed all. Our father Gilbert received those possessions with full great dread; and some was he in manner coax to receive; and some refused he and would not have them, because his desire was from the beginning of his order that his progeny should live in honest poverty.

Honest poverty call we that a man is not in harm for his daily need, nor he hath neither no great superfluity of good. This was the cause that he would not have over much when it was gave him, for often time it is seen that among great multitude of people and great plenty of richness rise full great spots of pride, as it is said by wise men. In the multitude of the people joy of the king. For his first purpose at his beginning was for to have kept no more but those seven which he had closed up, that as long as they lived there should be no more. But he say by the will of our Lord that rich men had multiplied many monasteries to increase of this order; he would not be contrary to God's will, nor let the devotion of the givers, nor by reckless of the sustenation to the servants of God, knowing well that this was God's virtue and not his; wherefore, he committed all this disposition to the profound counsel of our Lord which useth the service both of good and evil after his pleasance.

CHAPTER XVIII   AT THE CISTERCIAN CONGRESS AND MADE PRINCIPAL OF HIS ORDER

When our master Gilbert say thus the children of God grow so under his tuition and say them profiteth day by day in the way of God, unto the time in which they were greatly magnified, he deemed of himself, as it belongeth to good souls to have them self in little reputition, so deemeth he himself unworthy for to be in such height that he would put his burden and his honour from him, and commit his flock to one or else many which were able and mighty than he, that they should have it in governance.

He was in this case a follower of Moses which said unto the Lord: 'I pray the Lord send him that thou shall send', meaning hereby that he was not able to be sent. And in another place Moses said to God: 'Whom shall thou give, Lord, for to be Governor and principal over this multitude, which multitude thou hast made grow into a great people? Thou knowest that from that time that thou spoke to me, thy servant, that I should take upon me to be president over this people, since that time I am a man of lower life, that is to say a man of secular conversation, which should be holier than other, and I am not. I know full well that the judgement shall be full grevious to them which are prelates, for they must answer for them self and also for their subjects, and I am full evil afraid that if I be not better than my flock, I shall be turned from the first into the last'.

Such manner words had he often and such desires to leave his prelacy. In all this business he heard tell that there should be a great congregation of the order of Cistercians, which was newly begun that time by St Bernard. Where it was held, I read not, but the Pope Eugenius was there, which was sometime disciple to St Bernard. To this congregation went our Gilbert, proposing for to commit the care of his children to the keeping of these monks. For these men's conversation knew he best by great familiarity which he had with them, for often they came and were lodged with him, and to these only told he his counsel, for they were new and of harder rule that the black monks are. Wherefore he supposed that his order should be in most certainty of it were committed to them, for their new foundation and their strictness was more according to his ideas.

His answer had he of the Pope and of the abbots which were present: they said it was not convenient that prelates of their order should be preferred to the governance of another order, especially where women were. Thus frustrate of his purpose, he took leave, and, by the commandment of the Pope and counsel of the prelates there present, he was made master and principal over that congregation which he had begun. Our Lord would not that the congregation at Sempringham should want their own keeper which was better unto them than ten others, as Helchana said to Anna. 'For our Lord had disposed that same congregation to rise to the most perfect number which was at that time of another condition. This religion, which we call our sister, was but young at this time, for she had no tetes as yet, of prelates and sovereigns, to give such unto the tender age of subjects, nor for to give meat of substance to them which were to grow into more perfection, which also should dispose all the flock with protection outward and inwardly confirm.'

CHAPTER XIX   ST MALACHY AND ST BERNARD

Thus our holy father Eugenius has committed all authority to our master Gilbert in the keeping of this holy flock, for there was not found a better nor more sure keeper than that same man which was gatherer of that people, and also so jealous a lover of them and the first labourer in that holy vine. Never the less he held himself unworthy to the burden of such an imposition; he alleged the importance of his age, the unworthiness of himself to such dignity, the simpleness to that masterhood, his lowness also to so high a prelacy. All this dread had he in his soul that he was not worth to be preferred to such dignity; he dread also to lose the solitary rest of his contemplation, for while he waste that, those secret counsels which he was used to, and the busy contemplations, should often be interrupted with worldly occupation and busy over which belongeth unto prelates.

All these excuses of meekness were not admitted to the Pope, but the yoke of all his burden was laid in his neck, for the Pope committed all this cure unto him, because he say that he had no great appetite nor desire thereto. The purpose of our father Gilbert was ever to dwell amongst them that be humble, and the will of our Lord God is ever of custom to exalt them that most humble themself. Thus, when this God's own man knew well that the judgement of God had ordained he should take this charge, he was no more hardy to make any resistance against the disposition of God which had chosen him to that work. Thus would he not lose the great abundance of virtues which were within him with obstinacy, wherefore he meekly received this obedience of God and the commandments of God's vicar, the Pope, trusted for this obedience to receive sometime the more reward, because he had no great delight to be preferred to such an office.

He put his own will, his own profit behind, only for the welfare and health of many other. He was full, while learned before in the study of contemplation, and now began he to learn who he should profiteth in ministration of active life, for he would have the fruit of both lives, that is to say, both active and contemplative. He might also more lawfully be a dispenser of those worldly goods than another man, because the same goods were his sometime. For he gave them to poor men with which he dwelled as a poor man, not as a governor of his own, but as a procurator and a servant of other men's riches.

For this cause and many other holy tokens and many good reports which were said of him, the Pope Eugenius had in manner of and heaviness that he knew never our father Gilbert ere that time, for if he had known him, as he said, he would have promoted him to the archbishopric of York, which stood void at that time. Thus came our father home, in fellowship long time with St Malachy, archbishop of Ireland, and St Bernard, abbot of Clairvaux, to which two men he was so familiar in that voyage that in their presence, through his devout prayer, a certain man was made whole of sickness which he had. He received also tokens of love both of the bishop and the abbot, the staves of their crosses with which afterward were done many miracles; and in special, St Bernard gave him a kerchief, and therein a certain relic, as some say; but I understand that this kerchief was goodly bordered on the ends, for border soundeth so in grammar.

Thus is he come home again to Sempringham, frustrate, as we said of his purpose, in which, of very meekness, he had thought to have laid away the yoke from his neck, and have put this office on some notable man of the religion of those Cistercians; but our Lord thus with heavenly warning, as we suppose, kept him in this office as most perfect and able.

CHAPTER XX   MONKS AND NUNS

When he was thus constrained that he must keep this office himself, then chose he out of his own religion certain men to bare the burden of governance, with like as Moses did as we read by the counsel of Jethro, priest of the heathen law, he assigned certain men to have governance under him and all the great causes he would redress himself. Thus did our master; he chose men of sufficient learning, of holy conversation, ordered after the custom of the church, which should have under him this governance. Men were chose for this cause, for it is more convenient that men be preferred in governance than women. Learned men were chose and no unlearned men, that they should have cunning to teach others.

Ordered were they for this skill, for they might not else have cure of souls lest that they were in holy orders. Then chose he men for to govern women; learned men for to teach the way of Heaven both to men and women; clerks also, that they might be the better keepers of sheep which Christ bought with his blood. All this did this man by holy inspiration of our Lord God, and by good counsel of Holy men and wise men; for, as the decrees of our forefathers bare witness, the monasteries of maidens may not stand without help and succour of monks, or clerks, which must be spiritual fathers to such tender souls, to govern them in the sweet yoke of our Lord.

But for as much as the laws of the holy church forbid that no monks, no clerks shall dwell with women, but they shall be far removed, each of them from the other, so farforth that women should not come near the monastery than to the porch of the same, this same prohibition followed this man in the most straightest wise, in so much that he set the dwelling of the clerks far from the dwelling of the nuns, as a man should set in one city or in one town two divers places of divers religion. So were these canons far set from the nuns, that they should not come within the nuns in no manner but only for administration of the sacraments. In this matter may be said that habitation of men and women in one place was forefended in old time for great peril that, most speciallly for feign folk that used their sin under colour of holiness, as a man may read in diverse places of Saint Jerome Epistles.

Thus our Lord full mercifully and marvelously can make his saints to shine with great joy of conscience in this earth, for them that he justifieth he maketh full great; for he is not wont to light a lantern and hide it under a bushel, but to set it up in height on a chandelier, that all men which shall enter into the house of our Lord may see light. Our Lord will show often to the world what those men are which he loveth; for the great dignity which they shall rejoice afterward, our Lord showeth before are grace of miracles, that they which see all this thing may know the better are very way of truth and with certainty of hope come to the life that ever shall last. Such pity on his servant Gilbert hath the grace of God uses, first giving him good works with which he should shine, and afterward granting virtue of miracles to make his works open.

CHAPTER XXI HE AIDS THOMAS BECKETT

His patience among all other virtues was to him a very crown, for that was granted him of God that he should want no virtue but that he should be keeper of all virtues. God would that the ointment of virtue which was within him should be stirred and rolled with many triblulations, that after that rolling it should have the more odour. He would also that the small seed of mustard should be all broken to which should be the more poignant after that grinding. All this is said for our father Gilbert, which was accused to the King Henry II that he gave favour to Saint Thomas of Canterbury in his exile and sent him into France great plenty of money.

For which cause Gilbert was indicted and many of his fellowship for favouring of the king's traitor, and writs were sent out that Gilbert and all the priors of his order should be exiled. And in this cause our father was not guilty, that is to say, to send money over the sea; but before Saint Thomas's exile, while that he was hid in private in England, Gilbert gave him good and sent him sustenance. For as we read in the life of St Thomas, a canon of the Sempringham order led St Thomas from Northampton to the sea through many privy ways and fens unknown to many men.

In this same matter, because St Gilbert was of such reputation as touching holiness, he was required to come before the judges and make there a bodily oath whether he was guilty in this matter or not. But this refused he, for he said he had liefer be exiled than swear, for he would not leave a bad example to them that should come after him. Like unto this matter read we in the book of Machabees of the good old man called Eleazarus which would not eat swines flesh forbidden by law of Moses. He said he would rather die, and when he was counselled of his friends that he should pretend to eat it he would not, neither for fear of losing of his life, nor for counsel of his friends; he said that young men should not take example of old Eleazarus to break the law of Moses for fear of death. So was our old man also disposed that he would not leave the church undefended while he might leave it, nor he would not pretend to leave it; for if he had done so, he should have behold amongst men heartless; he should have been cautious that other men should have been more faint, and more over, before God he had run in great offence.

CHAPTER XXII   HIS MONKS REBEL, THEN BLINDNESS

In this same time while our father stood in this perplexity, our Lord changed the King's heart which was then in Normandy, and letters were sent from him over the sea to the judges of this land, that this cause touched Gilbert and his brethren should be differed from them to the King's audience. Merry and glad was our father in all this abiding, and when they all trembled for fear, as no wonder was when they had made them ready to forsake kindred and country and never to come again. His heart in all this time was trusting in God, for he thought as Saint James sayeth, 'A full great joy was come to him when he was assayed with divers temptations'.

Another vexation had our master which was not little. Certain brethren of his which he had converted from the world and nourished from their childhood, turned into malice, were weary of their order and of their profession, turning all their spiritual conversation to lust of eating and drinking and lechery, so farforth that they defamed our master and his fellowship of great vigour, and moreover writing and sent unto the Pope, complaining and allegations that many things which were not true. Upon this come certain bulls from Rome that this matter be indifferent persons should have his examination. Thus was our Gilbert called to appear into the farthest parties of this land, and to answer to these accusations, not withstanding his great age and feebleness.

But this man, full of constance, was not afraid of pain, nor labour, nor cost, nor threatening of the judges, nor fair suasions of others; all these might not make him to consent for to go out of the perfect way which he had begun, for he would say often he had liefer his throat were cut than anything be left of the first profession and the first institution which he had made. But when this matter was discussed, it was found that his accusers were false, and thus was the blessed man proved as metal in the furnace, and peace sent from heaven unto the church and his religion. For when his adversaries failed of their proofs and could with no craft have that they desired, they were compelled by God and shame in their conscience to pray him of forgiveness, in which prayer they desired that he should somewhat temper the great hardness of religion and suffer them not to be kept so straightly as they were before. The good old man without any difficulty received them to grace, and in token of entire love, he kissed them all; also, in that temperance which they desired of all sharpness of religion partly with authority of the Pope, partly with wise counsel of religious men, he promised them to fulfil much of their desire.

In the last end of his age, like another Job which was smit in his flesh with full grievous wounds, he was smit with blindness, for he lost the sight of his body. But this stroke was not smit of God as an enemy, but as a friend provoking a man to battle promising victory to him. For of that default of blindness in his body grew unto him a great perfection of understanding in his soul, and he was after that time replete with grace of the Holy Ghost more abundantly. For now grew he absent to secular things and more present to everlasting desires, as a man that after great labours had great delights of contemplations.

CHAPTER XXIII   HIS MANNER OF LIFE

His occupation by the day was in prayer, or in hearing of good lessons, or in spiritual comfort of his brethren, ever talking of virtue; of such occupation ceased he never, save such times as nature requireth his inclination; for, save those times, ever his mouth or his mind was not idle. If any man had interposed words which were not pleasance to God, nor sounding to virtuous life, they should greatly displease him. He himself spake but few words; he had more delight to hear than to speak, for all that he spake was sounding unto great prophet of virtuous governance.

He thought often of that verse of the prophet David, where he saith: 'Obmutui, et humiliatus sum et silui a bonis'. He was down, he saith, and humbled himself, and kept silence, that he should not speak good. It was the condition of David, and so hath been of many holy men, to speak but few words and but seldom, for they were ever afraid of that Solomon saith, 'That in much speech sin wanteth naught'. This caused our master to say but few words that he should use them well. Ever was his mind unto heaven and ever bidding soft prayers, often would he among his prayers say, 'How long Lord shalt thou forget me? And woe is me that my good dwelling place is kept so long from me!'

Sometime, when we supposed he had been asleep, his hands were covered with his mantel, but his eyes say we lift up to heaven, and ever soft words heard we of his mouth. Sometime also when he sat talking with other men, if the talking were long, he, as in partly afraid that there was some excess of speech, suddenly would burst out and say his confession, meekly asking absolution and then after he would assail devoutly them which were about him that time. By night time he was occupied most with prayers and full privily would he go to his rest, first kneeling long before his bed. And when his cubiculars would look if he lay well, then would blame them that they made his bed no better over night. These words were in manner of excuses, for he was loath that any man should see in what manner he rested, for to that private he desired no more secretaries but God and saints with whom he would talk the most part of the night.

What should we speak of his diet, with what scarceness of meat and drink he was fed? He loved so well the common refection that when he was in great languor, as it naturally follows age, he would not, for no prayer of his brethren, eat in the dormitory; he would never be absent from the same house where they all had their refection, not withstanding that the refectory was far and many steps there to, which was great difficult to an old man to climb. When he was prayed of his disciples that he should spare his great age and his sickness he would in a manner of a holy anger answer and say: 'Gilbert shall not be example to his successors for to eat delicacies in his chamber'.

For this cause were they fame for to bare him, one on the one side, another on the other; and with great labour thus came to the board, to which, when he was come, he pined his body with hunger rather than filled it, ever thinking of the vessels belonging to our Lord and ever having mind of his congregation. When he was bore from the board again to his couch, all the other part of the day he spent in the same use, that is to say, prayed or heard holy lessons, or commune in devotion. And that he should have the very end of all perfection, because he had ascended from one virtue to another, and also because he was greater in virtue that he supposed himself, for he knew well that a virtue is never the less though it defend not himself, for this cause he pervayed peace against all perils which might fall to those congregations made by him; also that debate which was among the lay people of his order for diversity of meats, this same debate with consent of all his chapter and in presence of Hugh, then Bishop of Lincoln, he set in rest and peace, and other means of peace ordained he, and made them to be written and kept in his congregations, without end to endure.

CHAPTER XXIV HIS MIRACLES

These be the miracles which our Lord wrought by his servant Gilbert while he lived in this bodily life. A canon of his that had been and was ever in his fellowship when he went from one place to another, which man's name was called Albyne, after a great feebleness that he had taken of labour in his journey, fell in a grievous fever, in so grevious that he might not go with his master as he was wont to do, so that our master was fain to abide at a place which they call the island; there abode he, abiding this man's recovery, and went no further. And when our good father had lay there long and grew weary, desiring to fulfil his journey, he sent a messenger unto this man, commanding him in virtue of obedience that he should no more suffer the fever to come unto him, but that he should without any cessation come unto his master in all haste. By the same messenger, also, he commanded unto the fevers that they should no more be bold to vex his servant. When this message was done, this same Albyne inclined his head to that precept, as religious men should do, saying that he was ready to obey his master in all things.

The next day came, and also the hour in which the fevers were wont to take him, and all the tokens were come, as shaking, aching of the head and such other; then spake this Albyne unto this sickness as to a living creature in such manner, 'What meanest thou that thou wilt now vex me again? Hast thou no mind who that my master forbade thee that thou should no more vex me? But now I command thee in my master's name that thou obey to his precept and busy thee no more to my vexation'. Immediately, as he had said these words, he blessed him with the sign of the holy cross, and soon after he fell in a sweet sleep, and after he woke he was delivered of that sickness, nor many years after was not he vexed with the fevers.

CHAPTER XXV   HIS MIRACLES

Another canon was there of the place called Sixhills which had in his feet a violent and intolerable pain. This man, trusting in the great virtue which our Lord had put in his master, made means to the minister of our master that he should keep him the water in which our master should wash his feet at eve. For that was his custom, as they say, to wash his feet every night. As the man desired, the water was kept, and he, with great devotion, washed there in his feet and thereby was made whole. The great faith of the one man and the clean living of the other, through the might of God, brought this miracle to end.

There was also a knight dwelling about Oxford, that, for health of his soul, was made a canon in the place of Osney. This man soon after his profession was made cellarer of that house, and not long during in that same office, he fell in that sickness which they called gout, which is a sickness, as they say, of them that have led their life in great delicacy; and it causes such pain in the feet that it deprives a man of his walking. This man thus hurt, heard tell of the great miracles wrought by our father Gilbert, and who many places and what number of persons were edified by his doctrine.

Of this fame he conjectures in his soul the very truth, that such things might not be done without virtuous living. Wherefore, with great trust of his soul, he converted him to God and to this Saint, and made means unto them that were dwelling with Gilbert, that he might have a pair of old socks, or thin shoes, which our master had often worn. He had such as he desired, and immediately, as he had used them awhile, his feet were whole. Along time after this the same pain that was in his feet fell to his hands, and more pain it was to him there than it was in his feet. Then took he the same socks and wore them on his hands, and from that day forth both his hands and his feet were whole.

CHAPTER XXVI   HIS MIRACLES

Our master had a cup of which he drank often, and, as it seems, it was of wood bound by silver, like as religious in this land use much. This cup was broke with some fall and sent unto Beverley, unto a goldsmith, for to repair it. This goldsmith, when the cup came, lay in the burning fever, for so happened it that, that same time was the hour of his sickness. And when he heard that this was our master's cup, and that of custom he drank often in the same, he desired greatly to drink of this cup. So was the cup filled with drink, and of that same drink this man had his health.

Another man, of the number of them that were now clerks in the same order, had in his foot a sore which they called a fistula. And so happened on Maundy Thursday when all the brethren should be washed, he desired greatly that our master should wash him. So was it ordained that he was set where our devout father should in his course wash all the row, that, by his touching, as he believed, verily the man might be whole. The good old man in his course of washing came to this sick man, and with both his hands constrained his sore foot, because he thought it was not clean. Thus he constrained it with washing, but in that same handling, corrupt blood ran out of the wounds and other matter such as sores have, and all this washed our father full clean with that same water of that holy ministry. What shall we tell long tale? By then he had washed away this blood and this other unclean matter, all the foot was whole.

There was also a prioress of his nuns that lay so sick that every man looked when she should die. He heard tell of her that she was so near death, and by a messenger commanded death that he should not take her at this time, for she was full necessary unto the religion. Soon after this he visited this woman himself, and his back was but turned from her in his going that she comforted immediately, for all the hurtful humours went out from her suddenly by a sweat, and also the great constriction of her womb was resolved marvellously.

CHAPTER XXVII   KING STEPHEN'S WARS

In that same time was a great debate between Stephen, King of England, and Henry, duke of Normandy, afterward king.

[Alternate] his debate was so great and the parties so strong that all this land at that time was nearly lost. For the fields lay without tilth, the small towns had no dwellers, the walls were fallen down and streets destroyed. Great towns were near desolate; there were nothing else but prey and theft, and burning, every man again the other. This made our master hurt greatly afraid because he say the land near destroyed, and in special for the new religion which he had begun was full likely to run desolation.

Upon this sorrow and heaviness the good man prayed night and day that our Lord should have mercy on his people and send an end to this desolation. Suddenly, as he lay and prayed, was shown unto him a book in which book was written the number of those years in which this desolation should last. When he had read this scripture he fell down flat and made great sorrow, for he supposed verify that all these years were for to come. For if it were so that this persecution should last so long, all this land should, by possibility be destroyed. Though he that shown him this book gave him comfort and notified unto him that these were the years which he say of that whole persecution; of which some were passed and some for to come. There he let him have knowledge how many were passed and how many to come; and as this vision shown, so followed the deed, for that same year marked in the book ceased that debate and that desolation. This revelation was a great comfort unto our father and unto other men to which he opened his counsel.

We knew also in that same time a noble woman of great richness, which, as often as she conceived, the children that she bear were born dead. Another woman dwelling beside had a girdle with which our father Gilbert had often been gird next his flesh. This girdle was taken by this woman to the other woman, which might not bring forth children one life, and she used it continually next her flesh. Soon after she conceived a child, and then another, which children lived on to man's age and were worthy men both in honour and richness.

CHAPTER XXVIII   A MIRACLE IN LONDON

There was a man, also, of Stamford, at that time had a wife that bore no children. So happened our master in a journey to choose his hostel at this man's house. When he was come thither, the woman heard great reports of his holiness, and thought that by his merits she might conceive like as the woman Shunammite conceived by the presence of Elisha. Trusting thus on this man's goodness, she made our father Gilbert's bed in that same place where her husband and she were wont to lie down. Gilbert went forth on his journey, the good man of the inn came home, and in that same bed, as the woman believed, the merits of our father Gilbert, she conceived a son, and called him, when he was born, after the name of the good old man Gilbert. And when our father heard of this chance, with great mirth he sent a cow to the woman, praying her to nourish well this child.

It happened on a time, also, our master to lie at London: happened so, that a place next to the inn where he lay was suddenly on fire. So when it came near his chamber, they that were about him cried upon him to go thence and flee such great peril. He would not himself remove nor suffer nothing in the house to be carried out, but commanded them that they should lead him and set him at the window which he might best see the fire. When he was set there he began to pray, sometime loud, sometime soft, sometime saying, sometime

85

singing. So the fire came so near that all other fled, but he sat still and moved not and suddenly the flame of the fire, as though it had dread the presence of our master, left that part and went to another place, sparing that house where he sat and all the houses which belonged to that inn. He that was lord of that inn and keeper thanked God often since, saying with great faith that through the merits of Gilbert his place was saved.

CHAPTER XXIX   POWER OVER ELEMENTS

Even as by the disobedience of the first man, Adam, mankind lost the due domination of himself and of other things that be under him, right so by the meekness of the second man Christ, they that follow his steps recover such right that they may have all things in subjection. Truth saith thus to us in the gospel: 'If ye have faith as great as mustard seed, or else, if your faith be as a mustard seed, ye shall see unto this hill, go from this place and fall in to the sea, and it shall be so'. And in another place he saith: 'I say you truly, what so ever ye ask in your prayer, believe, for ye shall take it'.

In our father Gilbert have we the exhibition of this precept. Because he was obedient to Him that made him, whom wind and water obey, therefore our Lord granted to him for to work many things, and to have commandment over these elements. For to his precepts were these elements buxom, wind, sea and fire, and all they bowed to the strength of his virtue. One special chronicle will we allege in this matter. Our father should once sail over the water of the Humber for visitation of his flock that was in the province of York, or else he came from York into this country and that is most likely.

The wind blew out of the south with such impetuousness and made the wave so for to rise, there durst no man go. He was compelled to abide at a grange which they called Hesslerkew Grange, abiding the end of the storm and comfort of fair weather. He lay there long and was weary of that life, and much more weary for he had great haste to see those persons which he went to visit. He asked of them that should lead him what wind was best to lead him over the water. They said the north wind was best, if it would blow. He answered that he supposed the north should be more gracious, but he commanded them in our Lord's name, in whom was all his trust, that they all should with a good devotion say the Lord's prayer to our Lord. This made he them to do that no man should deem that he trusted on his own merits, and that he should flee the praising of men, which was over his appetite.

After they had said this orison he commanded his horse to be saddled and all his men to make them ready. This they haste toward the brink of the water, and the tempest began somewhat to cease. The sailors said each to the other, let us take the water in Mary's name; we are likely to have a good freight. This said they of great certainty, for they trusted much upon this man's virtue. Thus make they ready their ships, and the same wind which our master desired, they had; they go into the vessels, draw up her sails and with a favourable wind they land where they desire. The most marvel in this matter was as they told that were present, that when our master was landed the same tempest rose again and that same wind in that place where he took his ship, that all men might know that the face of heaven was not changed at that time but by his merits.

CHAPTER XXX   VISIONS AT HIS DEATH

After that time that our master was passed out of this world, certain dreams were shown to certain virtuous persons, in which dreams the time and the hour of his death was notified and openly declared that this man was joined unto those saints in heaven. For that night in which he passed from the world such a vision was shown unto a prioress of nuns, not of his order, but of another, in the province of York. The woman say in her vision a great church standing in a fair place, and on the west side of the church a great house, in which house many men were busy to array all such things as belong to burying of a man, that is to say, a bier arrayed with clothes of silk, with candles and a cross and much other things, as belongeth to that solemnity.

And in this dream this same person, this prioress, had great marvel, for she had never in all her life seen no such solemnity about no dead man. Amongst the people, which were great, as she thought, she spake unto one and prayed him to tell her what manner man this was there dead for whom all this array was made. That same person gave her this answer, that master Gilbert of Sempringham was passed from this world, and our Lord would that he should be buried with such solemnity. After this he that lay on the bere rose up, as she thought, and took a cross in his hand and began to sing a song in Latin with a note of such melody that she had never heard no such. The letter to that same note was this: 'Pure mentis gaudia ostendamus eia in vocis melodia'. The English is this as I suppose: 'The joy of our clean mind let us show now all in fear with voice full of melody'.

When he had sung this verse all the people following sang the same, and so went they forth on procession into that same church. When this woman say this bishop thus singing and one live, she said unto him which told her that Gilbert was dead: 'Whence thou that I know not master Gilbert? I know him full well, and he is not dead, for thou said he was dead, and he is yonder in the procession'. Then the man said to her again: 'Know thou nought what fell to Saint John the Evangelist? Even as he had the mother of our Lord in keeping, so had this man in governance many persons which followed her virginity'. Then spake the nun to him again: 'I know well what fell to Saint John, for he is the advocate of our place, and I can his life nigh be hurt'. And then said the man to her: 'Right as our Lord hath done with Saint John, right so will He do with this man'.

In this meanwhile the procession went from the house, and she enquired of him whether it should go. He said that all the processions of the world should meet with that procession. Thus talking, they entered the church, and that procession stood still before the great cross. Anon she say many processions enter into the church, more than she could number, of which she knew many, and then she dread her for the great number that she should be trod under foot. In this dread she woke, and felt so sweet a savour in her nose that she had never felt before, for all that day and many days after that sweetness abound, with which sweetness she was greatly refreshed.

In this time of her waking her sister rang to mattins and she rose, gathered all her sisters, and told them plainly that she, to know by her dream that master Gilbert was dead. Not long after by a messenger that was sent to tell them of his passing, they knew verily that this was the hour in which he passed. It is full likely that this vision was truth, for we read that the death of St Martin was known to many sundry persons which dwelt far, in that same hour of his passing, as to Saint Sever, bishop of Coleyn, and to Saint Ambrose, bishop of Milan. Also Saint Benet say his sisters soul bore unto heaven the hour of her death. And Saint Jerome also appeared unto Saint Augustine in that same hour.

CHAPTER XXXI   VISIONS AT HIS DEATH

Like unto this vision was shown another to a noble woman of virtuous conditions and wife unto a man like in virtue unto her. She thought in her sleep that she saw a great multitude of angels, with great noise of praising and full sweet song, fly up into heaven. And after they were gone she saw two great companies of blessed spirits which were so ordained that each of them had face to face, like as they have that stand in a choir. They held amongst them a fair white sheet, and in this sheet were three naked children. One of them she might see from the navel upward; he was bald and yet he had a childs face; the other two saw she but the shoulders and the face.

She enquired of one in the company what manner things this might be, and it was answered to her that he in the middle was master Gilbert of Sempringham, which was dead to the world and thus born to God. She enquired also if these two were canons of his order, and it was answered no. They are not of his order, he said, but good and holy men which were taken out of this world and thus led to their Lord. This same vision saw this woman the same night our master died, and when she woke she told this vision to her husband; they both noted that day and found after that it was the same in which our master went from the world: wether he was born or where he was set, was shown after in a vision to one of his canons.

For a great time after that our master was dead, a canon of his order saw in his sleep one of his brethren that was dead long before. He thought that

88

enquired of him many sundry things, and had answered full convenient unto his questions. Though enquired he of the estate of their master, what he died of where he was, and his brother answered in this manner: 'He is not with us, a higher place holdeth him. For from that time in which he was taken from the world, immediately he was set amongst the dance of virgins'.

CHAPTER XXXII   HIS MIRACLES

Our blessed Lord, as he magnified Saint Gilbert in his life with great marvelous works, right even so would he shew the joy of him after his death with manifest tokens. And all these tokens, how that they came to the light of our knowledge, that they that live now and also they that shall come after us have no doubt in this matter, shortly, as they were doing, we will rehearse here. When this man, well beloved with God, was passed from the world, that man should know well his life and his merits were acceptable to God, in the first year of his deposition and so forth other years, where many miracles doing at his grave.

But at that time which he had left at Sempringham were men drawn into secret contemplation and had full little regard with great aquaintance of the world, and were negligent, if I should say so, to divulge these great miracles which were daily wrought amongst them. Thus thought they, of very humility, because they were his children, if they were the first that should publish these great miracles of their master, men might say of them, as Christ did of the Pharisees, that they magnified their own borders.

For this cause eleven years after his death was no great publication made, not withstand that in many places were wrought many sundry miracles; and then the brethren at Sempringham thought that the hiding of these glorious works were displeasure to our Lord, derogation unto saints, and wrong again the worship of the church; they as wise men and governed by the counsel of wise men, went up to the Archbishop of Canterbury, called that time Hubert, and told him all these things.

When the man heard all this he wept for very joy, and thanked God with full great devotion that he would show such miracles in his days. And though it were so that he had no doubt of the holiness of this Saint Gilbert, because he had known the man and heard great report of his holiness, yet to satisfy the opinion of other men, he thought best to put this matter in abeyance and tarry awhile, in which he might hear more to confirmation of his intention.

Upon this point this same archbishop sent down unto certain abbots of this same province, commanding them by his letters that in this matter they should make busy inquisition, and hear inquisition, in what form it was made, he would they should write it unto him, that he thus instruct by their information might write the more certainly unto our father the Pope to have leave of him for to publish the canonization of this Saint, after the Pope had done his part.

These abbots devoutly received this commandment, and joined unto them for more authority many other persons of the church, both regular and secular.

Thus came they all to the place of Sempringham, the ninth day of January, the year of our Lord 1201, and that same day the King of England, John, with many of his lords, visited the same place. There they did read the miracles and dicussed them with great diligence and straight examination, they wrote them in their letters both unto the said archbishop and to the Pope. All these letters sent to Hubert unto the Pope with his own epistles, in which he commended the great deeds wrought by this man, and prayed the Pope to grant leave that he should be lifted from the earth and laid in a more honourable place. Also, by exhortation of this same man, many notable persons of England and prelates written commendatory letters unto the court be seeking the Pope of the same. The King also wrote on his side and many of his lords that the Pope should the sooner perform their intentions.

CHAPTER XXXIII   STEPS TO HIS CANONISATION

Two of the lettered men of this order were sent with all these letters to the court in Rome, to whom fell a great miracle, that notwithstanding they went in the hot summer in full great distemper weather, in which much folk died of pestilence caused by that same heat, for all this these men went and came high and sound, not hurt with pestilence. Another thing fell also in that journey, that they went through an ambush of highwaymen, and not perceive for our Lord closed the sight of those theives with a sickness called acrisca, which is a feebleness that a thing shall lie before a man's eye and not be seen. Thus were they saved by merit of Saint Gilbert. Thus served our Lord the kings men of Syria that besieged Dotaim to kill Elisha, and he appeared unto them, and they knew him not.

Thus are they come home in good prosperity from the court, bringing with them the bull of our holy father the Pope, with his commendment to the Archbishop of Canterbury, to the Bishop of Ely, to the Abbot of Peterborough and the Abbot of Watton. In which bull was enjoined unto them that they should go to the place of his sepulchre and there should they command to that college of his order to fast three days solemnly, and in all those days they should pray devoutly to God that he should open in this matter to them the way of truth. And moreover, that these bishops with the abbots should ransack straightly the witnesses and the fame in the country, and some scripture authentic of the virtue of the manners of this man and the virtue of the miracles doing in his name. See this should they enquire busily, truly write it and after, send it up to the court sealed with their seals, the wise men and true, which men must swear in the presence of our father the Pope that all this information was true. All this commandment of the Pope was fulfilled indeed.

CHAPTER XXXIV   THE EMBASSY TO ROME

The sixth kalend of October, that is to say the day of Saint Cyprian and Justine, this same archbishop, with the bishops of Bath, of Ely, and of Bangor, with many abbots and priors, with some archdeacons, canons and officers of the church of Lincoln, with many famous masters and great people, came to the house of Sempringham; and they had fasted three days, they called first the Holy Ghost, as men do at elections, those called they the witnesses, religious and seculars, clerks and unlearned men and women, made them to swear that they should say the truth in which inquisition should be made.

And all their testimonies they write full truly in a due form, and sent them to the Pope closed under their seals. Furthermore, they write certain proofs of his holy life and conversation and of the same of the country. And while they tarried there three days the truth was opened of the matter which they sought, by a great miracle done at his grave, of a young man whose head with sickness turned round, and, for very pain, looked every hour to be dead. There was he made whole in their presence, and with the messengers went in good health to Rome, and in good health came home again.

For they sent in this embassy to Rome five of the same order, priests, six simple unlearned, of which number some were healed from certain sickness by the merits of this Saint, some were present when certain men were healed. For this cause were they in special sent, that the Pope should know by the men which were there that the suggestion of the letters sent were the truth.

The messengers go forth with great joy, trusting on our Lords help and the Saints prayer for whom they go, much more with the cheer, for they had merry dreams before their journey, and in their journey great prosperity in the way, and many other good tokens. And thus, with no great difficulty, though it were so that Sathamas would have hindered their way, yet, as we said, with out any great difficulty, they came to Rome on New Year's Eve, and after that the second day of January they came to Anagnia, where the Pope dwelt at that time.

Our Lord gave his so great grace in the site of our holy father and of the cardinals, that the tenth day they were come they were certain of all that ever they desired. For our father the Pope had his deliberation of this matter amongst the cardinals, and say the witness and the sworn men what they were, opposed then asunder, and found great accord between them, and though, as by man's reason, the Pope and the cardinals thought this matter might be performed anon, yet pleased it to the counsel of our Lord that it should be delayed, for he would that his counsel and his help should be called to this matter.

91

CHAPTER XXXV   THE POPE'S DREAM

One night within these ten days lay our father the Pope studied on this matter and might not sleep. He thought much of this man Gilbert, and was greatly in doubt what he should do in the matter. Then prayed he God that he would show him some token by which he might have knowledge of God's will. In this thought, sleep fell upon him, and that same sleep such a vision was shown unto him.

He thought he saw before him a great and a high tower, to which tower he had great appetite to go, and thither he went with many folk about him, as he was want. When he was come within the tower he saw a bed full of straw and arrayed at the best; about the bed a curtain of silk, precious enough, he saw hanging, and this curtain, as he thought, was embroidered with many images of saints. He stood and marvelled long on the beauty of this curtain, for he had no such about his bed, and for that cause he began to pull the curtain to him, for he thought he would sew it new and make it meet to his bed.

And in all this business he saw another camber more inward and much folk there. When he was come thither he enquired what he should do in the cause, for which the canons of Sempringham were come and in the canonising of this Saint. Then all suddenly he heard a voice crying thus: 'Michael the archangel, he shall be thy help in this business'. When the Pope had seen all this in his sleep, suddenly he woke, greatly comforted of this revelation, for he understood by this that our Lord's commandment and pleasence, was that this matter should be brought to a perfect end.

And anon, without cessation, he made a special orison of our father Gilbert with a secret and post communion after the form of a missal, and when he had made them he commanded that they should be said openly in his commemoration. Furthermore, the Pope, as a wise man desiring for to have certain interpretation of this matter, called unto him a full wise man and holy, an abbot, they called him Reynor, and commanded him, by virtue of obedience, that he should bethink him of his dream and tell him the conjecture of that same. The cause why that Pope uttered his vision to this man rather than to another, was for he led a solitary life in the mountains, and was in great opinion both to the Pope and the court.

Then answered the abbot again unto the Pope and said that this matter needed none advisement, for both the dream and his interpretation was open enough. So as another Daniel unto Nebuchadnezzar, or like another Joseph unto Pharoah, he expound it in such declaration: The fair tower he said, and the high, which thou say, sir Pope, is the great excellence of thy dignity, to which thou aspirest; not as dead many before thee, but by true election thou enterest into the same, and that is meant in thy dream where thou thought that thou were led into this place with the hands of many men.

The bed so well arrayed is a clean conscience, in which a man rests as in his bed, like as the prophet David said in the Psalm: 'I shall wash', he sayeth, 'or else, water my bed with my tears. For even clothes in which we rest be made clean with water, so is our conscience cleansed with repentence of our sins'. The curtains about this bed in which by impressed the fair figure of saints are the commemorations of holy saints used in the church, by which we be shadowed from winds of temptations. These curtains array full well our conscience when we, both with heart and work, fulfil their desire, either to honour them in God or else to follow their steps.

Then father Pope began to sew this curtain when thou thought first to set this man Gilbert in the kalender of saints, and I suppose, verily, he is full worthy to be anointed amongst them. Also such thing as then desired waking, thou asked in thy sleep and thine answer was gone, that Michael should be thy help.

Nothing again reason. Michael is the provost of paradise and prince ordained by God to receive those souls which shall be offered to God. This same Michael hath received this man's soul and led it to the high court of blessed spirits, and in that same court it is determined that this man Gilbert, from this time forward, shall be holden in honour and reverence as a Saint. Sew him in, therefore, with thy needle, with this power no man hath that in hand but thou. Join him into the fellowship of saints, for it is convenient that the church in earth follow the church above in heaven.

CHAPTER XXXVI   HIS CANONISATION

This interpretation of this dream, when it was thus expressed by the abbot, pleased the Pope greatly, for he, without any tarry, made call all the court of Rome, which was great at that time, and in special the archbishop of Rheims was there present at that time, and bare witness of the holy life of Saint Gilbert, for in his young age he had been in England and knew both the person and the fame. In this great congregation, when all men were set save these messengers of Sempringham, the Pope said a great and solemn sermon of the holiness and the miracles of Saint Gilbert, rehearsing the witness there present, and afer certain words which be pertinent to this office, there he solemnly and openly canonised Saint Gilbert with the common assent of all the church, and there also he made a decree that the feast of Saint Gilbert should be said and sung in the church like as the feast of the other saints be.

When the Pope in his seat had thus openly shown unto people this canonisation of this holy man, afterward he commanded that letters should be made of the same sentence to the Archbishop of England and to the chapter at Sempringham, in which letters he rehearsed all the matter from the beginning unto the end; with all the inquisition of his life and his miracles he rehearsed also discreetly, who sadly, with what circumstance, this matter had been treated, wherefore he commanded in the end of the bull that such thing as the

Pope with solemnity and with advise had ordained to be kept, they, as good subjects, meekly should fulfil and command the feast of this holy man to be solemnised by all their provinces. A special commandment sent he also unto the Archbishop of Canterbury, because the place of Sempringham stands in his province, that when so ever the brethren or canons of Sempringham required him, that he should go thither and lift up from the ground the body of this holy confessor, and with due reverence lay it there which as the same brethren had ordained it should be laid.

This commandment of the Pope was received of the archbishop and of the said canons as though it had come from heaven, wherefore they, desiring as good children to fulfil their father's commandment, all things that were necessary to such solemnity they pervade in all haste. And though the mind of this Saint, as have been of many others, was much out of remembrance, either for age or else for negligence of men, or ignorance, or some other cause; yet, as we hope, it was sufficient to us for to begin this work, because we had revelation first from God and commandment from our holy father the Pope, to whose commandment we be bound to obey as though it came from God. Also for the man in his life commanded us to do this thing and we also desired it should be done while we live, this was the great haste in this matter. For they that were sent for this matter thought it convenient to fulfil the Pope's precept while he was alive and they also.

CHAPTER XXXVII   HIS TRANSLATION

The year of our Lord Christ 1202, the foresaid brethren of Sempringham, in the vigil of the holy cross, with the most famous men of all that religion came unto the said archbishop with their master, making great instance that the next Sunday after the feast of St Denys, he would vouchsafe of his fatherhood to be at the translation of this holy confessor Gilbert. The archbishop received them not but in the best manner, and said he was glad of these tidings and ready to fulfil that solemnity which they all desired, and upon this he wrote to the bishops of his province that if they might have leisure they should come to him and honour this holy day.

Furthermore, he desired of them that this should be notified throughout their diocese, that all men which had devotion to this Saint might come to this feast if they would. Thus in the same day prefixed, that is to say, the 13th October, all this matter is put in execution. And beside all the miracles rehearsed before in the Pope's presence, also beside revelations had from heaven, and beside the said witnesses, new things fell that same day. The night of his translation, that is to say, the night between Saturday and Sunday, the noble men, the archbishop with other bishops and ministers came unto the grave where the holy members of Gilbert's body was hid, and with great worship they lift up that holy vessel of God, that, so washed and arrayed the next day afterward, he might with less tarrying be laid in his shrine.

Whilst that this service was done to the body with sweet hymns and songs, some religious men there present, and also some seculars, saw a great knot of fire all round, as though many candles had been joined together or else like a great shining star once, twice, thrice, come down from heaven and soon afterwards going up to heaven above the roof of the church, even over the sepulchre.

And at the third coming it seemed as though it had pierced the roof and fallen into the church. They that saw this sight without told it to them within, that they might go out and see the same, that is to say, the light of our Lord above the Church. Like things said other men which had woken at the grave certain nights in their prayers a little before this translation, that is to say, a great light enter through the roof and thrice enter the grave where the holy body was laid. Sweet savour also felt they there when the stones were removed by the masons for to make space where the new shrine should be set.

CHAPTER XXXVIII   HIS TRANSLATION

Nought only these miracles rehearsed were done at this time but many other testimonies were had in which men might know that this translation was pleasance to God. Thus when they had lifted the stone from the grave there was found fair red powder of his flesh, such as they say as virgins have when they are dead. The chasuble also in which the body was wound, of silk, was found whole without corruption. When all these relics were lifted from the ground and washed, the archbishop went again to the chamber for to take a rest, for it was far from day.

When he had lain a little time on his bed, suddenly fell upon him a grievous sickness, and the pain vexed him so sore that he stood in great doubt, and in manner dispair, that he might not fulfil that office for which he had called so many persons in special of such reverence. For this second cause was he more sorry than for his bodily sickness. He laid medicines to his body, such as they taught him, but although profited nought. Though turned he his trust and devotion to God and to St Gilbert, that our Lord at medication of that good Saint would send him might and strength to perform this office for which he was come and many other persons.

Immediately as his prayer was fulfilled so soon left him all this pain, for after that same pain was gone he felt his body more mighty and strong than it was before. At this same change came the hour in which the convent rang to mattins. Immediately as the archbishop heard the bell he rose himself and called all his clerks, and all in comradeship they go unto the canon's mattins, which, for the worship and love of that Saint for whom they gathered, were full solemnly sung. In the morning the archbishop rose highly and sound, and all that ever God and St Gilbert had shown unto him that same night, with great joy he told them, praising the virtue of our Lord and of this holy Saint, which virtue he felt notably fulfilled in him.

The hour is come of the day that this solemnity shall be done; the bishop is arrayed with his ministers; the water is hallowed that shall serve in the office; the shrine also is hallowed and born about on the shoulders of princes and lords which be there present; a solemn procession is ordained, in which procession first go the clergy, next the princes, lords and other, many bearing this hallowed vessel in which they will lay him; last of all follow the bishops. Certain sick men that were near and touched these relics were made whole that same hour, as was verily proved.

There said the archbishop a full notable sermon grounded all upon the holiness and the miracles of this holy man Gilbert, and there made he rehearsal of all the process, who it was sent unto the court of Rome, what answer they had from the Pope and much other thing. Then begun they a mass of this Saint with full sweet consent and in the last end of that man, after the bishop had received the holy sacrament, ere that they sang the post-communion, the said relics were wound in fair silk and then in a cloth of silk precious enough which our father archbishop had gave to that same intention, and all these thus wound were laid in that same vessel made for the same cause.

They laid also with him a great charter in which was written all his life, his canonisation also, and his translation sealed with the seals of the bishops and abbots which were present. There were put in with him also a plate of lead, on which was written all this thing more compendiously, as I suppose, that the remembrance of all this work should last for ever. Thus was that vessel closed and set upon a wall of marble in the same place where the Saint lay before. Then made they an end of the mass, and after they had refreshed their bodies every man with full great joy turned again unto his own place. Our master is laid now in his rest; let us follow therefore the steps of his good life that we may be translate from wretchedness to joy and through his leading come to that country where we shall have joy ever.

CHAPTER XXXIX   MIRACLES AT HIS GRAVE

Now of our father Gilbert, who holy was his life, who wholesome was his doctrine, who great rewards were sent from God unto his blessed merits, witness the great miracles which after his death were wrought by our Lord God. And of these miracles now will we tell all the manner like as they fell and like as our beloved father in God, the Archbishop of Canterbury, at the commandment of the Pope Innocent the Third with his suffragans ransacked and enquired. Like that inquisition in sentence and in terms, which inquisition they sent that time to Rome, through which messages this canonisation was performed, like that form will we write here.

There was a clerk whose name nor place is now unknown that used to go to school from one town to another as in this land is great custom. This clerk on his way to school fell in great heaviness, so that he must need sleep. He laid down and slept and after a sleep when he woke up he felt all his right leg, foot and all, so sered and dried that he might not go thereon in no manner. So with his staff and his other leg he hopped forth as he might till he came to the next town. From thence he was carried to a monastery which they called Haverholme, for there he dwelled he three months, ever vexed with the same infirmity. That leg, in all that time, down to the foot was so insensible and all might thereof go, that if men had pricked him with a needle or any other sharp thing, he felt no more thereof than a man had put this sharpness onto a stone or a tree.

Also the use of that leg was as lost, for when he should walk he should draw it after him as though it had by a branch of a sere tree, for he was more grieved with the burden than eased with the office. Because he might not lift that foot from the ground, but draw it ever from the earth, the toes were flayed and bloody to great pain of him and great pity to all that see him. The provost of that place did make him a hose all of leather, and that was wore immediately, in special at the furthest end which trailed so on the ground. After this he ordained him another remedy, for he tied his leg from the ground with a rope on to his shoulders, and thus borne he the leg which should have borne him.

To this same clerk sleeping one night a person of great worship, as he thought, and said thus unto him; 'If thou wilt be whole this same day, look thou visit the grave or else the sepulchre, of master Gilbert, at Sempringham'. At that same hour the man got him a cart and with one of the brethren of that same house he was brought to this sepulchre, and suddenly, as he prayed, he fell asleep. In his sleep, as he thought, the same person which appeared to him before, appeared again and said unto him such words: 'For what cause lie thou here so long? Behold thou art made whole'. With this vision he swet marvellously and began to wail five times, then woke he and rose by himself, looked on his foot and trod with it on the ground for to attempt whether he might go with that or not.

Because of the sudden change which was come so newly, he stood in great doubt what he should do. The sexton that stood by and procurator knew not of this sudden change made tokens unto him that he should rest again. He lay down soon afterwards, and after a little sleep woke again, and then he rose and felt both feet, thigh and leg all whole; thus he threw away his staff and forsook his cart, and with full great likeness went where he would. And in token that this health came to him by miracle, in that place which he might not feel a needle pricked before, now, when the natural heat is come again, he felt somewhat a pain in that same place where that wound was. Amongst all other that bore witness of the miracles done by Saint Gilbert this man was one, for he went to Rome and confessed all this before the Pope, and after when he came home, was made canon and priest in this same order thanking God all his life and Saint Gilbert of his gracious cure.

CHAPTER XL   A LAME CLERK CURED

A maiden was there also in the street at Sempringham, that in both legs in that part which is behind the knees, was so contract that she might not stand nor go, for instead of her feet when she would remove her body from one place to another, she crept with her hands and with her loins or buttocks. Also with great rancour of the sore her left foot was marvellously disfigured, for three great pieces of flesh grew upon her foot, each of them departed from the other, which seemed as though it had been cut. Moreover, her left arm had lost the virtue of feeling and the hand of that arm was like the left foot with such three cuttings of flesh as we said before. Thus hung it as a unprofitable burden from the shoulder downward.

This woman heard tell who that this clerk of whom we told last was cured and so cured that he was strong to take his journey to home. So made she great instance to them that dwelled in that street that they should lead her to this sepulchre of Saint Gilbert and leave her there. There she lay seven days continually perseveringly in her prayers, and as she slept on one night she thought that the stone under which Saint Gilbert was closed cleft asunder, and he rose up and sat thereupon with full great light. She thought also that he had in his hand many hosts and those multiplied fast, as to her sight so fast and to so great a number that he might scarcely hold them.

Two of those same hosts he put in her mouth, as she thought, and after that gave her his blessing. After this she awoke suddenly and found her body all on a sweat so abundant that it dropped from her body and made the pavement wet, she felt even at that time a new change in her body, for that which was heavy and contract before, now she feeleth it of such disposition that, as it seems to her, she might fly for lightness. In that same change she say who the lights that stood about the sepulchre of Saint Gilbert and burnt fell down suddenly, and though she began to creep as her use was for to amend those lights.

In her creeping the sinews which were contract before in her loins, they break and strained out to such largeness that she rose and stood on her feet and might walk and in that breaking she heard a great noise, who they cracked and had full great marvel who that the sinews when they began to extend themselves. In this same time that this woman standeth thus marvelling, the nun, the sextoness, rang to mattins; the sisters that come down and see this woman standing by the sepulchre; first they be afraid because many of them wished not that she was there, for she was not there at even when they went to bed, as it seems; they walk unto her and she confesseth all the circumstance of the miracle even as it fell.

There thank they God and Saint Gilbert all with one consent for the great cure which now is done. The woman was kept with them a certain time for declaration of the miracle and until her arm and leg had perfectly their use; after that time she went home to the street and lived there with her friends in good health of body, thanking our Lord of that sudden change.

CHAPTER XLI   VARIOUS SICK WOMEN CURED

A knight's wife there beside, a lady full noble fame, had such sickness and pain in special during in her left arm that she might not move that arm nor do with all no manner of work. This pain lasted upon her from the feast of Saint Peter, which they called in Latin, 'ad vinculam' in English 'Lammesse', unto the nativity of our Lady. Beside this had she other sores which we name not now. With all this infirmity she is come unto the sepulchre of this holy man, and after she had watched in devout prayers all the night she went home whole from both sores, evermore having great trust in this holy Saint.

Another woman there beside, contract and crooked which might not go, nor sit, nor stand, without help of them that were waiting upon her. The father and mother of her, having great sorrow for that disease, brought her unto the sepulchre of our master. The first night she was there, at instance of her friends, the canons put upon her the scapulary of Saint Gilbert and the woman confessed there before them all that in doing one of that cloth she felt great alleviance of her sore. The night following appeared unto her a fair old man with grey hair, as she thought in her sleep, and in his hand he had a staff as men walk for age. Thus he said unto her: 'Wilt thou be whole?' She answered that gladly she would. Then he blessed her and said, 'Thou shalt be whole'. She enquired of him what man he was and he answered that he was master Gilbert of Sempringham. After this dream she awoke and felt herself whole in every part and thus in health lived many years.

CHAPTER XLII   MORE SICK CLERKS CURED

A clerk was there also in that country that in his breast and in his womb had a marvelous rising which burned so within his breast that he feared greatly it should draw unto to dropsy. Thus all in despair of health he lay in his bed upon fifteen days without hope of any recovery. Certain men which came to visit him told him of great miracles which our Lord wrought at Sempringham through the merits of our father Gilbert. When the sick man heard of these new things he made a vow openly that, that place should he visit when our Lord would send him disposition and leisure.

Soon after this vow was made the man felt him somewhat amendable, that he might rise and walk. For which cause in great haste he took his journey unto Sempringham, and there in great devotion he leaned upon the grave and said such devotions as he could, praying with bitter tears that God should send him some release of his pain. In this time of prayer he felt that all the bowels of his body were greatly moved and turned, as they had drawn unto another kind that they were before. Then rose he from the grave and felt himself in other plight, for all the burning and also the pain is avoided. Thus walk he in the church, saying himself if all be well, and when he say verily that he was whole he took leave and walked unto his dwelling.

Another priest was washed in a bath upon a Friday and on the Saturday following he fell in so grievous sickness which continued a whole year and more, that all the members of his body had lost their office, he might not eat but if he were fed, not go but if he were led. Thus as a man all contract with a manner of a palsy, he kept his bed, never removing thence but with help. Thus was he fed and nurtured like a child with his servant ordained to his service, for he might nought do himself. This man was brought with great business unto the church of Sempringham in a cart, between the midday and evensong. There at the grave he made his devout prayer that our Lord be the merits of Saint Gilbert should relieve him. That same day was he whole, that without of cart or horse he went home to his own place.

CHAPTER XLIII   A LAME NUN MADE WHOLE

In that same country and in that same place at Sempringham was a nun which, at the commandment of her prioress, went unto the kitchen, and because she went with great haste and took no great consideration what thing lay in her way, she stumbled at a block which was hid with straw, and thus fell suddenly. In which fall she was so grievously hurt that her foot was broken from the joint, and thus she lay crying and wailing for great pain that she felt. Her cry was heard through the place and immediately her sisters came unto her, comforted her, lifted her up with many hands and great heaviness, and bear her unto the infirmary.

Thus burned the foot and ranked, that they were compelled to cut her shoe, else had they not got it off. Many remedies were ordained to this foot; it was drawn with great pain to bring it in joint again, but it availed not. They laid also to it plasters of divers herbs, but it profited not, for ever the pain grew more and more. Thus lay the nun in that pain all that year and the next unto the day which we called the anniversary of Saint Gilbert. Then was she so feeble that they thought best to give her the holy annointing which is last of all the sacraments.

Though she required then to make a candle of wax after her length, and that same candle and herself also she desired they should bear her unto the sepulchre of Saint Gilbert. This was done in deed, for when she was brought

100

there, the prioress took the same linen cloth in hand which lay upon the breast of this holy confessor such hour as he should die. In this same cloth wound the prioress the sore foot of her sister often rehearsed. Thus lay she waking there by the sepulchre all that anniversary day, the night following, and the next day till it was noon, for then fell she asleep.

In that same sleep she thought that she see many men, clad all in white, command into the monastery and busy to array the altar as though a priest should go to mass. Behind them all came Saint Gilbert, as she thought, arrayed like a priest, and his chasuble was all red. He turned himself to that woman which lay thus sick; he blessed her thrice, and at every blessing he made a token unto her that she should rise. She thought in her sleep that she rose and would have held him by the clothes, but her hold failed and she fell down face upon the ground. As she thought in her sleep, so found she when she woke, for she lay thus still on the pavement sore astonished.

In this meantime came the prioress and her sisters from mete with their grace, and anon this same woman told them how she was made whole by the help of Saint Gilbert also of all her dream and appearing of the Saint, she made at that time open declaration. Though the prioress took her by the hand and felt well that she was whole, for herself, with out any leader, she went again to the infirmary, and ever after was that foot as fair and as whole as any foot might be.

CHAPTER XLIV   CURE OF A PRIORESS

We read also that, by touching of the clothes of our father Gilbert, and also by drinking of that water in which his dead body was washed, that many virtues were wrought thereby and many sores healed. For there was a prioress of that same order which was vexed with sickness fifteen days and that grievous malady. Remedy could she non of no bodily medicines, wherefore she turned her trust to the help of God and this Saint, and with a great faith drank of that water in which his body was washed, and soon after was she whole, for the cup was not so soon from her mouth that her body was whole, as many of her sisters bore witness which were present.

Another woman also was there near by which travelled in birth of a child two days, so grievously vexed with pain, that every man had pity of her. She drank also of that water in which the tonsure of his beard was wet, and she was made whole.

Also the same year that our father died, one of the nuns, as she sat in the refectory and ate fish with her sisters, the bone of a fish left in her throat and stood so fast that she might by no way remove it, notwithstand that she might touch it with her finger. She drank often by the counsel of her sisters, but it amended nought, for the penance was so great in her drinking that she cast the liquor, but the bone abode still. Her fellows did all their craft to draw it out, and all availed not. This cure, as mine author saw it, was reserved to another manner drink and another work.

Thus lay she, her pain ever increasing from midday till even. Her sisters then, taking a sadder counsel, led her unto the church, brought her unto the altar and there all they fell down on their knees, devoutly praying to God and to Saint Gilbert for health of her. Then made her to drink of that water in which the body of that holy confessor was washed in. Immediately, as she had drunk that water, suddenly she was delivered of that pain, but she could never have knowledge where this bone became.

CHAPTER XLV   OTHERS CURED

Of that same order also a canon had such pain in his neck and the after part of his head that he might not suffer that place be touched, not with his own hands. This pain lasted eight days, that he might never turn his head but if he turned all his body. One of his brethren, which was his keeper, gave him this counsel, that he should wind his head with a certain cloth of linen which Saint Gilbert wore. I suppose verily it was his alb and a shirt, and in the first part of his life the same author said that this holy man wore next to his skin no hair, as for the hardest, nor linen, as for the softest, but he went with wool, as with the men.

When this man had wound thus this cloth about his head, which cloth Saint Gilbert had used at solemnity of mass, as we said, immediately and suddenly this man was whole. This was at even, for on the morrow he was purposed to enter the infirmary that he should not disturb his brethren with clamour which he made for pain. For this cloth was not so soon put about his head, and that wound it about his head was not gone from him three or four paces, ere he called him again, saying that all his pain was gone and he felt no manner grievance. He laid his hand to the place which was sore, groped it, and touched it with sad feeling, and he felt no sore. His head might he turn on what side he would, not moving his body; flesh, skin and neck, all was whole.

The same night he slept quietly, and to marvel of all his fellowship, rose to mattins, there fulfilled all his office in reading and singing as he of usage was wont to do. In the morning and immediately ere he told his bretheren all this miracle, how he was made whole by the linen coat of Saint Gilbert.

CHAPTER XLVI   VARIOUS PERSONS CURED

Also a woman of good report dwelled there beside, which in her knee and leg had such a passion that a month whole she might not go on the right foot, so burned and ranked was her knee. Thus with great business of her servants she was horsed, for in sickness this was her desire, that she would be carried to Sempringham trusting in the merits of this holy confessor through which she shall be whole. When she was come unto Sempringham after her desire, they brought her the hose of Saint Gilbert; she put her leg in that same hose and suddenly she was whole, so perfectly cured that she went that same day a mile on her feet home to her house.

Another woman also after the deliverance of a child had a grievous sickness forty weeks and two. For her womb was burned to such quantity men supposed she should die. Many holy places visited she for health and was not whole. So was she inspired at last to visit the sepulchre of our father Gilbert, and there was she made whole. For she was cured there soon after she was come, even in the feast of Saint Cruce, the ninth hour of the day. And then with full glad heart she went home, showing to her friends her body where they might perceived that all that swelling was gone.

CHAPTER XLVII   VARIOUS PERSONS HEALED

The throat and also the head of another man there beside was so risen and burned with sickness which they called the swinesie, and also so grievously knotted, that eight days continually he was compelled for very pain without meat or sustainance to keep his bed and suffer the malady. The last two days was his drink secluded from him, so closed were his pipes with violence of that sore. Then fell on him more grievance, for in the mid-hour of that last night of those eight days he lost his speech which privation lasted unto the even of that day following.

Then supposed they all which were about him that he should die. For to their comfort and consolation he might in no wise give no answer. The small issues of his throat might full evil receive wind into his body. Then, at great instance of his wife, the girdle of Saint Gilbert was brought, and water also, which he hallowed. With the girdle they gird his neck full devoutly, and the water they poured into his mouth. Also they washed the burning out of his throat with that same water, and then began the man feel somewhat released, for with that washing he voided wind, and after the wind one great bloody drop went out from his mouth. Thus began he to relieve in so much that or even he spake and eat, and within three days he received perfect heal, so suddenly cleansed of his pain.

CHAPTER XLVIII   VARIOUS PERSONS HEALED

One of the nuns of that same order thirty years continually twice or thrice in the year had marvelous sickness within her body, for about her heart, and in her left side was such pressure that when it came, the woman, near dead for very pain, lost her mind. And in this pain she had such strength that many of her sisters might not at that time hold her nor keep her in rest. Thus on a day when the sickness had caught her thus violently they sent after priests of the same order for to be about her in time of her death, for all look they when she shall pass.

Amongst these priests came in the master of Sempringham, that same master which was next successor after Saint Gilbert. There found he the woman bounden and holden as a furious person is wane to be served. Then he enquired of them that were there if any part of Saint Gilbert's water were in that house. They had it readily, and at the commandment of there prelate, they poured of the same water into her mouth. A great marvel was seen there, for that water was not so soon entered into her throat but she began to change all that would rage and her vile, which was pulled down to her shoulders, in full religious manner she redressed, and hid her face and her eyes as she want to do. And those in the presence of the master and many folk which stood with him, she cried in this manner: 'Oh mother of mercy, – what should we tell long tale?' – As though she had been in a trance she began to know herself, and by process of time she was restored to perfect health, for after that time had she never more that sickness.

Another woman was there with divers sickness. Vexed, that is to say dissentry, gout, and vomiting daily following. Dissentry the Greeks called this sickness when a man's guts be hurt so that they be slit or cut. Other sickness had this woman divers which she was ashamed to confess and for which she was compelled by debility to keep her bed from the feast of All Saints unto three days before Candlemas. Then was told her that two of her neighbours, women both, one deaf, another bedridded, infected with a manner of palsy, that they were led unto the tomb of Saint Gilbert and there were they made perfectly whole.

Of these tidings she caught a comfort, and anon she let make a candle after her measure, and in a cart with that same was she carried unto the sepulchre of our father. There woke she in prayer all that night, and the next day about nine o'clock was she made whole of all those maladies rehearsed before.

CHAPTER XLIX   MORE WOMEN HEALED

Another woman was there whose knee was so contract that two months she might not go. She was brought also in a cart unto the tomb of Saint Gilbert where she woke two nights in full devout prayers. The second night she thought in her dream that out of an image mouth which stood by the grave, made in worship of our Lady, fell a fair red flower and also that same flower as she thought, fell upon her sore knee. She awoke and felt her knee whole, for this sudden health, as she understood well, was gave her by the medication of our Lady and the merits of Saint Gilbert. Then with full great devotion she kissed the feet of that same image, and thus in perfect health she has gone home.

There was another woman also in that same country whose right eye began

104

to wax sick, that is to say, all red of colour with pain following. Soon after the left eye was in that same plight, for that eye in special burned so that three days she might see no light. In all this pain she came to the tomb of our father Gilbert, with a candle burning and a piteous heart. There abode she steadfastly in prayer whilst that the prior of that same place said mass there,. After she had heard that mass she went home in hope of health, and there fell she asleep. After her sleep she felt neither passsion in eye nor head, and ere the nun went to rest, that burning was dismissed and her sight restored. Day by day after this her sight was better and better till it came to the same perfection which it had before.

CHAPTER L   A CONVERT HEALED

A convert of that same order, in the vigil of Saint Mathew the Apostle, which was a weaver of cloth, after the evensong said of the same apostle, sat still in his craft weaving. Other of his fellowship warned him that at reverance of that feast he should cease, but he would not. The same night, after his first sleep, he felt that all the might of his right arm was lost from the elbow unto the hand; also the same right hand was turned wrong, and might in no manner have recourse unto his natural office. This pain lasted three weeks and three days.

So in the feast of Saint Benet he asked leave of the prior of that place in which he was converse that he might go visit, with other two fellows joined unto him, the sepulchre of our father Gilbert. Thither he came with a hand of wax, and made his offering; there abode he certain time in prayer and waking, living ever in hope that he should have release of his pain. The first night following, his hand was rather impaired than amended, so was the hand of our Lord agreaved upon him. The man he thought him and remembered that the sorely of his soul, peradventure, as often is seen, was cause of his bodily sickness; wherefore he thought best to throw away his sins, that he might the sooner purchase grace of his desire.

Upon this he went to a priest, and with good rememberance he confessed his sins from his young age unto that same day, took his penance meekly and fulfilled it devoutly. So after this, upon the night next the annunciation of our Lady, he set his hope only in him that would that same day be incarnate for our health, and in her also that blessed virgin, of whom he took both flesh and blood; moreover he put his trust in his father Gilbert, which in his life exercised the ways both of chastity and of meekness; in all this trust he desired with certain light for to wake all alone at the sepulchre of his father Gilbert.

There lay he and said his service such as is asssigned unto converses of the order. He prayed instantly for health unto his father and many other Saints, and in his prayer as he leaned upon the stone that lay over the grave, he fell asleep, and so rested a time. When he woke he felt certain pricklings in his arm near his elbow; he drew his hand unto him, and say well that the crookedness thereof was mended, for he might stretch it out as he would. All the sinews and all the fingers were so restored unto health that he might move them; also in his arm felt he no more pain.

CHAPTER LI   THE MAD CURED

There was a woman also, that for sickness fell in a frenzy, or else such manner passion which was like a frenzy. For as a mad creature she spake, gnashing with her teeth, and dismissing her spittle in other men's faces and women. So was she vexed in such wild rage that they bound her fast, and thus lay she bound fully a month. She was brought thus bound in a cart by labour of her husband and her friends unto the tomb of Saint Gilbert, and there abode in prayers three days and nights; then complete she went home high and sound, ever thanking God.

Like unto this miracle fell unto another woman that two months and a half was distraught, and when she was brought unto the grave and lay there two days and nights, the third day about the third hour she was made whole.

Also at a monastery called Watton a poor man, kept in the house made for poor men, had such a sickness two months that he fell into a manner of frenzy so was his mind alienate. The servants of that infirmary had full great pity and compassion upon him and laid him in an old horse bier in which our father Gilbert was carried sometime when he might not well walk for great age and feebleness. Many sick men had been laid in that same bier, and caught their health by the merits of this man which used it sometime. The man was laid therein, and because he was wild they bound him to the bier; so lay he two days and two nights, and on the third day he was made whole and turned unto health again.

CHAPTER LII   HARRY BISET HEALED

Also a noble woman, as they say, dwelled not far thence, and she had a grievous passion in her eyes, so grievous that she might see but little or else nought, especially in day light. Beside this had she other sickness, so that she was compelled to keep her bed. There had she a vision, that if she would go unto the tomb of this holy father, she should be relieved of that pain. She made a candle by the measure of her body, and to the grave she did come, where she drank of that same water in which the holy confessor's body was washed; soon after that drink she was made suddenly whole.

The son of this same woman also received health of his eye, which was nigh overspread with a web, by drinking of that same water.

Also another woman that might not hear no manner of things, not the sound of great bells, after she had woken in devotion at this sepulchre one night, first received comfort that she might hear the noise of bells, and after, the speech of men.

Another man of full great fame, called Harry Biset, a full long time was sick, and after that sickness had a great and grievous burning of his stomach. This same pain lasted him two year or more. The burning stomach rose unto such great quantity that when he was sat he might not see passing two inch of his thigh. Thus in despair of all health, for medicines might not help, he sent his wife and daughters to Sempringham, to dwell there and have aquaintance, for he supposed not else but for to die.

The wife came home again to see her husband and brought with her a linen girdle with which our father Gilbert was sometime girthed; she brought also of that same water in a phial in which the holy confessor's body was washed. And when the man had drunk of that water and was girthed with that girdle, immediately he began to quake and gnash his teeth, but he waxed nothing host.

Then fell he in a sleep, and in that same sleep, marvellous to say, he fell in a sweat for he had no sweat of all the time in which he was sick. But now sweated he horribly. His wife that sat by, say the yellow drops how they spilled from him and those were great and had full evil savour.

When he woke he espied this himself, and felt the same savour. He looked upon his stomach and say well that all his burning was fled downward from the girdle near half a foot. For the skin which was before his sleep so pressed out that he was afraid it would burst, now is it void as a empty bag. After all this, not long time the man recovered all this sickness and came to perfect health, might ride and go as man of arms for as it seems by mine author he was a knight.

CHAPTER LIII   VARIOUS WOMEN HEALED

A woman also was in that country which had a grievous sickness within her bowels all a whole year. Her womb burned not nor no manner rising had she of skin nor flesh, but fretting and pricking, especially about her heart and sometime in her sides, that she supposed verily for to die. Wherefore she was shriven and hustled and took all manner of observances which belong to men when they shall pass, and because she abode still in life after all this did, therefore her husband, of great devotion, carried her in a cart unto the house of Sempringham, trusting in the merits of this holy confessor.

When she was come unto that place she received the holy sacrament newly again, and then they made her to drink of that water in which the body was washed of this holy confessor, Gilbert. Thus abode she still praying at the grave of this Saint three days; on the third day she had a great vomit of corrupt blood, and with this corruption came out a great long worm. Thus three days and two nights had she this purgation. After this went she home, and thus day by day the vomit somewhat ceased, and the great pain was fully released.

CHAPTER LIV   A NUN HEALED

In that same house of Sempringham was a nun which our father Gilbert had received himself. This woman was infected with leprosy, which increased in her so horribly that all her body was infected. The hair fled from her head, her brow and her eyes were so infected that she might not lift her eyelids for to look. Her hands also so sore that she might in no manner put meat or drink unto her mouth. Thus lay she in the infirmary twelve year, ever served by a woman which was her bodily sister, which woman often would say that she saw never man nor woman so horribly infected.

Because that this same woman was so conversant with her and had often used to anoint her naked body with certain medicines, that the sorely should be more tolerable, for this cause, the nuns of that house fled the communication of this same woman, so were they afraid for to be infected. To this woman that lay thus grievously hurt with this horrible sickness appeared in her sleep a worshipful lady, commanding her that she should be carried to the sepulchre of Saint Gilbert, for there should she receive health.

Thus is she brought unto the grave and there, after devout prayers, she fell into a sleep, in which sleep the same honourable lady appeared to her and aid these words: 'Arise, for thou art whole'; and before these words the lady, as she thought, spread a fair mantle of purple about the grave, with which mantle she came in, and soon afterwards she said unto the sick woman: 'Arise, for thou art whole'. Then in that same dream appeared it to that sick woman that she was whole, and she heard the convent sing Te Deum Lauds for her health. Thus lay she dreaming unto that time when the convent rang to mattins, then she awoke and returned again to the infirmary. In her rising she voided great humour and in great quantity, but within three days she was perfectly whole, for all a week after, the sores fell from her body as they had been scales of a fish, and thus within few days after her flesh was restored like the flesh of a young child.

CHAPTER LV   A MIRACLE AT SEA

Certain men of this land sailed the sea which is between England and Normandy. In their sailing rose a great tempest which they escaped with our Lord's mercy. When the tempest was eased and down, then had they no wind for to sail, but likely were they all that night for to traverse the sea. Many that were there dread much the peril of the sea, especially by night cared much, but remedy could they none.

A man was amongst them called John, constable of Chester, a man of noble birth and great fame; he called a priest unto him whose name was Anceline, which was his chaplain, and prayed him that he should bring forth the scapular of Saint Gilbert which the successor of Saint Gilbert had gave him, and which he kept for a great relic. This Anceline full devoutly arrayed him in holy vestments like a priest, washed his hands, and out of his lord's coffer took out this scapular, lift it up in the air, and thus he prayed that they all might hear:

Lord God omnipotent, Lord Almighty, if it be so that the life and the conversation of Saint Gilbert were wrought unto the pleasance, shew now that through his merits we may come to some haven in which we may be safe from peril. Immediately, as these words were said, a fair soft wind blew in the scapular, and from the scapular it ascended unto the sail and ever multiplied, that in that same day they overtook ships that sailed with them and oversailed them, were also in Normandy long ere they; for some ships that were in that voyage came not to Normandy neither that day nor the next day.

Many other tokens were done by the miracles of our father Gilbert which was not touched in this present work, for some of negligence are forgotten, some were not approved by such notable witness as these were, some were also wrought after time that this book was made, wherefore they be not yet brought into this form. And because that we be in no doubt that these were done in the same form, therefore have we written them in such language as we could, to the praising and joy of our Lord God in whose name they were wrought, to the worship of holy church and profit of them that shall read or hear this life, for whom these notable things were done, to the worship also of this holy man by whom these miracles were done, which man with merits and prayers shall commend us to that Lord which is highest of all Lord's, and bring us also unto those joys that eternal, where we may rest from all labour without end. Amen.

CHAPTER LVI   THE POPE'S SERMON ON ST GILBERT

Our holy father, the Pope Innocent III, ordained that the canonisation of this same Gilbert should be solemnised in the church, and also his translation, of which canonisation he himself at Rome before all the clergy and the people, made a full solemn sermon, which sermon he commanded it should be written and sent unto the archbishops and bishops of England in bulls, and also unto the chapter of the house of Sempringham, of which sermon this is the sentence:

For as much as truth say in the gospel that no man light a lantern and hide it under a bushel measure, but set it upon height, that all that dwell in that house may have comfort of that light, for this cause, we think that it is a deed of great pity and of equity that those men whom our Lord God hath crowned for their merits and gave to them honour in heaven, that we on earth should worship them, praise them and make joy of their exaltation, especially when our Lord, for such worship as we do them, is magnified of us, because that scripture say it:

Our Lord is praiseworthy, or praised, and glorious in saints. To the great virtue of pity belongeth the great behest, nought only of this present life but of the life also that is eternal, as our Lord said by the prophet unto them that die in holy life: I shall make you that ye shall stand in such opinion of the people that they shall give to you praising and honour, the joy that ye have shall I give you. And in another place of scripture thus is said of saints:

Rightful men shall shine as the sun in the kingdom of their father. For our Lord ofttimes, that he should shew marvelously the might of his virtue, and that he should work mercifully the cause of our health, those same true servants which he rewards in heaven ofttime he honours in this world, and at the places where their bodies rest there raises he great tokens and miracles by which the wickedness of hearsay is confounded and the true christian faith confirmed.

CHAPTER LVII   THE POPE'S SERMON

Therefore we, as we may not as we should, send thanksgivings unto Almighty God that in our days to the confirmation of christian faith and confusion of wicked hearsay hath made now his tokens new and changed then marvelously, making the saints now in our days to shine with miracles, which saints as is now seen kept the true christian faith, not only with mouth but with work. Amongst which saints master Gilbert, founder and beginner of the Order of Sempringham, which in this world was mighty in great merits, now living in heaven, shines with great miracles, for it is full convenient that his holiness should be approved with open and manifest tokens.

And though it be so that final perseverance is sufficient enough to prove that he or any other that die in goodness should be a saint before God in that church above which has overcome her enemy, witness of truth that see: He that is persevering in goodness, unto the last end be safe. And in the Apocalypse where he said thus: Be true unto the last end, and I shall give thee the crown of life; yet that man should behold holy in the opinion of men, and here in this church which lives in continual battle with the enemies, two things to this matter be full necessary: Virtue of good manners and virtue of tokens, that is to say, good works and miracles, that each of them should bear witness to the other.

For good works be not sufficient without miracles, nor miracles sufficient without good works to bear very witness any men's holiness; for as we read, sometime the devil, which is called the angel of Satan, may transfigure himself like to an angel of light, and some men as we read all their good works which they do, they do them for this intention that they should be known amongst men as for holy liefers. Also of the witches that dwelled with Pharaoh read we, that they wrought marvellous tokens; and Antichrist when he comes shall work so marvellous things that, if it might be, those souls that he be chosen to heaven should be moved and led into error by the same tokens.

Wherefore we conclude that the testimony of good works by himself alone is sometime false and deceitful, as may be seen openly in these hypocrites, also the testimony of miracles by himself sometime is deceitful, as is seen in these witches that dwelled with Pharaoh. But when good works go before in any person, and after those following glorious miracles, then we have a very certification of man's holiness that those two things should lead us the right way to honour that whom that our Lord hath offered unto us to be worshipped, with good works going before and miracles following. These too are notably touched in the Evangelist Mark where he writes thus of the apostles: 'They walked forth in the world and preached, our Lord working, and helping their sermons and signs or else miracles followed after that'.

CHAPTER LVIII   POPE'S SERMON CONTINUED

And though it be soon that our well beloved children in God, the prior and the convent of Sempringham, have instantly made their postulation unto us that we should grant that master Gilbert should be written in the catalogue of saints and be numbered among saints, which Gilbert was beginner of their order, and which man, as they say, before his death had exercise of good works, and after his death wrought many great miracles, yet would we not grant their petition but we will be fully informed of his life and of his miracles, nor withstand that our noble and worshipful son in christ, John, King of England, with his lord's, and our brother Archbishop of Canterbury, Hubert, with his suffragans, also the prior of the said convent, with other abbots and priors, wrote unto us in this matter of the virtuous life of this man and of the tokens done at his grave.

Wherefore we will in this matter do great diligence to have the very truth, and for this cause we have written and commanded by our letters to our well beloved brethren, Archbishop of Canterbury, the Bishop of Ely, and to our well beloved son's, Abbot of Peterborough, and Abbot of Watton, they by our authority they shall go to that place of Sempringham and, in virtue of obedience, command all that brotherhood of men and women that they shall fast three days and cry on our Lord God which is the way, truth and life, that he will open the truth of this matter unto the knowledge of his servants.

Furthermore we will that they ransack the witness and the fame spread in the country, and make all this to be written by scripture authentic of the virtue of the manners, or the virtue of the miracles of this man and all this thing thus written, sealed with their seals, send up unto as by faithful and true men which may swear in our presence that all this thing be true, that we, thus plainly informed, may the more certainly proceed in this matter which is to increasing of the joy of Our Lord's name and a great confirmation of Christian faith. And if it be so that all these men assigned may not be at this examination, we will at the least that three of them shall fulfil this deed.

CHAPTER LIX   THE POPE WANTS EVIDENCE

Thus these same men fulfilled our commandment full truly, and because one of them might not be there for a great and a necessary cause, therefore three of them had this examination in our name, that is to say, the aforesaid archbishop, and the bishop of Ely, with the abbot of Peterborough; these three went unto that place and fulfilled all that was contained in our commandment, for with great diligence they examined all the witnesses and made them for to swear that they should no information make but the truth; they made also religious men, secular men, clerks, laymen, men and women generally, whose attestations and witness they written truly, and under their seals closed, sent all this thing to us, which messages though they were evident and certain, because they very many and divers, we will not at this time set them in our writing.

They made also great inquisition of his conversation and of his manners, which were open unto all men; they called in divers religious men, which were familiar with him at divers times, and which knew of his privy conversation; all these men with one accord bore witness that his life was undefiled and holy. For he was a marvellous man in abstinence, a clean man in chastity, a devout man in prayer, much used to waking, over that flock of his congregation with great provision discretion ever busy; certain hours when he might have any leisure in contemplation, quiet. So as it seems, while he was on earth he departed truly his life, sometime in good works of active life, some in holy rest of contemplative, like unto the patriarch Jacob that say, angels on the ladder going up and going down.

And when he had any conversation with his brethren or sisters, it might be said of him, as it was said of Samuel, there fell not a word of his unto the earth.For after the doctrine of the holy apostle, idol words were full seldom in his mouth, but those words which he spake were to edification of our faith, for he was good in that same, and therefore his words were full of grace unto the heavens. And though many other things made his life to be in great commendation, this was yet a principal thing belonging to his perfection, that he would choose wilful poverty, and all his possessions which were left him by heritage, he would assign for ever to maintain the brethren and the sisters which he had instituted and set under a virtuous rule of religion. For his succession in process of time grew, by the goodness of our Lord, to so great a number that he built nine monasteries of women and four of canons regular in which monasteries that time that he died he left, beside the religious men, a thousand and five hundred sisters that served God our Lord without villainy.

CHAPTER LX   THE EVIDENCE IS SENT, THE CHARTER AND CONCLUSION

Moreover, to strength of this matter and to a greater precaution five of those brethren of that foresaid order were sent unto our presence, we have charged them with great oaths that they should inform us with the truth, and they have told us much more, both of his meek works and of his glorious miracles. Wherefore we, of this man's life and miracles be sufficient witness thus inform and set in a manner of certainty, after the testimony of the angel that said to Tobie, it is good to hide the sacrament of the high King, but the works of God to open and confess is great worship, – also for the Psalm says that God should be praised in his saints, – for their causes have we ascribed and numbered St Gilbert into the catalogue of saints, and ordained that his memory shall be sung among other saints.

All these by the Pope's words; now follow with the author. Thus after the commandment of our father the Pope, when the translation of St Gilbert was brought to an end, and the holy relics were laid in the vessel arrayed for them, but before it was closed the bishops and the abbots that were principal fulfillers of this work, laid a charter upon his breast, in which charter was contained all the manner of this translation, of the miracles and of the canonisation, also they laid there a plate of lead, on which lead was written certain things which should never be out of mind.

The scripture of that plate was this: Here lies St Gilbert, the first father and founder of the order of Sempringham, which was translated into this shrine by our father and lord, Hubert, Archbishop of Canterbury, to the commandment of our holy father, Pope Innocent, the third ide of October, the year of our Lord, one thousand two hundred and one.

This is the writing of the charter laid by him in this shrine: In this shrine are contained the relics of St Gilbert, priest and confessor, the first father and beginner of the order of Sempringham, whose life, though it be so that many things made it commendable and honourable, this was the principal and most excellent cause why he should be in mind, that wilfully he chose honest poverty and all his temporal goods that God had sent him freely released to the neccessity and sustentation of those brethren and sisters whom he set under regular discipline and kept them full busy. And to this same Gilbert is process of time our Lord God granted such grace and virtue that he made four houses of canons and nine monasteries of nuns, in which houses that time that he died and went to our Lord, beside all those that were dead before he left of religious men unto a seven hundred, of sisters a thousand and five hundred, which full busily did service to God. He dies in his best age, more than a hundred year old, the year of the incarnation of our Lord Jesus, a thousand, a hundred, eighty nine, the day before the nones of February, the time of the worshipful King Henry the Second.

And thus because of his own merits and by testimony of many miracles followed, and revelations also, that came from God, he was canonised and written in the catalogue of saints of our holy father Pope Innocent the Third, by the general court of Rome at Anagnia, before the clergy and the people, the year of the incarnation of our Lord a thousand two hundred and two, the third ides of January, in the year of the kingdom of that worthy man, John, King of England, the third, president to the see of Canterbury the worshipful archbishop Hubert, which after the commandment of the said Pope, with his fellows as in that act, bishop of Ely, Eustace, and abbot of Peterborough, Acharius, had made diligent inquisition into the miracles wrought by this man, and written all this matter truly, and sent it up to the court. By which examination our father the Pope received the very truth, both of the holiness of this man Gilbert and also of his tokens, and for this cause he numbered him amongst saints, the year of his papacy, the fourth.

And that same year, by the commandment of the said Pope, he was translate of the said archbishop unto this shrine, the third ide of October, standing by, these worshipful men, bishop of Norwich, bishop of Hereford, bishop of Landaff, and other abbots and prelates and noble men of England, with much crowd of clergy and people.And to the perpetual memory of this thing done, the said archbishop and the other bishops and abbots set their seals onto this charter, and in this shrine they put it, to the praising of our Lord God Almighty which shall inform us with the examples of this man, and raise us from sins to grace with help of prayers of this man; and also the same Lord shall lead us from pain to joy where he liveth and reigneth evermore. Amen.

Thus ends the life of St Gilbert, translated into our mother tongue, the year of the incarnation of our Lord 1451 and now the second translation in 1987.

THE CONSTITUTIONS OF THE BLESSED GILBERT AND HIS SUCCESSORS

made by the General Chapters, and of the beginning, ordination and institution of the order of canons, nuns, lay-brothers and sisters of the Order of Sempringham; and of the election of the master, and his authority

From the Monasticon Anglicanum, *1717*

1. Having given the same account as above, of the original of the Nuns, Brothers and sisters, St Gilbert tells them, they are to vow Chastity, Humility, Charity, Obedience, in what is good, and Perseverance; renounce the world, and having anything they call their own, and other things that are proper for a religious life. Then he adds he had appointed for their food, a pound of bread, two messes of pottage, and a draught of water, and nothing more. The bread coarse, their garments and bedding mean; much watching and labour, and very little rest.

2. Having declared how the Canons were instituted, as before, he says, he had constituted four Procurators being the Prior, the Cellarer and two others unlearned, to take the charge of all their temporal concerns, as buying, selling, etc.

3. Upon the death of the Master of the Order, his Body to be conveyed to Sempringham, and there all the Heads of the Order, as well as the Canons as Nuns to meet, to elect another, not barely for his learning or high birth, but for his piety, and religion, and whosoever aspires to that dignity to be rejected. As to the manner of the election, the whole Chapter to name four persons, then those four to name nine others, and these thirteen, being first sworn to lay aside all favour and affection, to choose whomsoever they shall think fit for Master, whilst the Chapter assists at the Mass of the Holy Ghost, then the Chapter assembling with the aforesaid, one of these thirteen to declare the Master elected in these words: 'Behold this person we have in the fear of the Lord chosen for our Master'. Then 'Te Deum' to be sung.

4. The chief Prior of the Order not to travel with above six horses, with

which he might also make use of a carriage, as also one servant, and two Canons to assist. He to transact nothing without the advice of the Prime Brethren, etc.

5. The Master, with the advice of the Canons, to receive such as are to be admitted either as Canons, Nuns, Brothers or Sisters. No books to be sent from one place to another without consent of the Nuns and Prior. All that come into the Order to confess their sins to the Master, or whom he shall appoint; and if any shall omit doing so till Death, to have no office performed for them, nor be registered in their books.

6. Nothing above the value of three marks to be bought without the consent of the Prior, unless he be absent and necessity require. No writings to be sealed with the seal of the Monastery, but in the presence of the Chapter, and duplicates to be kept.

7. All to bow when the Prior passes by, and such as do not obey him, without showing sufficent cause, immediately to be looked upon as excommunicated; likewise respect to be shown to all others in the Office.

8. The chief Prior to appoint all others in Office, and upon occasion to dispose them; but the authority of the Head Prior to be above all others.

9. No money to be symoniacally taken for admitting of any into the Order.

OF THE CHIEF INQUISITORS

1. If the general Prior cannot visit the several Houses as often as is requisite, he may appoint two discreet Canons and one lay-brother to supply his place, as far as he shall direct, but they not to have power to admit any Novices,or depose Officers, or enter the Monastery of Nuns, without faithful Witnesses, in case of necessity.

2. One or two Canons fearing God and a Lay-Brother appointed by the general Prior, to go from House to House to correct what is amiss, instruct the ignorant and encourage the virtuous. The like to be done among the Nuns. The Men to visit their own Houses more than once a year, the Nuns only once a year.

3. Those who go from Monastery to Monastery by commission, the Master's Chaplains and the Father's Confessors to be appointed where to receive clothes and shoes when they have occasion, and to leave all there. No man to speak for himself, but one to declare the wants of another to such as have power to relieve the same.

4. A pittance may be added to those who go from one Monastery to another, if not, they to be satisfied with what the rest have.

5. The Inquisitor and Father Confessor to go together from Monastery to Monastery , the latter to stay in the Monastery whilst the other goes to inspect the barns, etc.,and to have a horse to carry his necessaries.

6. When Inspectresses are to go from one House to another, at least two

faithful persons of the Order to go with them, to attend them on the way, and to be punished for any neglect. The Nuns not to speak to the said persons by the way,without urgent necessity, and not in private. All things necessary for their progress to be furnished them by the Cellarer. The Nuns never to lodge where the men are, for fear of giving scandal.

7. The general Prior and Chief Inspectresses to appoint three or as many Nuns as may suffice, to correct what is amiss in any Monastery, or to improve what is good.

8. The Inspectresses to send out the books that are necessary, when the Canons shall require it, and so back to the Nuns.

9. The Inspectors and Inspectresses of good life and conversation to be yearly sent to each Monastery, and if they behave themselves amiss to be fed with bread and water, without a napkin, in the middle of the Refectory.

10. When Inspectors are sent from one Monastery to another, they are to take with them from their own House their clothes and other necessaries; and to have diet, needles, thread and what is requisite for mending their clothes and shoes, and to be satisfied with what will suffice them.

11. If the Prior, etc. shall not sufficently provide their Inspectors with clothes and shoes for the year, let the same be assigned them, when they come to the Chapter.

12. The Inspectors and Inspectresses are to take heed not to lay anything falsely to another's charge; and if any shall be convicted of so doing, they shall be liable to the greatest Punishment. And whosoever upon scrutiny shall be conceal any Offence, or Transgression of the Order, if the same shall be discovered to be most severely chastised, viz. to sit forty days in the middle of the Refectory to eat and drink, and to have the lowest place every where for a whole year.

13. All Inspectors, after the General Chapter, shall return to the House from whence they came, unless hindered by sickness, or otherwise ordered by the general Prior. And whosoever shall mutter against this, and shall attempt to stay in any other place on any pretence,shall hold the lowest place till he appears to be sufficiently penitent.

14. None of the Order to presume to persecute or slander a faithful Brother,who reproves those who act contrary to the Institutes; or for acquainting the general Prior or Brothers, with the Transgression of others, and if any Prior be guilty of the same, he to do Penance in the lowest place.

OF THE FOUR PROCURATORS OF MONASTERIES

1. Four men fearing God, discreet and peaceable, to be appointed in every Monastery to dispose of the substance belonging to the same, and nothing to be to be disposed of without them; and those to be the Prior, Cellarer, Procurator, and Store-keeper, who must diligently furnish all things that are

for the Nuns.

2. No Prior to go far upon the business of his House, without a Canon, or Lay-brother of good repute, unless obliged to it by extraordinary poverty. He is to acquaint the Sub-prior and other Procurators with the occasion of his journey, and never to take above two horses with him, unless there be an urgent necessity. Nothing of moment to be done without his advice, and he to act nothing considerable without acquainting the general Prior. When the Master is present, no Prior to give a Canon leave to go abroad, unless upon the business of the House, or to any woman to go into the Nuns. The Prior to give the Habit to the Novices. Priors if grown old not to be removed from the House they have governed well, but to be respected and cherished.

3. The Prior and Cellarer are allowed to discourse together of the business of the House abroad; that at home to be managed in the several Chapters. The Sub-Prior to do the like in the absence of the Prior, and to hold the Chapter, but not to give any Canon leave to go abroad. He is to visit the sick, and to give leave to Canons and Brothers to talk in the Monastery; to hear confessions for smaller offences, and correct daily failings. When the Prior is sick, the Sub-Prior not to grant leave for women to go into the Nuns, for men to talk to them, for the Canons or Brothers to go without the Monastery door, not to hear any confession, unless there be danger of death, and if he transgress these rules, to be twice reproved and the third time disposed.

4. The Prior, or in his absence the Sub-Prior or other person appointed by him, with two virtuous Canons, and some benefactors and other devout persons to be present in the Chapters of the Nuns, to go in and out all together, and not to talk to the Nuns.

5. No kindred of the Priors or other Chiefs of Monasteries to be received into the same to enter the Order, but in others, unless it be in danger of death.

6. The Prior and other Officers to have to examine into all things for the sustenance of the Monasteries, and the Nuns the same, and to presume to consume anything without their consent. Of all fruit or honey some part to be retained for the Brothers, and the rest to be sent to the Nuns.

7. Monthly accounts to be made up of all expenses,etc.,and transmitted in writing to the Nuns, and kept till the Yearly Chapter.

8. The Procurators to be careful to know the number of sheep and other cattle, and the wool not to be sold without general consent.

9. If the Nuns for want of beer be obliged to drink water, the Procurators for their neglect to be obliged to the same, unless it proceed from scarcity of grain, and care to be used that none drink any more than necessity.

10. Neither the Cellarer, nor the Sub-Cellarer to go abroad when the other is absent; and neither of them to carry about any money, unless for the expense of his journey; and in their absence no money to be expended without absolute necessity.

11. The Cellarer to keep exact account of the men hired to work, and their hire, and they to be paid their wages in the presence of the Prior, unless it be in very remote farms. If any be hired to comb wool, the Sisters not being able to perform the same, a trusty Brother to be set over such workmen, to prevent frauds and the admitting of Lay-Women to work among the Sisters.

12. The Cellarer to be assisted by a meek and provident Canon, to receive and distribute provisions, etc.,and he never to go farther than the farms. A modest Brother to be appointed to serve at the window, through which necessaries are served in to the Nuns; and another to serve the guests from abroad, who are to talk no more than is necessary. All iron and steel to be kept by the Cellarer for use. If he or his Deputy does not, in due time, give the hirelings their bread, he shall fast for his neglect.

13. Two to be appointed to look to the Appartment for strangers, one a Canon and a Lay-Brother, who know how to entertain guests; neither of them to retain to himself anything that belongs to the guests, nor to conceal anything from the Prior, which may be a loss to the Nuns. None of the Order to eat or drink with strangers in their appartment, unless by leave, to entertain the guests of great quality; viz. Archbishops, or Bishops. It is lawful to obey them, and to taste drink once or twice, if they command. Nor is flesh to be given to strangers, except Archdeacons, Bishops and sick persons; and in that case the flesh to be dressed by their servants; for in the Monasteries none are to eat flesh, except great men, sick persons and hirelings.

14. Care to be taken to provide lambskins for Nuns, Canons, and Brothers, and the neglect thereof to be punished by wanting the same in Winter, or fasting.

15. All are forebid under 'Anathema', any way disposing of the money of the Nuns, their provisions or cattle, without the consent of the Prior and the Cellarer, but in case of necessity, the same to be done with advice.

16. None to keep any boys, or horses, or saddles or the like, but such as the Prior shall assign, when they are to go abroad; the transgressors to be punished with many stripes; or else deposed if they are in Office. If anything considerable is to be bought, the proper Brother to receive of the Nuns at the window, and pay it away by direction of the person he is sent with, for the prelates are not to carry money, unless in case of necessity. When money is delivered into, or out by the Nuns, a discreet Brother to be present, who is to know all the expense, and an exact account to be kept both by the Nuns and the Brothers, to the end that when matters come to be examined, their vouchers may answer, and all things be plain and easy to the Examiner and Comptrollers appointed for the same.

OF THE CANONS AND NOVICES AND THEIR AGE: AND OF THE LAY-CANONS

1. Seven Canons at least to belong to every Monastery of the Nuns, if their possessions be sufficient, or more to the number of thirteen, if they can be maintained without burdening the Nuns. They to perform the Divine Office, but organs or other music are absolutely forbid. Punishments are enjoined for all Transgressors. Silence to be observed in the Cloister, Choir, Chapter, Refectory and Dormitory. The Canons to do what is necessary in the Cloister, Orchard, etc.,where they may not be seen by the Nuns, or disturbed by Lay-persons. Chiefly never to be seen or heard by the Nuns, unless at Mass, and such other occasions as cannot be omitted. None to be taught in the Monastery except Novices, to which none to be admitted till after fifteen years of age. Any person that desires to be admitted into the Order, to be received in the Chapter, and before his reception to dispose of all he has, never to recover the same, whether given to God or secular persons, though he should depart again, and none to be received without having first publicly declared to him, and a proper person to be appointed to instruct the Novices; none of them to serve or read at table, nor read lessons in the Church, but to serve at Masses, etc.

3. The garments of the Canons to be three tunics, one coat of full grown lamb skins, and a white cloak sewn before four fingers in breadth, and hairy furs to put on, if the cloak be not furred, and a hood lined with lamb skins and two pairs of stockings, a pair of woollen socks, and day shoes and night slippers; as also a linen cloak for divine service. At time of work to have a white scapular. Their beds like 'Cistercian' Monks. The Priors and other Officers to take care not to scandalise the rest by their clothing or diet.

4. No wool of several colours to be mixed in their Habits, nor any shorn cloth to be made, but if given or bought, may be worn with leave of the general Prior. The bed-clothes not to be fine, unless given.

5. If any refuse a garment misliking the colour or because short, or scanty, he must go without the same for a whole year. None to exchange those they have. Lamb-skin coats to last seven or eight years, or longer if it may be, they not being allowed for ornament, but for necessity.

6. If any one loses any garment, through neglect, he is to go without the same for a whole year.

7. The Prior and Cellarer to have boots reaching a little above their knees to ride in, the Dortorer to keep two or three other pair of boots for the use of such as ride out, and they to restore them at their return. All the shoes of the Canons to be of red leather of a moderate height. Any person using other shoes, or other bed-clothes than appointed, immediately to deliver up the same.

8. None to wash his own linen, but to leave the same to the care of those

appointed by the Prelates, to be washed by the Sisters.

9. Twelve Canons, with a Prior being the thirteenth, to be sent to new Monasteries, but not till books, houses and necessities are provided. The books, a Missal, the Rule of the Order, the Book of Customs, a Psalter, a Book of Hymns, one of Collects, the Antiphonary and the Gradual. The houses. an Oratory, a Refectory, a Dormitory, an Apartment for guests, and Porter's lodge.

10. The several times appointed for the Canons to be shaved.

11. A discreet Canon to be appointed to inspect every sort of workmen.

12. The method of performing Divine Office, of the holding Chapter, of reading the rule and expounding the same; with the punishment of such as reveal the secrets of the Chapter, and of confessing.

13. Silence to be observed in the Chapter House, except whilst the Chapter is held.

14. When gone out from the Chapter House, they are to sit and read in the Cloister. If anyone wants the book another has, he must deliver him his own and receive that, which must not be refused, or if it be who asks to take it patiently. None to look angrily upon another, or if any give signs of passion, to be twice admonished, and for the third time to be scourged in the Chapter.

15. All the Churches of this Order to be dedicated to the Blessed Virgin Mary, and some other Saint, unless necessity compel to the contrary; and for the preserving of unity, the rules of Saint Benedict and Saint Augustine to be interpreted after the same manner by them all. The same books relating to the Divine Service to be used in all Monasteries; as also the same diet, the same clothing, and the same customs. No superfluous paintings or carvings to be in their Churches, or Offices, lest they divert from prayer and meditation; but painted wooden crosses to be allowed.

16. Those who serve at the Altar to wear surplices, with hoods, to cover the head and naked part of the neck. The priests at Mass to wear a stole in the form of a cross. If there be a gold or silver chalice, after the service it is to be delivered to the Nuns.

17. Upon solemn festivals, a sermon to be preached in the Church of the Nuns, a cloth hanging between the men and the women.

18. Care to be taken to assist any Canon, or other that shall bleed at the nose, or to be otherwise sick whilst at the Altar, or Divine Office.

19. Those who are employed to write continually, to be considered as to sleep and other refections. Any one that writes anything to be concealed from the Prior, to be punished in the Chapter. None to presume to write, or procure to be written, any book, or other thing, without the consent of the Prior. None to presume to take to himself the book another has; but if it be necessary for him, it is to be cautiously asked of the Prior, or the proper person, lest the other take offence.

20. The Refectories of the Canons and Brothers to be built in such manner, that the meat may be delivered out to them both by the Nuns and Sisters by wheels; the height of them shall be a foot and a half, the remains to be returned the same way, and not otherwise disposed of. No one of the Nuns to serve there alone, but several at a time in their turns. None to go into the Refectory but at the appointed hours, of upon having leave to drink. Fire may be made in the Refectory in case of excessive cold.

21. Canons allowed breakfasts till thirty years of age, and not after, unless sick, or with leave. The breakfast to be no other than bread and beer, unless in case of necessity.

22. All to wash their hands before they enter the Refectory; to bow coming in, to stand till the Blessing is given, and then their messes to be served orderly, beginning at the Master, Prior etc. and so downwards. If any one cannot eat either sort of pottage, to be allowed another thing that is not more dainty, and if the revenues will allow it, some other pittance may be given.

23. If any one happen at table to bleed at the nose, or be taken with vomiting or any other infirmity, the servitor must not go out, but speak to the Cellarer to help him. The Convent not to stay for him, if he goes out, he may return and eat his meat.

24. All who are not present at the blessing of the table, to do penance for the same. The reader and servitors to dine as soon as the rest have done.

25. No wine to be bought for their own drinking, unless for want of beer, and in case of necessity; none to be drank but what is well mixed with water.

26. No white meats to be eaten of fasting days, unless in case of sickness, and even then no flesh without great necessity.

27. The fragments of the Canons to be returned to the Nuns by the same wheels the meat was given out, which is to be according to the number of those that are to eat, and nothing to be carried out of the Refectory.

28. None to eat out of the Refectory, not even the general Prior, unless there be some extraordinary guests to whom he must do honour. All strictly forbidden when out of their Monasteries, to drink above one measure and a half of the said Monasteries, of any liquor that can make a man drunk, because it is execrable to disgrace the Order by intemperance; therefore any person guilty of the same to drink nothing but water for forty days. Water and such liquors as cannot occasion drunkeness are not forbid in proper time and place. None to presume to eat flesh, even in the Refectory of religious men, unless commanded by an Archbishop, a Bishop, a Legate, or the King; but the sick to be allowed flesh in the Infirmary.

29. None to repeat what he has heard abroad against the Order. Any news carrier to do penance fifteen days.

30. None to go into the fire-room without leave, except writers to dry their parchment, the sacristan for coals for the thurible, and others for like

necessity. All to assemble in due time to collation in the Refectory, and strict silence to be observed after complin.

31. The Canons going to the necessary house to hide their faces, as much as they can, and never to sit down in the Dormitory, unless to put on or take off their shoes and stockings etc.

32. The beds to be searched by trusty persons appointed by the Prior, and if anything be found concealed in them, the offender to be punished with stripes and fasting.

33. If anyone goes out of the Choir on account of indisposition, yet he is, at his return, to kneel by way of penance, and to make his confession in the Chapter. The Imfirmary-Keeper to take particular care of the sick, and they to be indulged in all points according to their necessity.

34. Many rules prescribed about purging.

35. More of the same.

36. Ceremonies to be observed in processions going to meet the Bishop of the Diocese, Archbishops, Legates, the King, or the Master of the Order.

37. All things that have been written for the Brothers and Canons, and may be advantageous for the Nuns and Sisters, to be observed by them, and so vice versa.

THE WRITTEN RULES CONCERNING THE BROTHERS

1. When the Order of Sempringham was first instituted, there came some monks of the Cistercian Order, in a very low and humble manner, and with them Lay-Brothers very laborious, poor in habit, and satisfied with the most hard food, whom many of the labouring sort desiring to imitate, they were received into this Order of Sempringham, and ordered to follow the example of the Cistercians, and if any of them transgressed the rule, they were to be deprived of partaking of the Body and Blood of Christ, till they repented. The Lay-Brothers of what age so-ever, labouring under any great infirmity, were to be allowed a garment of rams skins, open before and tied together about the belly, like those worn by sucking babes, called in English, Flage. Every Brother to have three white tunics, and a mantle of grey cloth, reaching half way the leg, lined with coarse common skins, and a cloth reaching down not quite to the heels, with an hood only covering the shoulders and breast. The Prior may allow more to herds-men, carmen and shepherds. No regard to be had to the colour; they are to have two pair of stockings, and woollen socks.Only carpenters allowed to have black round rochets.

2. The shoes for the Brothers to be of the best part of the leather, and to last them a year, if possible, and to be mended when there is occasion.

3. If they have no scourers, the Brothers to wash their own clothes, or the porter to get some poor people to do it.

4. The new Brothers to be admitted at the Chapter, but none under twenty

four years of age, and immediately to be put to labour. The Novices to have an able Master to instruct them, and to attend at Church duties. The Brothers to take the usual Vows of Poverty, Chastity and Obedience. None of them to have any books, or be taught any more than the Lord's Prayer, the Belief, and the Miserere Psalm, with what else is requisite for them to pray. No Novice to be ever sent abroad.

5. Particular rules for their assisting at Divine Service, and behaviour there.

6. Not to work on any festivals, and to behave themselves as the Canons do, when with them.

7. The Lay-Brother to communicate eight times in the year.

8. The Lay-Brother not to go into any offices without leave, and to observe silence there, as also in the Dormitory and Refectory, and all exercising any trade to be silent in manner, only carpenters to have a place appointed to talk, in few words, about their business. A Chapter of Lay-Brothers to be held by the Prior weekly, and none of them to talk after it, but go to sleep, when complin is ended, without necessity.

9. Their Refectory to be as has been said of that for the Canons, and all other particulars much after the same manner.

10. All land to be sowed with that sort of grain which is most proper for it, and if the Brother farmer knowingly do otherwise, to be fed with coarse bread one day every week till the corn be reaped. Never to go into the Nuns enclosure, unless to help in case of fire, thieves, or the like. The Brother farmer may speak to all the Brothers about their labour,but not give them leave to talk, unless in case of necessity. Every Brother farmer to have an associate to inspect his behaviour.

11. No procurator, farmer, or other, to buy or sell, unless he has a Canon appointed by the Prior with him, and the said associates to be frequently changed.

12. Two Canons to be sent with a Lay-Brother, to buy what is wanting at fairs, and what is so bought to be shown to the Prior, and then delivered to the Nuns. No Brother of the Order at fairs to receive from another Order food for himself or his horse, but to live upon his own, as becomes his Order, not buying fish, or drinking wine, unless with much water, and contenting himself with two messes of pottage. They must never sell wine to taverns.

13. Nothing of silk to be brought by them, not even for the Church, unless absolutely necessary, the same of pictures, or images of the Blessed Virgin, or other Saints, which are only to be used at the Altar, when given gratis.

14. A Canon to be joined with the Lay-Brother for keeping of the wool, that no frauds may be used.

15. No Brother to talk to another of one that is present, of anything that may provoke or scandalise him; whosoever affends herein, to live three days upon bread and water, and be thrice scourged in the Chapter. All chests allowed for

keeping of necessaries, to have two keys, one of then in the custody of the Prior, to search the same when he pleases. Masons and carpenters, or such as ride, to be allowed breeches of such cloth as becomes religious men.

16. Beer and a pittance to be sent to the Brothers in the farms, at Christmas, Easter and Whitsuntide, with some allowance for strangers. In farms very remote from the Monastery, beer may be bought. The measure sent to the farms not to exceed what is prescribed in the rules. No beer to be brewed at the farms, unless some great person desire it, and then to be done by their own servants.

17. As soon as the Harvest is over, the corn to be threshed that is requisite to the Monastery for the year. Brothers to be sent yearly to look after the butter and cheese in the farms. In remote farms a certain number of sheep to be assigned the Brothers for the use of hirelings. The Brother at the farm appointed to entertain guests, to look after the geese, hens, eggs etc.,that they be carefully kept and sent to the Nuns, and to the Canons, from their farms. Brothers coming to the farms, to be treated like those who reside there, with many more particular rules for the preserving of all things and religious government there.

18. No women to come within the courts of farms unless by order of the Prior, and no Brother to talk to a woman alone. women to milk the sheep in the fields, and not in houses, and those that are young and handsome to be avoided; nor no Brother to come near them, but to have faithful servants to inspect and reprove those that do not milk well. Those that are hired to reap, not to be permitted to come within the enclosures, but to have houses with doors to them without. The Brother who is to find them meat, to keep a faithful hireling to give them what is requisite, and to have a small hole within the enclosure, to see how they are served, and not to speak there. The Brothers not to be joined with them in any labour, nor to work too near them. Any person laying violent hands on a Canon, or Brother, to be accounted excommunicate, pursuant to the bulls of the Pope's Alexander and Innocent.

19. Horses to be docked and their manes cut short, that they may look contemptable.

20. Whosoever shall hurt an Ox, or Ass, or horse, or colt, by over-working, so as they die or are disabled, to fast and be scourged.

21. Those who hurt themselves by carrying too much weight, or immoderate labour, to do penance with bread and water, and be scourged in the Chapter.

22. Those who upon the signal do not repair to the oven, to be punished.

23. Lay-men forsaking all they have, and repairing to the Monasteries, to be served in all respects like other Brothers, and to have the Office in like manner performed for them when dead.

24. None to be concerned in secular law-suits, nor to be bound for others, nor to visit their friends and relations, nor any Nuns of other Orders, but carefully

avoid giving any scandal.

25. The Procurators to visit men or women of good reputation well afffected to the Order, when they are sick, to comfort and give them spiritual advice.

26. When Canons or Brothers are to go abroad, a reasonable time to be allowed for them to return, and the transgressors to be punished.

27. Any Brother taken in theft, or other heinous crime, to be most severely punished or expelled; smaller offences to be more gently chastised.

28. If any man or woman of the Order should be guilty of sinning carnally together, the man guilty to be immediately stripped of his Habit, and cast into prison, or expelled, never to be re- admitted; but the woman, to avoid the scandal of her wandering abroad, to be shut up in a little house, separate from the rest, within the Nuns court, never to go out till death, but there to do penance all her life.

29. Any Brother or Sister that is obstinate and incorrigible, to be expelled by the General Chapter; but if not expelled, and shall happen to die in the same contumacy, to be deprived of all Offices performed for the dead.

30. Whosoever maliciously sows discord among the Brothers and Sisters, to be excommunicated.

31. Whosoever reveals the secrets of the Chapter, or falsely accuses the Brothers, to be excommunicated.

32. Any Canon, or Brother, taken in theft, or convicted of the same, to be expelled, never to be restored. Any one shedding blood of a Canon, or Brother, to be sent afoot to the Master; and any Brother convicted of uncleaness, to be expelled, never to be restored.

33. Those who flee from the Order, and commit theft, not returning within forty days, to be anathematised; but if a fugitive returns within a week, to do penance a whole year; but if he returns after forty days, then to do penance two years and in a much greater degree.

THE RULES FOR THE PENITENT NUNS OF THE ORDER

1. All the men belonging to the Order carefully to serve the Nuns, and care to be taken, that their houses be, in all respects, neater and better furnished than those of the men.

2. All the lambs of every Monastery to be yearly tithed, and the tithe-lambs put into good pasture, and care taken of the increase, and all the products of their wool etc. to be delivered to the Nuns, and what shall be to spare above supplying their wants, to be given to the poor. The Nuns also to have the keeping of all gold, silver, clothes, and other like things.

3. Three particular Nuns to be appointed by the rest to keep the common Seal, Gold, Silver, Etc.

4. Three marks to be yearly laid aside to make good the wall and ditch to shut up the Nuns, that no person may go in, or have the least sight of them. No

126

presents or messages to be sent to or from the Nuns or Lay-Sisters.

5. No Priest or Lay-Brother, having a Mother, or other kinswoman among the Nuns, ever to speak to her; nor to talk to any other, under pain of excommunication, excepting the Prior, Confessor, or others authorised.

6. The windows at which anything is delivered in or out, to be with wheels to turn, that the Sisters may not see the men, nor the men the Sisters; but there must be a gate for wains and great carriages to go in, the keys whereof to be kept by most faithful persons on both sides. The window where the Nuns talk to their kindred, to be the length of a finger square, and plated about with iron, and so the confession window. The doors and windows to be carefully shut up in good season. None to ask fire of the Nuns at night, without some urgent necessity, and then the same to be delivered out in the presence of three persons.

7. Two particular Nuns to be appointed to serve or speak at the wheels, and no others to come unto that room, unless commanded.

8. The Brother who keeps the window with the wheel not to enter the court of the Nuns, nor to talk to any of the handicrafts. Both he and the Sister on the other side, who are to deliver things and messages backwards and forwards, to be discreet and not talkative.

9. A discreet Brother and Sister allowed to talk to one another at the window upon adjusting of any accompt, with others standing by on both sides, who are not to speak to one another.

10. None to go into the Nunnery, whilst they are at their hours, or in the Refectory, or Dormitory; but in the case of absolute necessity, several to go in and out all together; excepting the cases of fire, robbery, or danger of death.

11. All to be served out of one cellar and kitchen, the care whereof to be committed to the Nuns.

12. If any of the three Nuns governing the Monasteries shall procure any thing peculiar for herself any way whatsoever, she is to be removed and do Penance. All the Nuns to pay respect and obedience to their chief, and she and the cellarer to have the entire disposal of their food and raiment.

13. If the Prioress goes out of the Dormitory after dinner, or complin, it must not be alone without some other Nun.

14. A certain place to be provided in the Nuns court for the Nuns and Sisters to talk to the Prioress and cellarer, and in all offices standing; and only two with them.

15. The Sub-Prioress not to be made Prioress, unless the general Prior, or the Inspectoresses shall think fit.

16. The cellarer not to talk to the yearly inspectresses of another house, in private, nor to another, so as they may hear it; nor to serve in the kitchen. A house to be made near the oven, to which the Sisters may go without being seen by the men, to carry away the bread. The cellarer to have the keeping of

all provisions.

17. The Nuns to have five tunics, three for labour, and two large, that is coules, to wear in the Cloister, in the Church, the Chapter, the Refectory and Dormitory, and a scapular for labour. All a coat of lambskins, and a shift of coarse cloth, if they will, and black linen caps, lined with lambskins. All clothes for their heads are to be black and coarse, and so their veils. Neither theirs nor the garments of the Canons to be made too long. The Nuns not to sew any work for abroad without the consent of the general Prior, or of all the Canons and Brothers; nor the shirts, or breeches of their Canons, or Brothers.

18. When the clothes of the Nuns and Sisters are to be washed at the same time, they are not to be divided, but each charitably to help the other. The same for those that belong to the Canons, to be delivered in once a month.

19. The Sacristan rising at night to ring the bell, to have at least two Nuns with her, appointed by the Prioress. It is her duty to ring the bell, to light the lamp, to provide coals for the censer. No care to be taken to have many lights in the Church, unless the three tenebrae nights, and the day of the purification of the Blessed Virgin; nor is the weight of the paschal candle on holy Saturday to be regarded; but in all cases superfluity, vanity and too much frugality to be avoided.

20. These Nuns not allowed to sing, but absolutely forbid it.

21. The Nun that is to read the Collect, is to provide the same before-hand, that there may be no disorder or confusion, if she mistakes.

22. All Nuns, not hindred by sickness, to attend diligently at all hours.

23. Several penances to be enjoined for faults. No Nun to communicate on Sunday, unless she has confessed publicly or privately during the week.

24. Fifteen solemn processions to be made every year in the Nunneries.

25. On holidays, and others, during the time of reading, all Nuns, except those in office, to be at prayer in the Church, and at the reading and meditation, sitting in the Cloister, not facing one another, but all on one side, and their backs towards the faces of the others, unless the Cloister be too small or that two are reading in the same book, or sewing the same garment. None to utter any words with an angry countenance. The Latin tongue is wholly forbid among them, unless there be a proper occasion. No Nun, or Sister, to take or keep any thing by theft, and all offences to be severely punished.

26. The washing of the feet on Maundy Thursday, how to be performed.

27. The manner how to perform the worship of the Cross on Good- Friday.

28. Nothing to be strewed on the floor of the Chapter House on Holy Saturday, unless it be wet, before the Chapter; but the same and the Cloister to be adorned between the hour of None and the Mass.

29. Nothing relating to the Chapter to be done during the time of work.

30. The cupboard for the books to be always locked, except at the time of reading. None to presume to take the book another has; but if she has great

need thereof, to ask it of the Prioress. None to presume to write, or cause to be written, any book or prayers, without leave, or to entertain writers in the Churches of the Nuns.

31. The rules to be observed in the Refectory, much the same as above for the Canons.

32. None to speak in the parlour without leave; other particulars much the same as above for the Canons.

33. Rules for the kitchen.

34. The Nun appointed to receive female guests, permitted to speak to them: the house for their entertainment to be within the Nuns court, but out of their sight , and none of them to go into it, whilst strangers are there. No flesh to be given to strangers to eat, without special leave from the Master; nor any to be allowed to bathe, or purge, or stay above one night, or be brought to eat or drink into the Refectory of the Nuns or Sisters: but if any guest be a relation to a Nun, to be permitted to speak to one another at the window or at the door, with an orderly witness. If the guest shall happen to bring a boy with her, no Nun or Sister to go into the house to her knowingly, and if she accidentally goes in, to come out immediately.

35. None to speak to young girls, who are not yet Novices, except the Prioress and their Mistress. None to be admitted among the Nuns till she has been some days in the house for entertaining of guests,that they may the better judge whether she is fit to be received. The Prioress before her admission to aquaint her with all the hardships of the Order. None to be admitted before she is full twelve years of age, nor to be a Novice till fifteen, nor to be professed till she has got the Psalter, Hymns, Canticles and Antiphons by heart, if when she came she was under twenty years of age: But if any are above twenty years of age at their entrance, not to be obliged to all those particulars, unless they have some peculiar genius for the same. Novices not to be continually sent to work till they have done and know their duty. Other particulars relating to Novices are much the same as have before been mentioned in speaking of the Canons and Brothers.

THE RULES FOR THE LAY-SISTERS

1. None to be admitted to the Habit of a Lay-Sister, under twenty years of age. To have one assigned to direct and inform the person so received; and if she be found to improve during her year of Noviceship, to make her profession before the Master. When professed to be diligent at their work and respect the Nuns, assisting them in all things. They are not to go about their work in the kitchen, brewhouse, etc., but to undertake the same in due season, and the Nuns at proper times charitably to help them. None of the Sisters to dispose or order things committed to their charge of any sort without leave or consent of the Prioress. The Sisters to be clad like the Nuns, excepting the

couls and scapulars, instead whereof they are to have cloaks of full grown lambs-skins and hoods covering their breasts. All of them to have caps of black linen coarse cloth, or very old, lined with lambs-skins.

2. All things relating to the Sisters to be brought into the Chapter, after the Nuns have done what relates to them there.

3. If Brothers or Sisters are professed on a weekday, they may receive the Eucharist the next Sunday, unless something obstruct.

4. The Sisters not to sit down to table till their chief sits. If any of them transgress at table, to be corrected as the Nuns. They may have drink and other allowances like the Nuns on festivals.

5. The Sisters attending the brewhouse may say their Mattins there.

THE RULES FOR THE SICK NUNS AND SISTERS

1. A discreet, chaste and religious Priest to be appointed to go about to Monasteries to hear the confessions of the Nuns and Sisters, at the confession-window. Whilst one confesses two others to sit at a distance in the room, to observe her behaviour, and the Priest not to ask any questions of curiosity, remote from the business of confession, and one to be at a distance to see how he behaves himself. The confession-window to such another as that above described for talking to kindred. All houses to supply him with necessaries, and he to hear all confessions.

2. In every Monastery a proper window to be provided for the Nuns and Sisters to communicate at; as also a place in the Church, or in the Infirmary for administering to them the Extreme Unction, so that the sight and near access of men may, as much as is possible, be avoided, excepting him who is to perform that office. Four Canons and a Brother to go into administer this sacrament, the rest staying in the Church. Three grave Priests, of whom there can be no jealousy, to be appointed in every Monastery to administer Extreme Unction to the Nuns and Sisters, and to talk of confession, if there be occasion. The Priest officiating at the Altar, not to give the Holy Eucharist to the Sisters, but one of the three above mentioned. Two Nuns to hold the Communion cloth before her that communicates. The sick that can may go and receive the Sacrament; but if they cannot go, then two modest Priests, and a grave Brother to carry the Viaticum to them, cautiously avoiding to see or be seen by any of the Nuns in the Monastery.

3. When any Nun is sick another to read the Hour to her, if there be enough that are learned, if not she must do it as is done by the Sisters.

4. The Infirmary Nun may have a Lay-Woman assistant in a white veil, who according to her direction may serve the sick, dress their meat, wash their linen, and do whatsoever else shall be necessary, and this woman to communicate as a Novice and have the office said for her when dead. The Infirmary Nun not to be put to any other office.

5. Weak Nuns out of the Infirmary, though they cannot be present at the Night Service, they may be at the other Hours, and no such to be put to work with the rest, till she can assist at Divine Office. Those who work may do it in their Scapular and sleep so in the day, but at night in their Coul. Nuns or Sisters who labour under continual diseases, not to eat flesh daily, but during fifteen days, twice, thrice or four times in the year, at great festivals.

THE RULES CONCERNING THE OFFICE OF THE DEAD

1. When the hour of death draws near, let every one hasten to the dying person, and by the way say the Creed, and repeat it twice of thrice. When they are all come, let one read the Passion and Gospels, and say the Penitential Psalms and the Litanies with other usual and proper prayers, if he lives so long. When he is dead, the bell must be rung thrice, and none then to go abroad till the body be interred. Whilst the body is washing the Canons to sing Psalms, with the Placebo and Dirige. When a Nun, or Sister dies, the Priest to perform the office at the Altar, and the Nuns about the body. The bodies of Nuns, Sisters and all women to be placed in their choir till the office is performed; but in the Church before the Altar at Mass, that the Canons may come to perform their part. The bodies of Canons to be placed in their Choir, those of the Brothers in theirs, those of Lay-Men before the second Altar. The rest is the particular prayers, ceremonies, and other particulars till the laying of them in the ground.

2. The hours for burying the dead, which was always the same day, if they died in the morning so that Mass could be said; for none of the Order was to be buried without.

3. After every yearly Chapter an office to be solemnly performed in every Monastery for all the dead of the Order, and such as the Priors had engaged for. Also a three years office, and then every Canon to say the Psalter ten times, and the Brothers and Sisters their way, and every Priest twenty Masses, for those of the Order. Also the office for the dead after every Chapter held yearly in each Monastery.

4. Every day in the year, on which the Convent does not say office of the dead the Hebdomadarius of the week past with his assistants shall say it after dinner in winter, and after the hour of Nones in summer. Every week in the year Mass to be likewise said for the dead.

5. Any person received as a Canon or a Brother at his death, to have the office performed for him in the same manner as the Canons or Brothers.

6. The fathers, mothers, brothers, sisters and relations of the brethren of the Order to have commemorations made of them by name, and a solemn Mass for them all in general to be said once a year throughout all Monasteries.

THE RULES BELONGING TO NUNS AND SISTERS IN COMMON

1. None to be admitted among the Nuns without their consent, nor any to compel them to receive any such.
2. No Nun or Sister to go abroad to work, not even to gather flax, or to reap; nor to receive any Cordovan shoes to wear, or bestow.
3. The Sisters to have their heads shaved at least three times a year. The Nuns to wash their heads but only seven times a year. None to wash their feet without leave, unless they have fouled them by working in the mire or marshes.
4. If any one shall desire to remove to another house, she shall do fifteen days penance, be thrice scourged, and be forbid going any whither. The same for Brothers.
5. Any one refusing to do what is enjoined her, to do penance with bread and water. The like to those who enjoin anything that ought not to be.
6. If any one contract a particular familiarity with another, to be punished.
7. The rules to be read four times a year to the Brothers, Sisters and Nuns, but not to them all together; by the Canons to the Brothers, and by Nuns to the Sisters.
8. No purses to be made by the Nuns or Sisters, but of white leather, and without any silk ornaments, unless for the body of our Lord, Hosts, Chalices, etc., for the Divine Service, and adorning of books.
9. The Nuns and Sisters to behave themselves humbly and meekly, and to avoid all that tends to discord and strife.
10. None to bathe, unless for health, or great necessity, and when done in such cases not to be naked, but covered with some linen.

THE RULES RELATING TO PRESERVE THE UNITY OF ALL HOUSES

1. No house of this Order to disturb another, or its possessions, or acquire anything so near as to straighten the same. But if anything should be given it is to be yielded up to the other house, near whose possessions it is, and that house to make a suitable return according to the judgement of other houses; unless the house near which it is shall consent that the other retain the same. If anything to the contrary shall be attempted, the possession to belong to the house that is molested.
2. If any house of the Order shall labour under want, the other houses charitably to relieve the same; unless the charity be obstructed by their own sloath, or relaxation in the observance of their rules.
3. No lands to be bought, farmed, or taken upon mortgage, without permission of the Master, and no lands to be farmed by the year, unless in

case of extreme poverty, no debt to be upon interest, without the Master's leave, nor any churches, or altars to be set to farm, nor any chaplains to be hired, who have women servants, or if they have, to be immediately put away.
4. No fine bread to be made in the Monastery, unless upon great festivals, with an exception for the sick, as also strangers, who are to have white bread, as also those of the religious who are purging.
5. The Prior and Procurators to be acquainted with anything that is given to the Sisters, by strangers, or by the Sisters to strangers, and the Brothers on their side to acquaint the Nuns with anything given them; because none are to possess gold, silver, or clothes, or shoes, or knives, or girdles, etc. without leave, and transgressors to be punished.
6. None of their own accord to fail in point of obedience. No Canon or Brother, Nun or Sister to receive anything in trust, or to borrow or lend anything without leave, and such as do to be treated as guilty of theft.

THE RULES CONCERNING THE GREAT CHAPTER

1. All the Priors, and Cellarers of the several Monasteries, and two heads of each Nunnery, and the great visitors to assemble yearly at Sempringham to treat about the affairs of the Order, for keeping up of unity and strict discipline; where the rules of the Cistercian Order are to be observed.
2. The Nuns when they travel to be carried in a waggon, but never to ride; but the sick may be carried in a horse litter. None of them to take anything for their journey, but to be supplied with all necessaries, by the Heads. The like to be understood of the men. None to go along with the Nuns but such sober persons as are appointed by the Superiors. When the Nuns get into, or come out of the waggons the men must be remote from them. No Nun to eat or drink at a religious house of another Order. If any Nun goes to the Chapter, without being ordered, to be punished in another house. Neither Nuns nor religious men to talk with their kindred at the yearly Chapter.
3. Two sorts of pittances allowed those that go to the Chapter, viz. butter and cheese, or the like, if there is no fish. Those who stay at home to have one, with their pottage; and those of the Chapter, there to be content with their usual diet and one pittance to avoid giving scandal.
4. All the Canons and Brothers, Nuns and Sisters, excepting those in Office, to enter into the Chapter, to be edified by the word, and then all to go out, except those who according to the rules belong to the chapter, which when ended, all to meet again, to receive absolution.
5. At the yearly General Chapters, the candles being lighted, all are to be Anathematized who conspire against the Order, and sow discord among the Houses. The same to be done in each house, at the return of the Prior, in the presence of the Canons and Brothers. Incendiaries, thieves and such as have

anything of their own to be yearly excommunicated in the General Chapter, and every Monastery.

6. The following number of Brothers never to be increased, viz. at Sempringham 60; Chicksande 55; Watton 70; Malton 85; Lincoln 16; Haverholm 50; Catley 35; Bullington 50; Sixhills 55; Ormesby 50; Alvingham 40; New Place 13; Hospital 55; Mattersey and at St.Leonard's 10. The total 594. If one be under a continual distemper, another may be received. Also the number of Nuns not to be increased in any of the aforesaid Houses, and the Sisters to be included in the said number, viz. at Watton 140; Chicksand 120; Sempringham 120; Haverholm 100; Catley 60; Lincoln 20; Bullington 100; Sixhills 120; Ormesby 100; Alvingham 80.

A Gilbertine Canon and a Gilbertine Nun

GILBERTINE PRIORIES FOR CANONS AND NUNS

DOUBLE FOUNDATIONS IN ENGLAND

SEMPRINGHAM. Lincolnshire. Foundation. *c.* 1131. A small convent was built besides the parish church by St Gilbert for seven maidens who wished to live a strict religious life, lay-brothers being soon added to do the land work. Numbers quickly increased, and *c.* 1139 a large monastery was built on a new site with double church, cloister and buildings. The monastery of Sempringham held three carucates of land of Gilbert de Gant, on which the priory was founded, being the gift of Gilbert de Gant, and that they were not geldable; also three carucates in the same town, the alms of Reginald de Ba, worth £20 per annum; one carucate at Kirkby, the gift of Adam St Leonard; one hundred acres of wood, in the manor of Aslackby, of Hubert de Ria; half a fee at Horbling, of Roger Goylin; fifteen plough lands at Stow of Richard Pikeson; and one carucate at Welthorpe worth 30 shillings a year of Laurence Preston.

Hugh de Bajocis gave to the nuns at Sempringham lands at Sempringham and Billingborough; King Henry III, in the 12th year of his reign, the church of Fordham, Cambridgeshire. John Daldedry, Bishop of Lincoln, confirmed to the monastery of Sempringham the donation of Robert Luteral, of his manor in the parish of St Peter at Stamford for the increasing of the number of the scholars studying Philosophy and Divinity there, and the maintenance of a secular chaplain, yet saving all the dues of the parish. The prior and monastery of Sempringham, by their deed, own themselves obliged to Robert Luteral aforesaid, in consideration of the lands he gave them at Ketton, Cottismore, and Casterton, in the county of Rutland, and at Stamford, in the county of Lincoln, to maintain three chaplains to say Mass for his soul, one in the parish church of St Andrew at Irnham, one in the chapel of St Mary in the manor of Stamford, and one in the conventual church of Sempringham, also to increase the numbers of scholars, studying Divinity and Philosophy at Stamford, in proportion to the number of their monastery.

Numbers limited to: Nuns 120, Brothers 60. The mother house at Sempringham was never wealthy considering the number of inmates, there being two hundred women here in 1247 who often lacked the necessaries of life. The order suffered perhaps more than any other order from the changed labour conditions of the fourteenth century. The Black Death also grievously reduced their numbers, and the lay-brothers and sisters who had been the

135

KEY TO DISTRIBUTION MAP

No.	Priory	County	Single(1) Double(2)	Date Founded	Date Dissolved
1	Sempringham (i)	Lincs	1 (nuns)	1131	1139
	Sempringham(ii)	Lincs	2	1139	1538
2	Bridgend	Lincs	1	-1199	1538
3	Haverholme	Lincs	2	1139	1538
4	Catley	Lincs	2	1148	1538
5	Lincoln	Lincs	1	1148	1538
6	Bullington	Lincs	2	1148	1538
7	Sixhills	Lincs	2	1148	1538
8	Alvingham	Lincs	2	c1148	1538
9	North Ormsby	Lincs	2	1148	1538
10	Tunstall	Lincs	2	-1164	1189
11	Newstead	Lincs	1	1171	1538
12	Mattersey	Notts	1	c1185	1538
13	Ellerton	E.R.Yorks	1	-1207	1538
14	Old Malton	N.R.Yorks	1	1150	1539
15	Watton	E.R.Yorks	2	1150	1539
16	York	Yorks	1	c1200	1538
17	Shouldham	Norfolk	2	1193	1538
18	Marmont	Cambs	1	-1203	1538
19	Fordham	Cambs	1	-1227	1538
20	Cambridge	Cambs	1	-1219	1539
21	Hitchin	Herts	1	c1361	1538
22	Chicksands	Beds	2	c1150	1538
23	Clattercote	Oxon	1	1253	1538
24	Poulton	Glos (was Wilts)	1	1350	1539
25	Marlborough	Wilts	1	-1189	1538-9
26	Ravenstonedale	Cumbria	1	c1336	1538

Mainly taken from Monasticon Anglicanum, *1717*

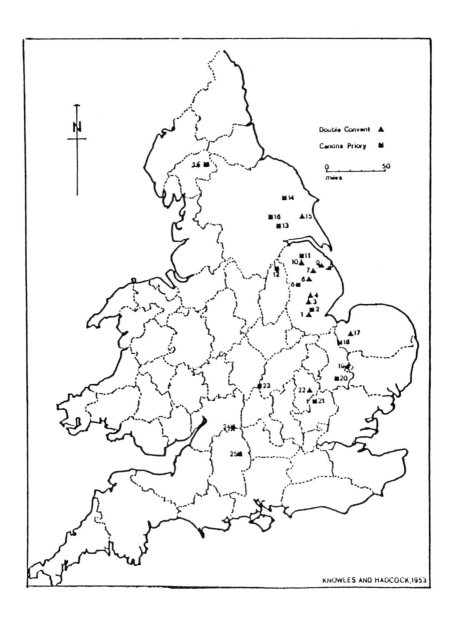

Distribution of the Gilbertine Priories (taken from D. Knowles and R. N. Hadcock, Medieval Religious Houses in England and Wales, *by kind permission of the publishers. Longman Group)*

137

mainstay of their mode of life almost ceased to exist. In 1538 eighteen canons surrendered, including the master and the prior, the prioress and sixteen nuns being included in the pension list.

HAVERHOLME. Lincolnshire. Founder, Alexander, Bishop of Lincoln. *c.* 1139. This had been intended for Cistercian monks from Fountains.

Numbers limited to: Nuns 100, Brothers 50. There were seven canons in 1381. In 1538 the house was surrendered by the prior and six canons; the prior, four canons, the prioress, and seven nuns receiving pensions. Henry II, Roger Mowbray, Roger de Lacy, Constable of Chester, were among the benefactors of Haverholme.

ALVINGHAM. Lincolnshire. Founder unknown: *c.* 1148–54. May have been William de Friston, Hugh de Scoteny, or Hamelin the Dean.

Dean Hamelin gave to the nuns of St Mary at Alvingham, three parts of the church of that town, belonging to the lands he held of the Earl of Brittany, the fourth part being granted them by Roger Gocelin, Robert Cheney, Bishop of Lincoln, investing them in the whole. Peter de Melsa gave them his manse, and the west side of their copse; his wife Beatrix the one half of the demesne; their son John the lands of Alvingham and Cockerington, 1232. Robert, Bishop of Lincoln, confirmed those donations.

Henry, Bishop of Lincoln, by order of King Henry III, in the year 1401, certified to the Barons of the Exchequer the names of all the churches appropriated to the monasteries of the Order of Sempringham. Henry Scoteny gave to this priory the third part of the church of St Mary at Alvingham, as also the whole church of Cockerington, one plough-land there. Master of the Order of Sempringham, ordained, that all the alterage of the churches of Cockerington and Alvingham, whether offerings, or other profits, as well as the tithes of lambs and wool, and arrears of money arising thence, should be assigned to the infirmaries of the nuns and sisters of Alvingham.

King Edward I, in the eleventh year of his reign, sent a mandate to the prior and prioress of Alvingham to admit to their habit, such of the children of Llewelin, Prince of Wales, and his brother David, as he should send to them. Walter Bec gave these nuns the church of St Peter at Newton. This Walter came over with King William the Conqueror; his own estate was in Flanders, and the King gave him Eresby and many other manors.

The Bull of Pope Innocent III confirmed to this monastery and all others of the Order their several possessions, particularly reciting the same. It also established their rules, forbidding all persons to impose any master upon them, and ordaining that he be chosen, according to the rule by all the priors of the Order, or to build any monasteries, nunneries, hermitages, churches, or chapels within their precincts, without their consent, and adding many other privileges of the same nature as have been mentioned in speaking of other monasteries, as may be seen in the Monasticon.

Numbers limited to: Nuns 80, Brothers 40. There were eight canons in 1377, five in 1381. The prior and seven canons surrendered in 1538, the prioress and eleven nuns being included with them in the pension list.

BULLINGTON. Lincolnshire. Founded *c.* 1148–54. Simon Fitz-William founded a religious house in his park of Bullington, in honour of God and the Blessed Virgin, and gave it to the nuns of the Order of Sempringham, and their brethren, priests and lay-men, and endowed the same with part of his park and wood, and lands on the north and east sides of the house, the limits whereof are assigned in his deed. William de Kime confirmed to the said monastery all their lands, and the patronage and advowson of the churches of Bullington, Langton, Fulnetby, Haveringham, Burgh, Wynthorpe, Prestwold, Ingham and Spridlington, with half the churches of Friskney and Hackthorn,etc.

Robert Putrel gave them the church of Houtun; Andrew Prestwald, that of St Andrew, at Prestwald; William Sceggeneffe three acres of land at Burgh. Philip de Kyme confirmed the grant made by his grandfather Philip, of lands at Hutoft and Sutton. Alexander Crevequer forty acres of arable land at Hackthorn, with ten acres of meadow, and two near the mill, with pasture for five hundred sheep, ten cows and as many calves; as also all the Island of Tunstal, in the territory of Redburn, etc.

Reginald Creuker was a great benefactor to this priory, as were several of his successors, Barons of Redburn; the last of whom, Alexander, left five daughters, among whom the Barony was divided. The deed of Philip de Kyme entitles him and his Father Founders of this Priory, and recites several donations of theirs; and two other deeds of his give twenty acres of land for the clothing of the religious men and women, and confirm the grants of the churches of Bullington and Langetun. That of Simon Crevequer confirms the donations of his father Reginald. There is also another of the said Reginald repeating the gift of the island of Tunstal, etc. The prior and monastery of Sixhills, of this same Order of Sempringham, yielded up to this priory of Bullington, one plough land at Nettleton, in the county of Lincoln, with the advowson of the church of St John there.

Numbers limited to: Nuns 100, Brothers 50. There were ten canons in 1377, eight in 1381, and also two lay-brothers. The prior and nine canons surrendered in 1538, the prioress and fourteen nuns being included with them in the pension list.

CATTLEY. Lincolnshire. Founder Peter de Belingey. *c.* 1148–54. The deed of Peter, son of Peter Belingey, confirms to the monastery of Cattley all the donations of his predecessors in the territories of Billinghay and Walcot, and of his own gift, confers on them one acre of land at Billinghay. A small priory on an island in the marsh of Walcote. This was one of the poorest houses, the income from temporalities being under £35 in 1291 so that it is doubtful if the number of inmates can ever have approached the limited figures.

Numbers limited to: Nuns 60, Brothers 35. There were four canons in 1377. The prior and two canons surrendered in 1538, the prioress and four nuns being included with them in the pension list.

NORTH ORMESBY. Lincolnshire. Founder Gilbert of Ormesby with the consent of his lord, William of Albemarle. *c.* 1148–54. In 1144 William turned the canons of Bridlington out of their house and defiled the church: 'By generous and frequent alms given to the poor, and by the building of fair monasteries, he expiated his crime.'

Gilbert of Ormesby endowed it with half the churches of Ormesby and Utterby, with their appurtenances, and the third part of all his land in both those towns; as also the land called Crigdale, described in his deed; and ten acres at Durewardethorn. Robert, sewer to William Percy, gave to this monastery the church of Elkington, Robert, senischal, or steward, pasture for sixty sheep at South Elkington, and all his common pasture. William de Kyme confirmed the donation of Robert the sewer, above named.

Numbers limited to: Nuns 100, Brothers 50.There were six canons in 1377. The prior and five canons surrendered, four other canons then serving as parish priests, and nine nuns were included in the pension list.

SIXHILLS. Lincolnshire. Founder ....de Gresli. *c.* 1148–54. The indenture between Thomas de la Warre, clerk, and the canons of Sixhills, shows, that ....de Gresli, predecessor to the said Thomas, was founder. The charter of the seventh year of King John, recites and confirms the donation of Agnes Percy, of the manor of Ludeworth. Haldon gave to these canons five plough lands at Melton, Herywike and Wycham, and Haco gave five more.

King Richard II, in the twelvth year of his reign, for ten shillings paid him by these canons, granted leave to John Thymilby, parson of the church of Nettleton, Albin Enderby, and William Langholm, to give and assign to these nuns and canons the manor of Hotham, worth forty shillings yearly.

Numbers limited to: Nuns 120, Brothers 55. There were eleven canons in 1377, five in 1381, and twenty-eight religious in 1462. In 1538 the house was surrendered by the prior and seven canons, the prioress and fourteen nuns being included with them in the pension list.

WATTON. East Yorkshire. Founder Eustace Fitz-John. *c.* 1150. Watton is said to be called Wet-Town, being a place beset with waters and marshes, which Bede says was once renowned for a multitude of holy women. The founder of the Gilbertine monastery here was Eustace Fitz-John, who gave to it the town of Watton, with all the lands, meadows, etc., within and without the town; as also all the land of Hor of Feriby. All this was confirmed by Henry, Archbishop of York, and William Fossard, the lord of whom the founder held in fee; and by Agnes, wife to the same founder; four plough lands at Hilderthorpe by Robert Constable of Flamborough, and Robert, constable to the Earl of Chester, whether they be two persons, or one and the same, but there are two distinct deeds. Roger Lacy, constable of Chester, in like manner confirmed the donations of Watton and Hilderthorpe.William Fossard gave three carucates at Howald, and Alexander Santon some lands at Sancton, confirmed by his son Richard. The charter of King John, dated the first year of his reign, confirms to this priory all Langdale, with its appurtenances, and the pasture between the said Langdale and Butresdakesbec, as the water, called Tybbey, comes down, with all the liberties and customs as mentioned in the charter of his father King Henry.

The founder, Eustace Fitz-John, above mentioned, had, by his wife, the daughter and heir of Ivo de Vescy, his son William, who was cut out of his mothers belly and then died; and from her, as an heiress, the said William took the name of Vescy, which descended to his posterity, till, as appears by inquisition ninth year of Edward II, Warin, the last of them, left only two daughters, Maud and Marjory, coheirs; one of them married to Gilbert de Aton, from whom lineally descended the Gilbert living at the time of the said inquisition.

Numbers limited to; Nuns 140, Brothers 70.There were apparently fifty-three nuns here in 1326, the number of canons, and lay- brothers and sisters not being recorded. Some canons were accused of taking part in the Pilgrimage of Grace, but none were condemned. In 1539 the prior, seven canons, and fourteen nuns surrendered.

CHICKSANDS. Bedfordshire. *c.* 1154. Founders, Pain de Beauchamp and his wife Roese, the Countess, gave to the nuns of the church of St Mary of Chicksand, under Gilbert de Sempringham several lands there, four hundred acres at Hagues, with the wood at Appeley and the church there, besides other

Watton Priory,E.R.Yorks.

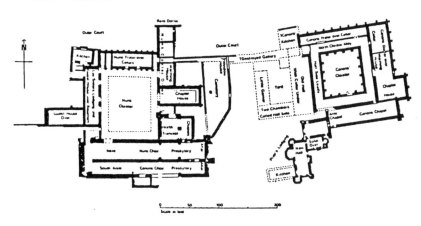

Plan of Watton Priory

Chicksands Priory, Beds.
From VCH Beds.,II,272

Scale in feet

Key

Medieval

Modern

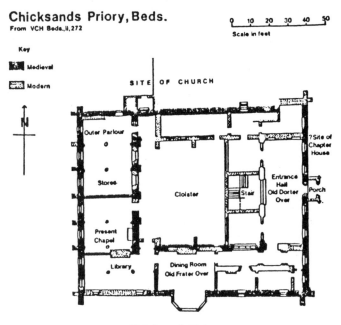

Chicksands Priory

smaller parcels. The deed of William, son of Simon Beauchamp, recites and comfirms all his father's grants to this priory, and the charter of the tenth year of King Edward II, gives licence to John Blondel, to confer his manor of Chicksand on the monastery of that place.

Numbers limited to; Nuns 120, Brothers 55.The house was surrendered by the sub-prior, six monks and eighteen nuns, the priorship being then vacant; and in 1553 seven canons and eight nuns were still receiving pensions. It appears doubtful if all the canons surrendered, comparing the names in the pension list.

TUNSTALL. Lincolnshire. c.1164. Alexander de Crevequer added to Bullington the island of Tunstall, near Redburn, on which his father had founded a Gilbertine Priory in the reign of Stephen. The priory was united to Bullington before 1189, possibly because the endowment was not enough to support a double house.

SHOULDHAM. Norfolk. *c.*1190. Founder Geoffrey de Fritz Piers. Geoffrey, the son of Peter, Earl of Essex, founded this priory, endowed it with all his manor of Shouldham, with all its appurtenances, as also the churches of All Saints and St Margaret at Shouldham, and those at Carbystorp, Stoke Ferry, and William, and translated the body of his wife, which had been buried at Chicksand to this church.

In 1321 one of the canons was playing football when a lay-friend ran up against his sheathed knife, dying later from the wound. There were six canons and two lay-brothers in 1381. In 1538 the house was surrendered by the prior, nine canons, the prioress, and six nuns; while the pensions were later granted to the prior, eight canons, the prioress and eight nuns.

HOUSES OF THE GILBERTINE CANONS IN ENGLAND

LINCOLN. Lincolnshire. c. 1148. Robert de Chesney founded the Priory of St. Catherine. The charter of King Henry II, confirms to the canons of this church, founded by Robert, Bishop of Lincoln and his Chapter, the prebend of Canwick, and five plough lands at Wigsley, with the churches of Newark, Norton, Marton, and Newton. and all their appurtenances.

The priory was founded for canons, who were granted the custody of the older hospital of St.Sepulchre here. Lay-sisters were probably soon introduced to look after the sick, and the numbers were limited to twenty sisters and sixteen brothers; and the priory was presumably for the usual thirteen canons. In 1536 the prior is said to have been deprived for promoting the Lincolnshire Rising and other offences; but he reinstated himself forcibly expelling the new prior, and he was later granted a pension, with twelve other canons, after the surrender in 1538, there then being five sisters.

CLATTERCOTE. Oxford. c.1148-66. Clattercote Priory, near Banbury, founded in, or before the first year of John, had a leper hospital attached to it. It was a hospital for members of the order, limited to fifty-five, who contracted leprosy. Between 1258 and 1279 it ceased to be a hospital for lepers, and became an ordinary Gilbertine priory. About the time of the suppression it consisted of a prior and four canons, and in 1536 there were three canons besides the prior.

MALTON. Yorkshire. c.1150. Founded by St.Gilbert. Eustace Fitzjohn gave to the canons of Sempringham the church of Malton, on the south side of the Derwent, with lands and other possessions. One carucate of land and the copse there, as also the church of St.Peter at Wintringham, the little town of Linton, etc. and by another deed he gave them the church of Brompton. William de Vesci conferred on it the hermitage of Spaldingham, with lands therin described, etc.

William the son of Eustace aforesaid, confirmed all his father's donations, and added of his own the church of Watton, with the town, and by another deed the church of Ancaster; likewise by a third deed confirms all as above, with the additions of the places called Kerlote, Cowhouse at Knapton, and Depeher.

His wife Burga confirmed the grant of the church of Langton, which was hers by marriage. Iveta Arches confirmed the gift of the church of Norton, which was her dower. The prior and Chapter of St.Mary Newburgh, gave to these canons certain lands by Norton Bridge, to be held upon payment of twelve pence yearly, and giving them and their men lodging, when they should pass that way; confirmed by William Flamville, who was lord of those lands. Roger Flamville gave the church of St.Mary at Morton with all its appurtenances, pasture for two hundred sheep at Morton, with place for a sheep-fold and for two hundred more at Hutton, and forty loads of turf, etc. for maintenance of the poor entertained in the hospital at the head of the bridge of Norton, and the persons attending them.

Hugh Flamville confirmed the same. The great Prior and Chapter of the Order of Sempringham yielded up to the canons at Marton, the church of Marton with its appurtenances. Hugh, Bishop of Lincoln, cofirmed to them the church of Walden, of the gift of Walter Nevil and Alan Hayrun. John, was the father of Eustace above mentioned, as founder of this priory. This Eustace begot William on the daughter and heir of Ivo de Vescy, which William came into the world by ripping open of his mother, who accordingly died, and therefore he took the surname of Vescy, because of the inheritance he had by her.

The Charter of King John confirms to these canons the possession of one hundred and sixty acres of land in several townships. Pope Innocent III, having by his Bull authorised the abbot of St.Mary at York, the prior of the Holy Trinity there, and William Priest of Gilling, to oblige W.de Laceles to

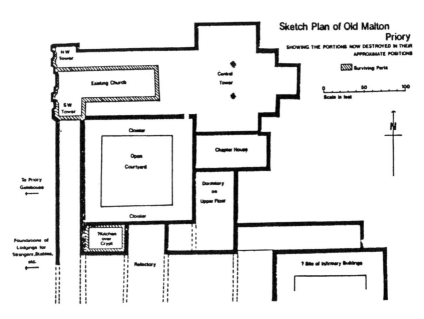

Old Malton, Yorkshire

do right to the monastery of Malton in relation to their tithes at Saureby, belonging to their church of Wintringham, this affair was amicably adjusted between the said two parties, in the presence of the Commissioners, around 1200, the aforesaid W.de Laceles at Old Malton, nearer to their own lands in lieu of the said tithes.

This was founded by St.Gilbert as a "retreat-house" for his canons, and perhaps originally contained more than the usual thirteen canons, and the number of brothers was limited to thirty-five. There were ten canons in 1381. Prior William Todde was arrested for taking part in the Pilgrimage of Grace, but nothing is known of his fate except that he ceased to be prior about that time. The house was surrendered in 1539 by the prior and nine canons.

NEWSTEAD-ON-ANCHOLME. *c.* 1171. Founder King Henry II. The Charter of the thirteenth year of Edward II, recites and confirms the Foundation-Charter of this abbey made by King Henry II, wherein the latter says, he had granted to the canons of the Order of Sempringham, in the island of Rucholm, in the territory of Cadney, called Newstead, the place of their habitation, and two carucates and a half, and a plough-land and a half, and an acre, called Grovie-Acre, and a plough-land at Hibaldstow, and the place of their dwelling their, besides five plough-lands at the Herdewych, etc.

It was agreed between the Cistercian monastery of Longville, and that of Newstead, that the latter should for ever hold all the lands the former had at Kicketon for one hundred shillings per annum. King John himself granted to them the lands called Howsham at Cadney. The possessions above-mentioned were ascertained to them, third year of Edward I by inquisition taken of the same. A record in the Exchequer, eighth year of Henry IV gives Peter, the son of Henry Bilingey, the title of founder of this monastery, and says he bestowed on it all he had, or might have, in the island called Catley, and the marsh of Walcot, as far as the old water-course by Digby Marsh, etc. The number of canons and lay-brothers was limited to thirteen; there being thirteen in 1377, seven in 1381, also a lay-brother, and the house was surrendered in 1538 by the prior and five canons.

MATTERSEY. Nottinghamshire. *c.* 1185. Founder Roger, son of Ralph de Maresay. The Charter of the fourth year of Edward III recites and confirms the donation of Elizabeth Chauncy to this monastery of St Helen, in the isle of Mattersey, being all the lordship of the towns of Mattersey and Thorpe, and confirms it to all the lands and possessions they had of the gift of her predecessors in the towns of Mattersey, Thorpe, Gamston, Elkesley, West-Retford, Misson and Bolton. The priory was for six canons, the number of brothers being limited to ten. The buildings were badly damaged by fire in 1279 causing great loss to the canons. The gross income in 1291 was £52. The prior and four canons surrendered in 1538.

MARLBOROUGH. Wiltshire. King John took this house under his protection in 1199-1200. This was a small priory, with probably never more than five to six canons. There were at least two canons besides the prior in 1538, as two were still receiving pensions (other than the prior) in 1553. Dependancy: the Hospital of St Thomas M. Marlborough (from 1393-4).

BRIDGE END. Lincolnshire. *c.* 1199. Founder Godwin, a citizen of Lincoln. It appears by inquisition taken the seventh year of Edward I, that Godwin, a rich man of Lincoln, was founder of this priory, and gave to it the place of St Saviour at Pont-Aslac, with other lands and tenements, obliging them to apply what was over and above their own maintenance to the repairing of the said Bridge; and therefore the said King reversed the judgement given them to repair the said Bridge or Causeway, alledging that according to the foundation their own maintenance was first, for which reason he ordered the cause to be brought over again to inspect the value of the lands, and thence judge how far they might be liable.

This was a very small priory with probably never more than three to four canons and a few lay-brothers, part of whose duties was keeping in repair the causeway and the bridges here. The church and buildings were burnt in 1445, and some time after this and before the suppression the priory became a cell of Sempringham, probably for two canons. The prior received a pension in 1538.

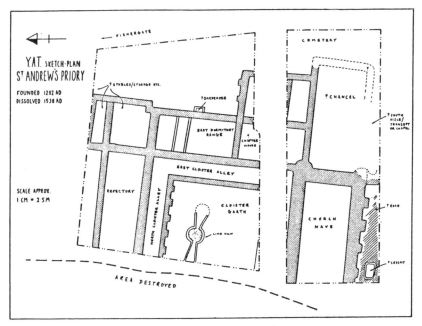

St Andrew's Priory, York

YORK. Yorkshire. *c*. 1200. Founder Hugh Murdac. Priory of St Andrew in the suburbs of York, founded by Hugh Murdac at the Fisher-Gate, and endowed with the church of that place, and the adjacent lands, and a perpetual revenue of twenty-one marks, the several particulars in houses, etc. to make up that revenue, mentioned in his foundation-deed.

It was agreed between the Dean and Chapter of York on the one part, and the Master of the Order of Sempringham, and the monastery of St Andrew, at the Fisher-Gate, York, on the other; that the said Master and monastery, and Hugh Murdac, should resign to the Dean and Chapter that piece of ground before the West Door of the Great Church, which they had of Hugh de Virly; and in exchange for the same, the said Dean and Chapter should secure to the said monastery a revenue of two marks and a half on two carucates of land at the town of Cave; and the aforesaid Hugh Murdac gave to the said canons of St.Andrew, the revenue of one mark, upon the mill at Thorpe, in exchange for the said land, before the said agreement had been made between the Chapter and canons.

The priory was built next to St Clement's Benedictine nunnery, and was intended for twelve canons, though it is doubtful if this number was ever reached. In 1380-1 there were three canons besides the prior, with the same number in 1538, the prior and three canons receiving pensions.

WELLES. Norfolk. *c*. 1203. King John, by Charter of the 5th of his Reign, confirms the foundation of this Priory by Ralph Havil, and the grant to all his lands in the territory of Welles, on both sides of the town, with all their appurtenances, and of the churches of Dunton, Deketon, Kettlestone and Acuneby; for which the canons to say one mass for ever for the soul of the said King John's Queen Ellenor, and to pay the said founder and his heirs five shillings yearly, besides the service due from the said lands.

This was a small cell for only three canons, one being prior. In 1535 it was called a cell of Watton, and it was surrendered in 1538 by the prior and one canon.

OVERTON. Durham. *c*. 1204. At Hertnes priory. The charter of the 9th of King John confirms the grant of Alan Wilton, founder of this priory, of his town of Overton, twelve plough lands at Hoiton, one carucate at Huplin, two plough lands at Wescote, and half a carucate at Midleton in Cleeveland.

The charter of John is the only record of this house which was in the county of Durham. It is doubtful if there was ever a priory was ever established here, though there may have been a grange.

ELLERTON. East Yorkshire. *c*. 1209. William Fitz Peter founder. William, son of Peter, gave for the founding of this monastery of the Order of Sempringham and the maintaining of thirteen poor persons there, all his lands at Ellerton, and all the wood of Lathingholm, etc. Peter de Malolacu confirmed to these canons all grants of any possessions within his lordship;

147

and Adam Linton confirmed all the donations of William, the son of Peter.

In the year 1387 it was agreed between this monastery of Ellerton, on the one part, and German Hay, patron of the said monastery on the other, that whereas the said patron had the presentation of only one of the thirteen poor persons to be maintained there, he and his heirs should for the future present nine of the said thirteen, as the Lords of the Manor of Aughton; and if the monastery should refuse to admit any of the same, or should be deficient in any part of the allowance due to those received, and not redress the same within a month, at remonstrance of the said German, or his successors, then the said German and his successors to have the presentation of the whole number of thirteen. And after the death of the said German and his wife Alesia, the said canons to be obliged for ever to perform an anniversary service for their souls. And in case the said canons shall not within a month after presentation of any poor person admit the same, or omit to perform the office for the dead aforesaid, then the canons for every such omission to pay to the said German, or his successors, the sum of ten pounds sterling.

Henry de Puteaco gave to these canons, the meadow at Cliffe towards the maintainance of the aforesaid thirteen poor persons. The master of Sempringham and the prior and the canons of Ellerton, by public deed, confessed their obligations to maintain the said thirteen poor persons, and empowered the Archbishop of York to compell them to the same, whensoever they should fail therein. Alan Wiltun gave these canons, for the maintainance of themselves and the aforesaid thirteen poor persons, twelve plough lands at Howm, the nearer to Watton, and seven plough lands at Brech.

William, the son of Nicholas, the son of Patrick Habbeton, conferred on this priory twelve plough lands at Habbeton, reserving only to himself the right of scutage. Alan Wilton, six plough lands at Habbeton, besides two others elsewhere, and his mill at Marston to defray the light at the altar of St Laurence, and maintain a chaplain to say mass for ever at the said altar. It was found by Inquisition 24 Edward III, that it was no damage to the King, or any other, to grant leave to Gerard Salvayn of Herswell knight, to give twelve messuages and twenty four plough lands at Little Thorp, near Hayton, to the monastery of Ellerton, for those canons to find four of their number to perform the Divine Office for ever for the souls of the said Gerard and his wife Agnes.

It was founded as a priory and hospital for the entertainment of thirteen poor persons. In 1380-1 there were four canons besides the prior, with the same number in 1538.

FORDHAM. Cambridge. *c.* 1227-8. Foundation unknown. There were probably never more than four to five canons here, the income from temporalities being under 32 in 1291, and a hospital, founded before 1279 for fourteen poor persons, was also then maintained. In 1538 the prior and three canons signed the deed of surrender.

CAMBRIDGE. St Edmund's. *c.* 1290-1. Founded on the site of the Friars of the Sack in 1290, the Gilbertines came in 1291. The priory was apparently for a few resident Gilbertines and student canons studying at Cambridge. Surrendered 1539.

STAMFORD. Lincolnshire. *c.* 1292. Robert Lutteral of Irnham founder. This was merely a hall or house of studies in the quasi-university which had been growing up here since 1266; and it was doubtless closed in 1334, when the students were dispersed, if not earlier.

RAVENSTONEDALE. Westmorland. *c.* 1336. Torphin gave to the Gilbertine canons of Watton (Yorks) all the lands of the dale.

POULTON. Wiltshire. *c.* 1348. Thomas Seymore founder. By Inquisition taken 21 Edward III, it was found that it was no prejudice to the King to grant license to Thomas St Maur, knight, to give his manor of Poulton to the canons of Sempringham, to found a monastery of their Order, the said manor being held of the King in Capite, for half a knight's fee, and the yearly value thereof ten shillings and that of the advowson of the church one hundred shillings.

The charter of the 28th of the aforesaid King Edward III, confirms to them all their possessions whatsoever, and exempts the canons and their men from all tolls and other usual burdens whatsoever, throughout all England, and allows them a court with all other usual Royalties, as they have been here before specified in other Charters of the same nature, and therefore need not be repeated; and the said King takes the said canons and all that belongs to them into his special protection.

This was a small priory for some four to five canons at most, and apparently a prior and two to three canons at about the time of the suppression in 1539.

HITCHIN. Hertfordshire. *c.* 1361. Founded by Sir Edward de Kendale. This appears to have been a very small priory, with possibly never more than three to four canons. Two canons in 1381.

SEMPRINGHAM PRIORY
EXCAVATIONS 1938/39

When the excavation of Sempringham Priory was first suggested by Capt Cragg of Threekingham, it was thought that the Priory site lay to the north west of the Parish Church, as shown on the twenty-five inch Ordnance Survey maps, and by kindness of Air Vice-Marshal Baldwin, air photographs were taken of this site.

As soon, however, as Mr Hugh Braun, who had been responsible for the excavation of Bungay Castle, Norfolk, and had undertaken to superintend the work at Sempringham, had examined the site and the air photographs, he expressed the opinion – confirmed by the excavations – that the Priory lay to the south of the Marse Dyke near the spot marked on the ordnance map 'Site of Sempringham Hall' and that the site previously mentioned was probably that of the medieval village of Sempringham.

This meant that the site, instead of being – as far as was known – unworked, was one on which the house erected by Edward Fiennes, Lord Clinton – the grantee at the Dissolution in 1538 – had stood for some one hundred years. The work of the excavation was made possible by the kindness of the Crown who are the owners and occupiers of the site.

The thanks of the Committee are due to Mr Braun who gave his services gratuitously to work which he carried out under most discouraging circumstances and whose report and plan follow.

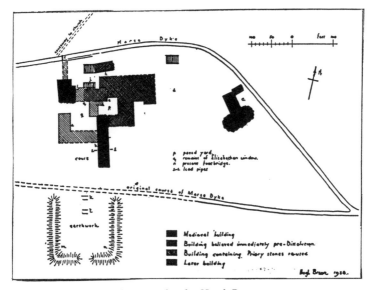

From a plan by Hugh Braun

REPORT BY HUGH BRAUN

When work was begun on July 12th 1938, nothing was visible above ground except the rectangular earthwork. The arrangement of mounds appearing, on the axis of this feature, to the north indicated that the post-Dissolution house was situated in that area.

Three men were engaged, and it was necessary first to train them as excavators. On the assumption that the best walls would be found on the house site, the men were put to work at the points a. and b., where the post-Dissolution walling, full of re-used medieval stones, was soon exposed. The angle at b. showed a junction with older work containing no such stones.

Having showed the men how to follow walls, it next appeared best to get away from the house site to try to find medieval walls. Assuming that the nucleus of the great house had originally been the Prior's lodging, the obvious place to explore seemed to be a high mound away to the east at c., where the remains of a medieval building were then exposed, a large room running north-west to south-east and having thick walls. It had not stood alone, but the walls to the east, west, and south when followed, were found to have been completely removed, and excavation at this point had to be abandoned as fruitless.

Trenches were then dug in all directions from this site for some distance, all proving disappointing. Towards the west, a few thin enclosure walls were exposed, and at d. was found a broken stone coffin (now in the parish church) which was not *in situ*, and had probably been used as a horse-trough. Trenches in all other directions showing the area to be free from buildings, exploration was continued westwards towards the site of the house. Adjoining this on the east were found the remains of a series of buildings, built in rubble and not incorporating any recognisable Priory stones, but not apparently forming part of a monastic plan.

Eventually, at c., the excavators exposed the well-preserved remains of a small house, consisting of a small hall with parlour to the east, each room having a fireplace. This house was on the axis of the earthwork and obviously formed the nucleus of the post-Dissolution mansion. The little house appeared to be a farmhouse of early 16th century date, was built of rubble without any re-used Priory stone, and had the stops to the chamfered openings uncut, suggesting that some event had prevented their completion. It may be that the little farmhouse, with its complementary buildings to the east, had been in course of erection at the time of the Dissolution, and had subsequently formed the nucleus of the great house.

The western end of the farmhouse kitchen had apparently been extended with Priory stone to meet a medieval building (at f.) the purpose of which is uncertain, but which had an elaborate 'garderobe' tower, with two shoots, to the east of it. The stonework at the base of these two shoots was the only medieval dressed stonework found in situ during the whole course of the work.

The enlargement of the farmhouse kitchen was probably effected to enable it to form a 'great hall' suitable for the post-Dissolution mansion. A second fireplace was constructed to the west of the earlier one, and a porch-like projection at the opposite corner. This last served to shut off the farmhouse yard to the east of it from the new courtyard which was then constructed in front of the old farmhouse (g).

The walls forming the house-complex were being followed in the hope that they would echo the monastic plan, but this hope was not realised, although a number of thick walls, deeply buried, were discovered to the north-east, at h. The depth, six to eight feet, and the badly robbed condition of these walls, made it unprofitable work to follow them, especially as no plan could be found by which to work.

North of the house, at j., was found a projection probably built for an Elizabethan staircase, and northwards again were further uninteresting walls of indeterminate date. The long building to the south-east seemed to be unconnected with any cloister, although attempts were made to find buildings which could be complementary with it.

Throughout the course of the work, quantities of fine medieval detail were discovered, as well as a considerable amount of 14th century glass. A coin of Edward III and jettons of the 14th and 15th century had been found, as well as medieval potsherds, all of which seemed to point to the fact the Priory buildings could not be far away.

While medieval walling had been found in several places, nothing had been found which suggested claustral buildings, so it was still to be hoped that the cloister site had yet to be found. The presence of the pre-Dissolution farm building suggested that the cloister was away from this area, but the trenches to the east of it had been so unprofitable that it seemed useless to continue to explore there.

The earthwork had been investigated at the commencement of the work and been found to consist of rubbish of all descriptions, clearly piled there to form a sort of walled garden. A brick wall ran along the crest of the banks.

On September 26th, while the filling-in of the trenches was being completed, two trenches were dug within the earthwork immediately to the south of the original course of the Marse Dyke. At k. and l., these trenches exposed foundations of thick walls, apparently medieval, crossing the enclosure from west to east. This suggested the possibility that the earthwork covered the site of the cloister, the west, south, and east ranges of which had been filled with rubbish and utilised for landscape gardening, and the north range removed to open up the area on the house side.

The cutting of two exploratory trenches, at m. and n., which have demonstrated that the mounds at these points are in fact bounded by walls. It would therefore seem desirable that the earthwork should be fully investigated, as it may contain the remains of the claustral block of the Priory. Once a clue to the arrangement has been found, the remainder of the exploration will be much less arduous and expensive. It was recorded that the Lincolnshire weather, which throughout the course of the work has been of the very worst quality.

Work was begun again on June 26th 1939, with three of the four men trained last year. Wright (forman), Davey and Cyril Wesley.

First was investigated the large 'earthwork' which lay to the south of the old course of the Marse Dyke, and which, it was believed, might contain the remains of the claustral buildings of the Priory. It was discovered, however, that the banks were bounded by the walls of a large mansion, built round three sides of a courtyard, and having projecting towers at four outer angles.

The architectural detail of this building showed it to have been constructed about the year 1625. Stones from the Priory were used in the foundations, but the walling itself was all in newly-quarried stonework, suggesting that the remains of the monastic buildings had practically all disappeared before the erection of the mansion was begun. The remarkable feature connected with the house was the fact that it appeared to have been pulled down deliberately to the level of its plinth, and the residue filled in with earth, which was then banked up to bury the whole structure completely. The 'earthwork' thus formed was finished with carefully laid brick paths along the crest of the banks, which suggests that the intention was to provide a garden feature for the house further north, described in last year's report.

It is clear that this smaller residence had a much more intensive occupation from the time of its foundation as an early sixteenth century farmhouse to its abandonment, which occurred, apparently, during the late eighteenth century. The great house to the south, however, shows no signs of having ever been occupied, and one is tempted to suppose that it was never completely finished, although there is definite evidence that the walling was completed to the coping, and that an elaborate drainage system was constructed.

It was during the course of the exploration of the outline of the great house that the first definite evidence came to light that it had been founded on the site of Sempringham Priory. The discovery of a fourteenth-century respond base in situ was speedily followed by the exposure of a complete column from the thirteenth-century crypt which had apparently been filled in at some time during the medieval period, doubtless because its floor was beneath the level of the valley's water-table.

Spurred on by these truly exciting discoveries, the excavators soon found themselves working eastwards along the face of a formidable wall, having on its southern side large projections, clearly the foundations of vaulting-shafts of considerable scale. This wall was, in fact, the north aisle wall of the great church, and, this fact once established, little time was lost in exposing the whole plan of this fine building.

While nothing whatever remained above pavement level, the foundations were in excellent condition and hardly robbed at all except for the five eastern bays of the south side of the southern, or nun's, choir and the southern half of its east wall, together with the south-east angle, all of which had entirely disappeared.

The small mound to the east of the earthwork is a mound of rubbish and broken roofing tiles of post-Dissolution date. It is situated exactly over the south-east angle of the church.

The orientation of the mansion is slightly different from that of the church, but the north wall of the central block is roughly upon the foundations of the south wall of the church, and the east wall of the eastern wing is approximately on the site of the west wall of the transept. That some portion of the church was still standing when the great house was begun is suggested by the presence of most of the tracery of a large window in the foundations of the north-east tower.

The eastern line of the garden wall of the post-Dissolution mansion is built in part upon the foundations of the east wall of the Priory Church, the west front of which was a little inside the western bank of the "earthwork". It is perhaps interesting to note that, if the site of the Priory is viewed from the Parish Church, the length of the large 'earthwork' roughly represents the length of the nave of the Priory Church, the choir of which would have occupied the space between this and the small eastern mound. With these points in mind, a good idea of the size of the Priory Church can be formed.

The original church of the Priory was about 250 feet in length internally. The nun's portion was about 35 feet wide, and that of the canons, which lay to the north of it, was some five feet narrower. The site and arrangements of the transept have not yet been investigated. There is some indication that the canons' nave was at some time enlarged by the addition of a north aisle.

West of this, lying east and west, stood a curious building, 105 feet long and 30 feet wide.The purpose of this building is not at the moment clear. It has on its southern side, a wide vaulted passage or aisle of fourteenth-century date, two of the respond bases of which were found in situ.

The church as we see it to-day is the building begun by Prior John de Hamilton in 1301. Vaulted throughout, and of cathedral proportions, it must have been a magnificent structure. In a district which has produced so many fine contemporary parish churches, it is indeed a tragedy that the finest achievement of all should have perished so utterly.

With its great span, its length of some 325 feet over-all, and the vision of a towering loftiness suggested by the remains of its vaulting, Sempringham

Priory Church may well have been one of the finest creations of its era. Forty years after it was begun it was still unfinished.

While exploration of the building is as yet far from complete, it appears that the whole of the canons' church, save its west and south walls, was entirely swept away. The new nave and choir were some 38 feet in span and fifty feet longer. The former, which had five wide bays, had an aisle twenty feet wide, to the north. There was a large north transept of three bays, having in an eastern aisle three chapels. There were probably the successors of the chapels of SS. John, Stephen, and Catherine, which existed in the earlier church. In 1291, visitors to the Priory were being encouraged to contribute at these chapels towards the cost of rebuilding the church.

The length of this exceptionally large transept brought it across the course of the Marse Dyke, which had therefore to be diverted to its present route. The east and west walls, where they crossed the old watercourse, were carried on strong arched foundations. At the north end of the west wall are to be seen indications of a porch. It seems probable that here was the canons' entrance to their choir.

The sub-base of one of the transept piers was completely cleared, and upon it was found the mason's trace of the pier-base itself. It was possible to deduce that the pier had large shafts, about a foot in diameter, at the angles, with two smaller shafts, of about half the size, on each face. The shafts rose from semi-octagonal bases. The plan is unusual in that one secondary shaft is more normal. Exeter Cathedral has three, but no church, at the moment discoverable, has two.

A Sub-Base of one of the Transept Piers

The eastern arm, close on 150 feet long, of the canons' church had its six wide bays separated by vaulting shafts, the sub-base of one of these being still in situ. The arrangement of the shafts is not clear, but it seems probable that there was, in each case, a large main shaft, flanked a short distance away, by lesser shafts, as may be seen at Bourne Abbey. The nave of this church was apparently to have been rebuilt on the lines indicated by its west front, and the lower part of the north-west vaulting shaft may be seen.

The nuns' church has not yet been completely explored, partly owing to the far worse condition of its remains, and partly due to the premature stoppage of the work at the Declaration of War. Although extended in length to match its neighbour, the southern building, constricted as it presumably was by the adjacent cloister, does not appear to have been enlarged laterally. There is ample evidence, however, that it was embellished to some extent to match the rest of the building, as the same huge foundations for vaulting shafts can be seen added to the earlier walling.

At the west end of the canons' nave may be seen a few stones (each with its 'mason mark') of original twelfth-century west front. The southern end of this wall, however, has been reduced to below this level. A gap near the west end of the south wall of the nuns' nave indicates the site of the western doorway into the cloister.

The medial wall has not as yet been fully explored, but up to the present no doorways have been found in it. It is interesting to note that the architectural evidence supports the view that the wall was a solid division throughout its height, and not, as has been suggested, a comparatively low screen wall, open above as an arcade.

At least a score of interments have been unfortunately disturbed by the excavations, and, in the third bay of the canons' choir from the crossing a stone coffin was found in situ, its contents being left untroubled. A bay to the west of this the medial wall showed evidence of considerable disturbance. The rebuilding work of the fourteenth century had stopped short of a section where the earlier wall had apparently been preserved intact for a short distance, after which the new additions continued.

Base of Shrine of St Gilbert

This section had subsequently been widened, the new foundations incorporating a piece of fourteenth-century vaulting rib. The position and appearance of this section of the medial wall leaves little doubt that here was the tomb of St Gilbert, who, on the seventh of February, 1189, was buried with much honour 'between the altars of St Mary and St John'.

It is greatly to be hoped that a suitable memorial will one day be erected to mark the spot, which may otherwise pass once more into oblivion, perhaps for yet another four hundred years.

The church has as yet not been sufficiently explored for it to be possible to state with any degree of certainty the ritual arrangement of the choir. There are, however, indications that there was a screen across the north crossing arch, and another, across the aisle arch, which may have been extended across the unexplored western arch of the crossing.

It thus seems reasonable to suppose that the choir-stalls occupied the crossing and the bay east of it, immediately west of the bay containing St Gilbert's Shrine. There are indications of a step crossing the choir in line with the wall of the transept. There are also indications of steps separating the two eastermost bays from the remainder, so it seems probable that these two bays formed the Sanctuary. This would leave a presbytery of three bays, the westernmost containing the founder's tomb, for burials and ceremonial.

Sempringham Priory, after four centuries of oblivion, has now been rediscovered.

I sincerely trust that steps will be taken to mark the site, once and for all, with a suitable memorial to the founder – St Gilbert of Sempringham.

HUGH BRAUN F.S.A.,F.R.I.B.A.
3/11/1939

Left:
nave responds

Right:
crypt column

157

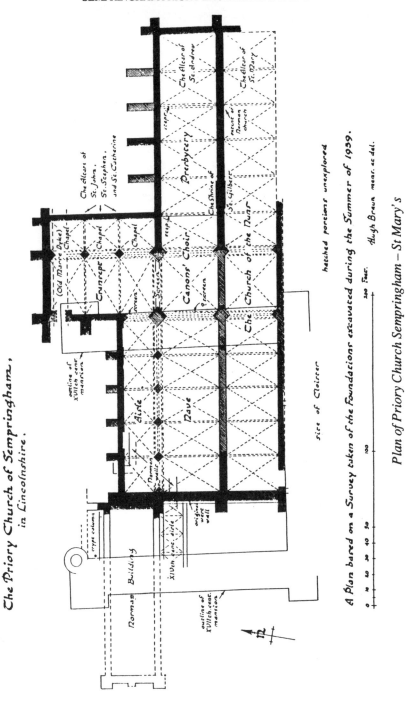

The Priory Church of Sempringham, in Lincolnshire.

Plan of Priory Church Sempringham – St Mary's

A Plan based on a Survey taken of the Foundations excavated during the Summer of 1939.

Hugh Braun maor. sc del.

Passage? with threshold and adjacent door
Part of domestic building north of Priory

Pair of doors into pair of narrow chambers
?Garderobe shafts in tower of building north of Priory

Moulding from the drain of the Clinton House

Carving of lion from the Clinton house

Stone carving found during excavation

The men who did most of the excavation at Sempringham
Left to right: Cyril Wesley, Fred Wright, and ——— Davey

SEMPRINGHAM PRIORY CHARTERS
from the *GENEALOGIST*

CHARTERS ENROLLED ON THE EXCHEQUER
MEMORANDA ROLL 12 HENRY IV

1. ROGER SON OF GOCELIN to Sempringham Priory with the assent of Lord Ranulf de Bayeux
  Nine bovates of his land in Sempringham and Billingborough and a mill in the territory of Cockerington
  Later he gives the residue of his land in Sempringham and Billingborough, viz four carucates and three bovates complete [with all appurtenances] in free alms of all services
  Given in the hands of Bishop Robert II of Lincoln
  Witness list: Walto, Abbe de Kirkestede; Johe, Abbe de Bardenaye; Johe de Boleby; Brien de Pointon; Thorald de Billingburc; etc.
  Date: *c.* 1150-60

2. GODWIN THE RICH DE LINCOLN to the nuns of Sempringham and their brothers both clerical and lay, with the consent, will, and encouragement of his lady Countess Alice de Gant
  One carucate of land in the territory of Sempringham which he once held from the Countess, with a quitclaim to all rights
  For the souls of himself and his wife Alice and the fraternity of the house Master Gilbert and the community have agreed to take them, both alive and dead, into the community of the order in all things
  Warranty clause [agreeing to be responsible for any burdens on the estate]
  Witness list: Willo Basset, Sheriff of Lincolnshire; Alexand de Pointon; Rico filius Jacobi de Lincoln Hugon, monk; etc.

3. RALF DE BADUENT to Master Gilbert and the nuns of Sempringham
  One carucate of land in Sempringham quit which Richard de Baduent, his father, gave to them for his soul, and those of his own, and with his body [ie in return for burial in the priory]
  Viz that carucate called 'the carucate of the girls' which Agnes de Bellofago gave to his father
  Witness list: Pagano de Horbling; Andrea Burnell; Toroldo de Pointon; Math filius Sebbe; etc.
  Date before 1189

CHARTERS

4. ADAM DE MUNDEVILLE to Sempringham
Eleven bovates of land in Sempringham with in the vill as without, as with men as with other things [ie a grant of villeins and possibly sokemen], quit
Be it known that Gilbert de Gant, once his lord, gave the land to him for his service
Warranty clause
Witness list: Rogo Burnele; Robto Coffin; Gocelino filius Robti de Horbling; Nigell de Ingoldesby; Andrea Burnele; Willo Mustele; etc.

8. COUNTESS ALICE, daughter of Gilbert de Gant, gives and confirms to Sempringham [ie this is the confirmation of gifts made by tenants]
Inter alia, confirmation of 1 and 2
Warranty clause
Witness list: Philippus de Kime; Petrus de Scremby; Helias persona de Helpringham; etc.
Date after 1184

22. ROGER MUSTELA, with assent of mother Agnes and brother Hugh, to Sempringham five and a half carucates in Sempringham and Billingborough with the wood which is called Fastolueshaga, and all other things which Roger son of Gocelin his great uncle gave to them, viz whatever rights he had in the said vills, the church of Torrington, and the mill in Cockrington.
In the presence of the bishop
Warranty clause
Witness list: Baldric de Sigill; Robtus de Burnham; Radus Prior de Markeby; Radulf de Howton; Alexander de Pointon; etc.
Date before 1168

26. BRIAN DE POINTON AND HIS SON ROBERT confirm to Sempringham
a. whatever their men gave to God and St Andrew when the chapel was built
b. that half bovate given with Hugh his [Brian's] brother
c. Foxhou Furlong which Brian gave along with one of his daughters,
d. ½ acre meadow and 12 acres of arable land, with two other daughters, which he has assigned in various places in the territory of Pointon
e. ½ acre land next to Hestcroft and Hefdland and pasture in the same territory for 200 sheep when they took him and his wife Ivet into their fraternity
Warranty clause
Witness list: Alfredus de Poynton; Ricus de Milnetorp; Johes de Lincoln; Ricus de Sco Marco; Walterus de Navembi; Thoraldus de Pointon, etc.

ADDITIONAL CHARTERS (page no. given)

226 Inspeximus charter [royal confirmation] of Richard I to Sempringham

a. whole vill of Sempringham with the church and chapel of Pointon and other appurtenances

b. grant no. 1 plus the church of Torrington noted in no. 2

c. grant no. 4

d. gift of Ralf Bathuent (no. 3) one carucate in Sempringham gift of Godwin the Rich (no. 2) and with the permission of Alice de Gant (no. 8)

e. their cowshed, meadow, pasture, turbary [peat-diggings], fisheries, ditches, and parks in their own marsh of Sempringham

f. many other churches, parcels of land, and rights

Witness list

Rotuli Hundredorum

154 They [the jurors of the wapentake of Aveland] say that the prior of Sempringham holds in alms three carucates of land from Gilbert de Gant on which the priory was founded of the gift of Gilbert de Gant some 160 years before. They are not taxable, and they know not by what warrant. Gilbert de Gant holds them from the king in chief, but what service is not known, and they are worth £20.

The same prior holds three carucates in alms in the same vill of the gift of Reginald de Badeunt some hundred years ago. They are not taxable, by what warrant they known not, and are worth £20, Reginald held them from Gilbert de Gant for service of one knight's fee and Gilbert holds [sic] them in chief from the king, service and warrant unknown.

Date 1275/6

156 The prior of Sempringham claims to have the assizes of bread and ale in Sempringham and warren and a fair from the vigil of the feast of St John the Baptist at the church of Stow [Green]. [Marginal notes indicate that the prior showed his charters, and he was therefore allowed his liberties.]

Date 1275/6

THE PARISH CHURCH OF ST ANDREW

Parish church. *c.* 1170, mid C14, *c.* 1400, restored and chancel rebuilt 1868–9 by Edward Browning. Uncoursed pale yellow limestone rubble, limestone ashlar. Plain tile and slate roofs with coped west gable with kneelers and cross finial. Nave with north aisle and south porch, crossing tower and apsidal chancel. C12 west front with moulded plinth and flanking pilaster buttresses reaching up to string course, with angle shaft on south buttress with cushion capital with Caryatid figure above. Rubble wall beneath string course. Pointed window above, restored in C19, with 3 pointed, cusped lights and hood mould with ornate label stops. 2 human heads in gable above. C12 north aisle to west with moulded plinth, rubble walling reaching up to string course and pilaster angle buttress with angle shaft with cushion capital. Mid C14 window restored in C19, with triangular head, 2 cusped ogee headed lights, and breaks through head of pointed fragmentary, blocked C12 window to right.

St Andrew's, Sempringham

North side of north aisle rebuilt in 1868-9 and extended to cover area of former north transept destroyed in 1788. Regularly placed pilaster buttresses with moulded string course and Lombardic-style corbel table. Doorway to right with semi-circular head, continuous, roll moulded surround, hood mould and plank door. Segmental relieving arch above. Small semi-circular headed window to right with 3 similar windows to left. East end of north aisle with re-used pilaster buttress with angle shaft with cushion capital, and small semi-circular headed window.

C12 crossing tower re-modelled in late C14 with clasping pilaster buttresses, the south-east buttress containing a stair turret with C19 narrow doorway with triangular head, chamfered surround and plank door; 2 slit stair lights above, and 2 grotesque sculpted figures. Late C14 bell openings on all 4 sides, each with pointed head, 2 cusped, pointed lights, mouchettes, hood mould and ornate label stops. Moulded eaves with large corner gargoyles and central corbel heads supporting angular shafts rising to base of central pinnacles. Battlements with 8 ornate pinnacles.

C19 apsidal chancel with plinth, moulded string course and Lombardic style corbel table. 4 regularly placed windows, each a lancet with ornate flanking shafts with stiff leaf capitals and hood moulds running into string course. South side with segmental relieving arch.

Truncated south transept, destroyed in 1788, with blocked, pointed archway with pointed window inserted with 2 pointed, cusped lights, panel tracery, hood mould and re-used C14 label stops. 2 plain roof corbels above and narrow rectangular light. South side of C12 nave restored in C19. Moulded plinth and Lombardic style corbel table. Single tall, narrow semi-circular headed window to east with pilaster buttress to left. Mid C14 window to west with segmental head, 3 cusped ogee headed lights and hood mould. Gabled C19 south porch built over pilaster buttress to left. Plinth, corbel table and small semi-circular headed windows in east and west walls, both with hood moulds running into string course on either side.

Round headed south doorway with moulded head and single semi- circular jambs with geometrically decorated scalloped capitals and glazed doors. Porch interior with fine south doorway of c. 1170 with 3 orders of shafts with ornate foliate capitals including ribbed leaves, beaded tendrils and incipient waterleaf. Roll moulded, chevron, billet and incised scalloped semi-circular head, with hood mould and ornate label stops. Early C13 door with ornate iron scrollwork. Another C12 doorway re-set in west wall of porch with semi-circular head with tympanum decorated with large fan of scallops, outer orders with beaded ribbon, circle, and petal decoration. Capitals supporting head with ornate, beaded scallop decoration. Aisle to west of porch with pilaster buttresses flanking tall, narrow semi-circular headed window, heightened in C19.

North arcade of nave of c. 1170 of 4 bays. Responds with clusters of keeled shafts. Round pier to west with cruciform abaci and large rectangular pier to east with single keeled shafts to north and south and pairs of small keeled shafts to east and west, round pier beyond with plain scalloped capital. Semi-circular moulded heads in 2 orders with string course above. Easternmost arcade bay with fragmentary remains of red painted decoration on soffit. Late C14 crossing arches to west, north, east and south, all with semi-circular responds, polygonal capitals and abaci and richly moulded, pointed heads. 3 eastern windows of C19 chancel flanked by 6 slender shafts with shaft rings and stiff leaf capitals, and ornate corbel table. C19 roofs.

C19 pulpit with traceried panels. 10 ornate late C15 bench ends with rich traceried panels and large, beaded finials; the design copied in C19 for remainder of pews. C15 octagonal font with quatrefoil panels containing blank shields. Medieval chest. Fragments on window ledge of north-west window of north aisle include a gargoyle head, a C15 jug from burial ground and a cresset stone with 7 hollows for holding oil and wicks. Another octagonal font bowl with narrow roll mouldings at each corner. North-west crossing pier with inscription in north side: 'Sing Prayses unto the Lord O Ye Sans of His 1581. N.Edone. Sperni. N.C.I.EER' and a small carved panel below. In vestry at east end of north aisle, 2 moulded C15 heads of window embedded in wall 2 fragments of Lombardic style corbel table. C16 wooden altar table. White marble monument with coat of arms on apron to John Hubbard, died 1783.

A proud Norman church, unfortunately shorn of its chancel and transepts and provided with an apsed chancel of 1868-9 (by Browning). In the porch part of an Anglo-Saxon cross which was found in the church-yard. Monuments – many slate headstones, mostly signed, as they are to be found in this whole neighbourhood.

The well in the church-yard. C12, C19, C20, containing salts of iron.

A SERVICE FOR ST GILBERT'S DAY
13th OCTOBER

COLLECT
O, Eternal Saviour, effect in us the full need of Thy virtue, that we, who venerate the renowned merits of Blessed Gilbert, Saint and Confessor assisted by his prayers may be delivered from all the diseases of our souls. Who liveth and reigneth........*(Collect written by Innocent III for St Gilbert Canon - 11th January 1202)*

EPISTLE
Eccles. 45: 1-5.

GOSPEL
St Mathew 19: 27-29.

SECRET
May this salutary oblation be acceptable to Thee O Lord that as it may rebound to honour of Thy Confessor, Blessed Gilbert, so it may assist us Thy servant to salvation. Through Jesus Christ Our Lord. *(Innocent III 1202)*

POST COMMUNION
We beseech Thee O Lord that what has descended from Thee to us, may also ascend from us to Thee, that by the intercession of Blessed Gilbert Thy Saint and Confessor it may these whom Jesus Christ Thy Son hath redeemed. Through Jesus Christ our Lord. *(Innocent III 1202)*

Saint Gilbert's Hymn
(to the tune Sempringham)

How great the promise of his birth
The Church rings out its joy
The faithful English folk were taught
By this weak, holy boy
Send forth O fruitful Sempringham
This child to Christ's High Court
Join Gilbert with those citizens
Who, that same peace, have sought.

He wiped a leper's stains away
And heat of fire anneale
On pleading with Almighty God
The poor man's sores were healed
He stilled the waves, made fever cool
Helped ailing wife bear child
The woman, so relieved from pain,
Gave birth in manner mild.

O Jesu, glory of the Saints
Your grace in us increase
May we enjoy the fruits of Heav'n
And everlasting peace
Praise be, and honour still, to Thee
Most Holy Trinity
And may eternal ages show
Your Power and Unity.

Fr Hilary Costello OCSO
Music: Peter Yelland 1986

A Poem by M. Benton,
from the Sempringham Log Book

White-hooded, scarlet-slippered, swift
Through swirling winter snows
'Neath hawthorn boughs with berries red
The sainted Abbot goes.

Along the cart-track's rutty way
Where fragrant blossom foams
In spring's sweet air with saintly grace
Saint Gilbert's spirit roams.

By summer time, the ripened corn
In glory stand erect
Red poppies blow where scarlet feet
Have stood in watch elect.

When chilly mists of autumn rise
From dyke and loamy fen
On leafy carpet, rustling red
Treads ghostly Gilbert then.

Though age to crumbling age succeeds
And years relentless roll
In quiet fields, where passed his life
Immortal dwells his soul.